INTELLIGENT VIDEO SURVEILLANCE

Edited by **António J. R. Neves**

Intelligent Video Surveillance
http://dx.doi.org/10.5772/intechopen.71342
Edited by António J. R. Neves

Contributors

Ying-Jen Chen, Agha Husain, Mritunjay Rai, Ravindra Kumar Yadav, Tanmoy Maity, Fozia Mehboob, Muhammad Abbas, Shoab A Khan, Abdul Rauf, Richard Jiang, Hakil Kim, Chengbin Jin, Trung-Dung Do, Mingjie Liu, Radu Danescu, Diana Borza, Razvan Itu, Ricardo Ferreira Ribeiro, Daniel Lopes, Antonio J. R. Neves, Carlos Flores-Vázquez, Marcelo Flores-Vázquez, Daniel Icaza, Nelson Federico Cordova, Shaufikah Shukri, Latifah Munirah Kamarudin, Mohd Hafiz Fazalul Rahiman

First published in London, United Kingdom, 2019 by IntechOpen
IntechOpen is the global imprint of INTECHOPEN LIMITED, registered in England and Wales, registration number: 11086078, The Shard, 25th floor, 32 London Bridge Street
London, SE19SG – United Kingdom
Printed in Croatia

British Library Cataloguing-in-Publication Data
A catalogue record for this book is available from the British Library

Additional hard copies can be obtained from orders@intechopen.com

Intelligent Video Surveillance, Edited by António J. R. Neves
p. cm.
Print ISBN 978-1-78985-027-7
Online ISBN 978-1-78985-028-4

For EU product safety concerns:
IN TECH d.o.o., Prolaz Marije Krucifikse Kozulić 3, 51000 Rijeka, Croatia,
info@intechopen.com or visit our website at intechopen.com.

Meet the editor

Prof. António J. R. Neves received the Ph.D. in Electrical Engineering from the University of Aveiro, in 2007. Since 2002 he is a researcher at Institute of Electronics and Informatics Engineering of Aveiro and since 2007 an Assistant Professor at the Department of Electronics, Telecommunications and Informatics of the University of Aveiro. He is an IEEE Senior Member and member of several other research organizations worldwide. His main research interests are computer vision, robotics and image and video processing. He participated or coordinated several research projects and published 145 publications, including books, book chapters, journal articles and conference papers. He has also a vast experience as a reviewer of several journals and conferences. As a professor, he supervised several Ph.D. students and Master students in the referred areas. Moreover, he has been head Professor for several courses in the areas of computer science, signal processing, image processing and robotics. Over the last months I have been coordinating the restructuring of the Master's Program in Electronics and Telecommunications Engineering, as he has been recently nominated as director.

Contents

Preface IX

Section 1 Video Surveillance Systems 1

Chapter 1 **Particle-Filter-Based Intelligent Video Surveillance System 3**
Ying-Jen Chen

Chapter 2 **Video Surveillance-Based Intelligent Traffic Management in Smart Cities 19**
Fozia Mehboob, Muhammad Abbas, Abdul Rauf, Shoab A. Khan and Richard Jiang

Chapter 3 **Advance Intelligent Video Surveillance System (AIVSS): A Future Aspect 37**
Mritunjay Rai, Agha Asim Husain, Tanmoy Maity and Ravindra Kumar Yadav

Section 2 Human Activity Recognition 57

Chapter 4 **Real-Time Action Recognition Using Multi-level Action Descriptor and DNN 59**
Cheng-Bin Jin, Trung Dung Do, Mingjie Liu and Hakil Kim

Chapter 5 **Human Activity Recognition without Vision Tracking 77**
Carlos Alberto Flores Vázquez, Joan Aranda, Daniel Icaza, Santiago Pulla, Marcelo Flores-Vázquez and Nelson Federico Cordova

Chapter 6 **Device-Free Localization for Human Activity Monitoring 95**
Shaufikah Shukri, Latifah Munirah Kamarudin and Mohd Hafiz Fazalul Rahiman

Section 3 Face and Expressions Recognition 121

Chapter 7 **Access Control in the Wild Using Face Verification 123**
Ricardo Ribeiro, Daniel Lopes and António Neves

Chapter 8 **Detecting Micro-Expressions in Real Time Using High-Speed Video Sequences 141**
Radu Danescu, Diana Borza and Razvan Itu

Preface

Intelligent video surveillance is a multidisciplinary field related to computer vision, pattern recognition, image processing, networks, embedded systems and image sensors.

The goal is to efficiently extract useful information from a considerable number of videos collected by surveillance cameras by automatically detecting, tracking and recognizing objects of interest, and understanding and analyzing their activities. The widespread availability of digital cameras and processing equipment, together with a growing need for public safety have shifted the attention of researchers in video surveillance, becoming one of the most active research areas in computer vision.

Video surveillance has a huge amount of applications, from public to private places, such as homeland security, crime prevention, traffic control, accident prediction and detection, monitoring patients, elderly or children in different environments. These applications require monitoring indoor and outdoor scenes of airports, train stations, highways, parking lots, stores, shopping malls, offices, just to name a few. Nowadays, there are a considerable number of digital cameras in the referred places collecting a huge amount of data on a daily basis. Researchers are urged to develop intelligent systems to efficiently extract and visualize useful information from this big data source.

The exponential effort on the development of new algorithms and systems for video surveillance is confirmed by the amount of effort invested in projects and companies, the creation on new startups worldwide and, not less important, in the quantity and quality of the manuscripts published in a considerable number of journals and conferences worldwide.

This book is an outcome of research done by several researchers and professionals who have highly contributed to the field of video surveillance. The main goal is to present recent advances in this hot topic. I would like to thank all the authors for their excellent contributions and to all those people who helped in this project.

This book contains of eight chapters divided into three sections. Section 1 consists of three chapters focusing on the development of systems and algorithms for video surveillance. Section 2 presents three chapters focusing on people, namely human activity and action recognition. Section 3 consists on a couple of chapters related to algorithms for face and expressions recognition.

Finally, I hope that all the readers of this book will find it interesting and informative, considering it as a good tool for their research or project.

Prof. António J. R. Neves, Ph.D.
Department of Electronics
Telecommunications and Informatics
University of Aveiro
Portugal

Section 1

Video Surveillance Systems

Chapter 1

Particle-Filter-Based Intelligent Video Surveillance System

Ying-Jen Chen

Additional information is available at the end of the chapter

http://dx.doi.org/10.5772/intechopen.76960

Abstract

In this study, an intelligent video surveillance (IVS) system is designed based on the particle filter. The designed IVS system can gather the information of the number of persons in the area and hot spots of the area. At first, the Gaussian mixture background model is utilized to detect moving objects by background subtraction. The moving object appearing in the margin of the video frame is considered as a new person. Then, a new particle filter is assigned to track the new person when it is detected. A particle filter is canceled when the corresponding tracked person leaves the video frame. Moreover, the Kalman filter is utilized to estimate the position of the person when the person is occluded. Information of the number of persons in the area and hot spots is gathered by tracking persons in the video frame. Finally, a user interface is designed to feedback the gathered information to users of the IVS system. By applying the proposed IVS system, the load of security guards can be reduced. Moreover, by hot spot analysis, the business operator can understand customer habits to plan the traffic flow and adjust the product placement for improving customer experience.

Keywords: intelligent video surveillance (IVS), Gaussian mixture model, particle filter, Kalman filter

1. Introduction

Video surveillance systems are often utilized at some specific places such as exits, entrances, parking lots, convenient stores, etc. for management. Traditionally, security guards watch screens of monitored places for surveillance. However, according to statistics, one security guard can only watch four monitors at the same time, and the concentration can last only for 10 minutes such that more than 50% of key information is lost. Moreover, it is not economically worthwhile to hire multiple security guards to monitor one video surveillance system. Therefore, intelligent video surveillance (IVS) systems have become more and more important in commercial sector and have attracted a lot of attention in research area as well [1–3].

IVS system can be defined as the real-time monitoring of both persistent and transient objects within a specific environment. IVS is also referred to as video analytics (VA) which involves the use of software to automatically detect the objects of specific interest and analyze their behaviors. For finding the objects of interest, it is usually done by detecting the movements or changes in the image that can be achieved by background subtraction technique. To do background subtraction, an effective way to build up the background is the Gaussian mixture model [4, 5]. After the object of interest is detected, the goal is to analyze their behavior that sometimes can be done by tracking them. Usually, particle filters and Kalman filters are employed for the purpose of tracking objects in IVS systems [6–10].

IVS systems have been applied for different kinds of purposes. Ref. [11] presents an architecture for a perimeter security system dedicated to critical transport infrastructure protection. Ref. [12] addresses a framework for event decision of vision-based intelligent surveillance system based on the fuzzy model. A shape-perceived algorithm using the building block-based matching method is presented in [13] for object tracking of intelligent surveillance applications. A way of unification of flame and smoke detection algorithms by merging the common steps into a single processing flow is proposed in [14] for IVS systems.

The aim of this study is to design a IVS system based on the particle filter. The designed IVS system can gather the information of the number of persons being in the area, the number of persons having been in the area, and hot spots (places of more than usual interest, activity, or popularity) of the area. The Gaussian mixture background model is utilized to detect moving objects by background subtraction in the designed IVS system. The moving object appearing in the margin of the video frame is considered as a new unit (person). When a new person is detected, a new particle filter is established and assigned to track the new person. For saving the computational load, the particle filter is terminated when the corresponding tracked person leaves the video frame. Moreover, the Kalman filters is utilized to estimate the position of the person when the person is occluded. Information of the number of persons in the area (having been in the area) and hot spots is gathered by tracking persons in the video frame. Finally, a user interface is designed to feedback the gathered information to users of the IVS system. By applying the proposed IVS system, the load of security guards can be reduced. Moreover, by hot spot analysis, the business operator can understand customer habits to plan the traffic flow and adjust the product placement for improving customer experience.

2. Preliminary

In this section, three well-known techniques, i.e. adaptive Gaussian mixture model, particle filter, and Kalman filter, are presented for constructing the IVS system.

http://dx.doi.org/10.5772/intechopen.76960

2.1. Adaptive Gaussian mixture model

The recent history of each pixel, $\{X_1, X_2, \cdots X_t\}$, is modeled by a mixture of k Gaussian distributions. The probability of observing the current pixel value is given as Eq. [4]:

$$P(X_t) = \sum_{i=1}^{k} \omega_{i,t}\eta\left(X_t, \mu_{i,t}, \Sigma_{i,t}\right) \tag{1}$$

where k is the number of distributions, $\omega_{i,t}$ is an estimate of the weight of the ith Gaussian distribution in the mixture at time t, $\mu_{i,t}$ is the mean value of the ith Gaussian distribution in the mixture at time t, $\Sigma_{i,t}$ is the covariance matrix of the ith Gaussian distribution in the mixture at time t, and η is a Gaussian probability density function:

$$\eta\left(X_t, \mu, \Sigma\right) = \frac{1}{2\pi|\Sigma|^{\frac{1}{2}}} e^{-\frac{1}{2}\left(X_t-\mu\right)^T \Sigma^{-1}\left(X_t-\mu\right)}. \tag{2}$$

The updating rules for the parameters of the adaptive Gaussian mixture model can be found in [5]. After the Gaussian mixture model is established, the foreground pixels (representing the moving objects) can be obtained by applying the Mahalanobis distance:

$$D_i(X_t) = \sqrt{\left(X_t - \mu_{i,t}\right)^T \Sigma_{i,t}\left(X_t - \mu_{i,t}\right)}. \tag{3}$$

The adaptive Gaussian mixture model has been applied for different kinds of applications, such as automatic speech emotion recognition [15], tracking targets on long-range radar systems [16], fast sampling-based motion planning [17], etc.

2.2. Particle filter

The key idea of particle filtering is to approximate the probability distribution by a weighted sample set [18]:

$$\mathbf{S} = \left\{\left(\mathbf{s}^{(n)}, \pi^{(n)}\right) \middle| n = 1, \cdots, N\right\}. \tag{4}$$

Each sample consists of an element $\mathbf{s}$ which represents the hypothetical state of the object and a corresponding discrete sampling probability π where $\sum_{n=1}^{N} \pi^{(n)} = 1$. The evolution of the sample set is calculated by propagating each sample according to a system model. Each element of the set is then weighted in terms of the observations, and N samples are drawn with replacement. The mean state of the object is estimated at each time step by

$$E(\mathbf{S}) = \sum_{n=1}^{N} \pi^{(n)}\mathbf{s}^{(n)}. \tag{5}$$

Particle filter provides a robust tracking framework.

The particle filter has been successfully applied to many applications. An algorithm to track the vehicle with the adaptively changed scale based on particle filter is propose in [19]. The vehicle guidance with control action computed by a Rao-Blackwellized particle filter is proposed in [20]. The localization of indoor robot based on particle filter with EKF proposal distribution is proposed in [21].

2.3. Kalman filter

The Kalman filter [22] addresses the general problem of trying to estimate the state of a discrete-time controlled process that is governed by the linear stochastic difference equation:

$$\mathbf{x}_t = \mathbf{F}\mathbf{x}_{t-1} + \mathbf{w}_t \tag{6}$$

with measurement equation

$$\boldsymbol{\varphi}_t = \mathbf{H}\mathbf{x}_t + \mathbf{v}_t \tag{7}$$

where $\mathbf{x}_t$ is the state vector, $\mathbf{F}$ is the transition matrix, $\boldsymbol{\varphi}_t$ is the measurement output, $\mathbf{H}$ is the output matrix, $\mathbf{w}_t$ is the process noise, and $\mathbf{v}_t$ is the measurement noise. The process noise and measurement noise are assumed to be independent of each other, white, and with normal probability distributions:

$$p(\boldsymbol{\omega}) \sim N(0,\ \mathbf{Q}) \tag{8}$$

$$p(\mathbf{v}) \sim N(0,\ \mathbf{R}) \tag{9}$$

where $\mathbf{Q}$ is the process noise covariance matrix and $\mathbf{R}$ is measurement noise covariance matrix. Moreover, $\widehat{\mathbf{x}}_t^-$ is defined to be the a priori state estimate at step t, and $\widehat{\mathbf{x}}_t$ is defined to be the a posteriori state estimate. Then, $\mathbf{e}_t^- \equiv \mathbf{x}_t - \widehat{\mathbf{x}}_t^-$ is defined to be a priori estimate error, and $\mathbf{e}_t \equiv \mathbf{x}_t - \widehat{\mathbf{x}}_t$ is defined to be the a posteriori estimate error. The a priori estimate error covariance is then

$$\mathbf{P}_t^- = E\left[\mathbf{e}_t^- \left(\mathbf{e}_t^-\right)^T\right] \tag{10}$$

and the a posteriori estimate error covariance is

$$\mathbf{P}_t = E\left[\mathbf{e}_t^- (\mathbf{e}_t)^T\right]. \tag{11}$$

The equations for the Kalman filter fall into two groups: time update (predictor) equations and measurement update (corrector) equations. The time update equations are given as

$$\widehat{\mathbf{x}}_t^- = \mathbf{F}\widehat{\mathbf{x}}_{t-1} \tag{12}$$

$$\mathbf{P}_t^- = \mathbf{F}\mathbf{P}_{t-1}\mathbf{F}^T + \mathbf{Q}. \tag{13}$$

http://dx.doi.org/10.5772/intechopen.76960

The measurement update equations are given as

$$\mathbf{K}_t = \mathbf{P}_t^- \mathbf{H}^T \left(\mathbf{H} \mathbf{P}_t^- \mathbf{H}^T + \mathbf{R} \right)^{-1} \tag{14}$$

$$\hat{\mathbf{x}}_t = \hat{\mathbf{x}}_t^- + \mathbf{K}_t \left(\varphi_t - \mathbf{H} \hat{\mathbf{x}}_t^- \right) \tag{15}$$

$$\mathbf{P}_t = (\mathbf{I} - \mathbf{K}_t \mathbf{H}) \mathbf{P}_t^- . \tag{16}$$

Figure 1 shows the operation architecture of Kalman filter.

The Kalman filter has been widely applied to time series analysis and statistical modeling problems. This study [23] improves the navigation performance, when refraction starlight is used to compute the position and velocity of a satellite in unscented Kalman filter. An anti-spoofing algorithm based on adaptive Kalman filter for high dynamic positioning in global positioning system is proposed in [24]. In this work [25], the robust Kalman filter is applied to the people occupancy estimation problem, and an iterative algorithm is developed to handle the state-dependent model uncertainties.

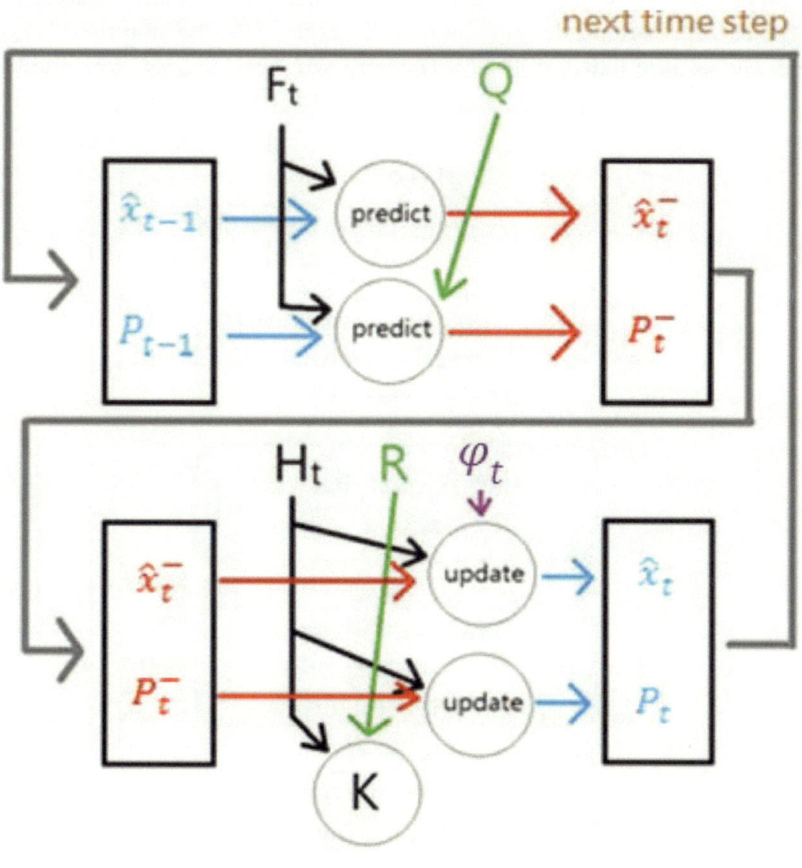

Figure 1. The operation architecture of Kalman filter.

3. IVS system design

The IVS system design is presented in this section. **Figure 2** shows the operation process of the IVS system. Firstly, the adaptive Gaussian mixture model is applied for constructing the background model to detect moving objects in the video image frame. The moving object appearing in the margin of the video image frame is considered as a new unit (person), and then a new particle filter is established and designated to track the new person. Moreover, the Kalman filter is utilized to correct the position obtaining by the particle filter and to estimate the position during occlusion. After that, the information of the number of persons in the area, the number of persons having been in the area, and hot spots are obtained by analyzing the tracking paths. Finally, the information is fed back to the user by the user interface. Each block of the IVS system design shown in **Figure 2** will be illustrated in the following subsections.

3.1. Gaussian mixture model for detecting new units

By applying the adaptive Gaussian mixture model described in Subsection 2.1, the moving objects can be detected by using the Mahalanobis distance of Eq. (3). **Figure 3** illustrates the foreground pixels representing the moving objects obtained by the adaptive Gaussian mixture model. Here, we assume that a new unit (person) will appear only from the border of the

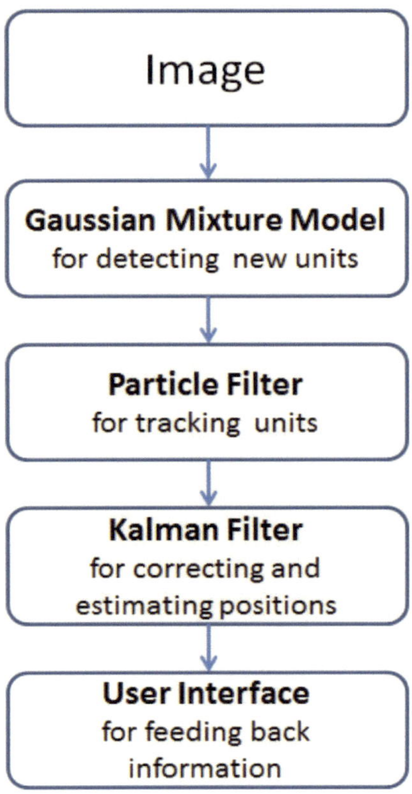

Figure 2. The operation process of the IVS system.

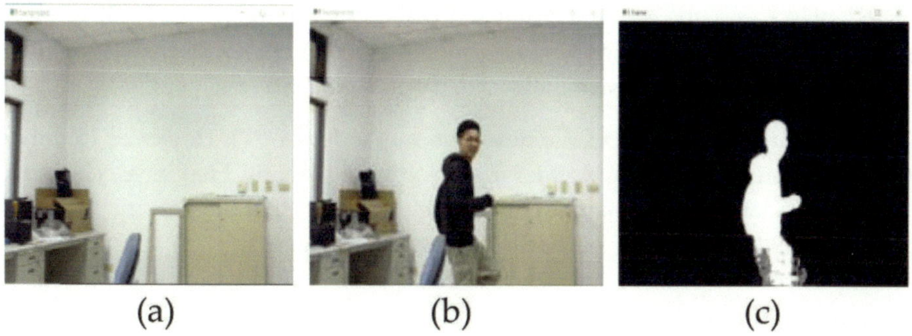

Figure 3. Foreground pixels representing the moving objects obtained by the adaptive Gaussian mixture model: (a) background, (b) moving object, and (c) foreground pixels.

monitored place. Therefore, for a moving object detected in the margin of the monitoring video frame, we need to determine that it is a new person or not.

Figure 4 shows the checking process for determining the object detected in the margin of the monitoring video frame as a new person or not. At first we need to check the size and ratio of the detected object to identify that the detected object is a person or not. If the size and ratio of the detected object are identified as a person, then we have to check that the detected person is new or not. In the case that there is no tracked person in the video frame, the detected person in the margin of the video frame is determined to be a new person. In the case that there has (have) been tracked person(s) in the video frame, we need to calculate the distance(s) between the detected person and tracked person(s) to check that the detected person is new or not. If the distance(s) is (are all) longer than a predefined threshold T_d, the detected person is considered as a new person. If some distances are shorter than T_d, we need to apply Eq. (18), which will be described in the following subsection, to calculate the similarities of color distribution between

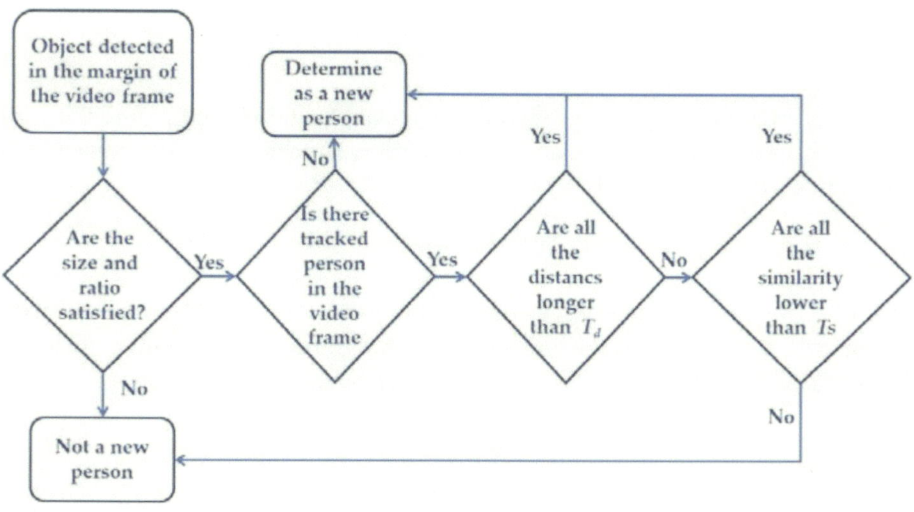

Figure 4. The checking process for determining the object detected in the margin of the monitoring video frame as a new person or not.

the detected object and the tracked units with distance shorter than T_d. If all similarities between the detected object and the tracked units with distance shorter than T_d are lower than a predefined threshold T_s, the detected object is determined as a new person.

It is noted that there are several people detection methods [26, 27]. However, in the designed IVS system, we assume that the only moving objects are persons. Hence, we choose a simple method, which is adaptive Gaussian mixture model, to detect that the persons appear from the border of the monitored place for reducing the computational load.

3.2. Particle filter for tracking units

For a new detected person, a new particle filter is established and designated to track the new person. In the design of the particle filter, the target model of target region (the detected person) is the color distribution which is represented by histograms calculated in the HS (Hue, Saturation) space using 8 × 8 bins. A popular measure between two color distributions is the Bhattacharyya coefficient. Considering discrete densities such as two color histograms

$$p = \left\{p^{(u)}\right\}_{u=1\ldots m}, \quad q = \left\{q^{(u)}\right\}_{u=1\ldots m} \tag{17}$$

the Bhattacharyya coefficient is defined as

$$\rho[p, q] = \sum_{u=1}^{m} \sqrt{p^{(u)}q^{(u)}}. \tag{18}$$

The larger ρ is, the more similar the two distributions are. For two identical histograms, we obtain $\rho = 1$ indicating a perfect match. The target region of the detected person is represented by a rectangle so that a sample is given as

$$\mathbf{s} = \left[x \ y \ H_x \ H_y\right]^T \tag{19}$$

where x and y represent the center location of the rectangle and H_x and H_y are the width and length of the rectangle, respectively, as shown in **Figure 5**. The sample set is propagated through the application of a dynamic model:

$$\mathbf{s}_t = \boldsymbol{A}\mathbf{s}_{t-1} + \boldsymbol{w}_{t-1} \tag{20}$$

where $\boldsymbol{A}$ is an 4×4 identity matrix and $\boldsymbol{w}_{t-1}$ is a random vector drawn from the noise distribution of the system. Assuming that the target histogram is q and the histogram of the sample $\mathbf{s}^{(n)}$ is $p_{\mathbf{s}^{(n)}}$, the observation probability of each sample is given as

$$\pi^{(n)} = \rho\left[p_{\mathbf{s}^{(n)}}, q\right]. \tag{21}$$

The tracking result can be calculated by Eq. (5). During filtering, samples with a high weight may be chosen several times, leading to identical copies, while others with relatively low weights may not be chosen at all. **Figure 6** illustrates persons tracked by particle filter.

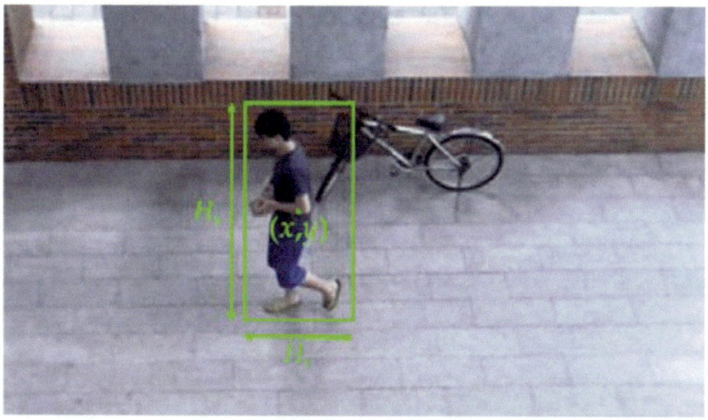

Figure 5. The target region of the detected person represented by a rectangle.

Figure 6. Persons tracked particle filter.

Although the particle filter is a robust method for tracking objects, it cannot deal with some special cases. Since we use color distribution for the target model of the particle filter, it may lose tracking when the color of the background is similar to the color of the tracking object. Moreover, if the tracking object is occluded, still the particle filter will lose tracking.

3.3. Kalman filter for correcting and estimating positions

In the IVS system design, the Kalman filter is utilized to correct the position obtained by the particle filter and to estimate the position during occlusion. Here, the uniform linear movement is considered. Hence, the linear stochastic difference equation is given as

$$\begin{bmatrix} \widehat{x}_t \\ \widehat{y}_t \\ \dot{\widehat{x}}_t \\ \dot{\widehat{y}}_t \end{bmatrix} = \begin{bmatrix} 1 & 0 & 1 & 0 \\ 0 & 1 & 0 & 1 \\ 0 & 0 & 1 & 0 \\ 0 & 0 & 0 & 1 \end{bmatrix} \begin{bmatrix} \widehat{x}_{t-1} \\ \widehat{y}_{t-1} \\ \dot{\widehat{x}}_{t-1} \\ \dot{\widehat{y}}_{t-1} \end{bmatrix} + \boldsymbol{w}_{t-1} \tag{22}$$

and the measurement equation is given as

$$\begin{bmatrix} \hat{x}_t \\ \hat{y}_t \end{bmatrix} = \begin{bmatrix} 1 & 0 & 0 & 0 \\ 0 & 1 & 0 & 0 \end{bmatrix} \begin{bmatrix} \hat{x}_t \\ \hat{y}_t \\ \dot{\hat{x}}_t \\ \dot{\hat{y}}_t \end{bmatrix} + v_t \tag{23}$$

where $(\hat{x}, \hat{y})$ is the estimating position and $\dot{\hat{x}}$ and $\dot{\hat{y}}$ represent the estimating speeds on x and y directions, respectively. In the measurement update equation of Eq. (15), the measurement $\varphi_t = \begin{bmatrix} x_t & y_t \end{bmatrix}^T$ is obtained from the tracking result of the particle filter.

For improving the tracking results of particle filter, after propagation by Eq. (20), the estimating speeds $\dot{\hat{x}}_{t-1}$ and $\dot{\hat{y}}_{t-1}$ of the Kalman filter are added to the position of each sample of the particle filter such that

$$\mathbf{s}_t^{(n)} = \left[x_t^{(n)} + \dot{\hat{x}}_{t-1}, \; y_t^{(n)} + \dot{\hat{y}}_{t-1}, \; H_x, \; H_y \right]. \tag{24}$$

When the tracked object is occluded, the Kalman filter is applied to estimate the position of the occluded object. Therefore, for the case that all the similarities between samples of particle filter and the target are lower than lower than a predefined threshold T_p, the Kalman filter doesn't use the measurement correction and only takes the filter prediction as object position. Moreover, all samples of the particle filter are uniformly distributed around the estimating position such that the particle filter can retrieve tracking after the object recovering from

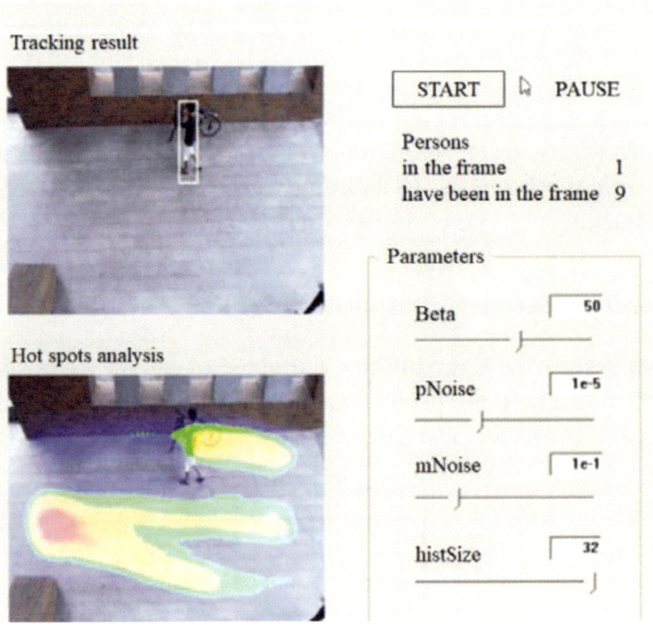

Figure 7. User interface of the IVS system.

occluded. However, if the occluded object is stayed in the back of obstacle without moving, the Kalman filter will still lose the tracking.

3.4. User interface for feeding back information

Finally, by analyzing the tracking paths, the information of the tracking result, the number of persons in the area, the number of persons having been in the area, and hot spots are obtained and then fed back to the user through the user interface as shown in **Figure 7**. Furthermore, several parameters can be adjusted through the user interface for adapting different environments.

4. Experiment results

The experiment is done in the San Shia Campus of the National Taipei University, Taipei, Taiwan. **Figure 8** illustrates the operation process of the IVS system. In **Figure 8**, the up-left frame is the original image; the up-right frame is the background subtraction binary image applying Gaussian mixture model; the left-down frame shows the tracking result by applying particle filter (green rectangle) and the result corrected by Kalman filter (white rectangle), and the right-down frame is the final tracking result. **Figure 9** makes a comparison to show the

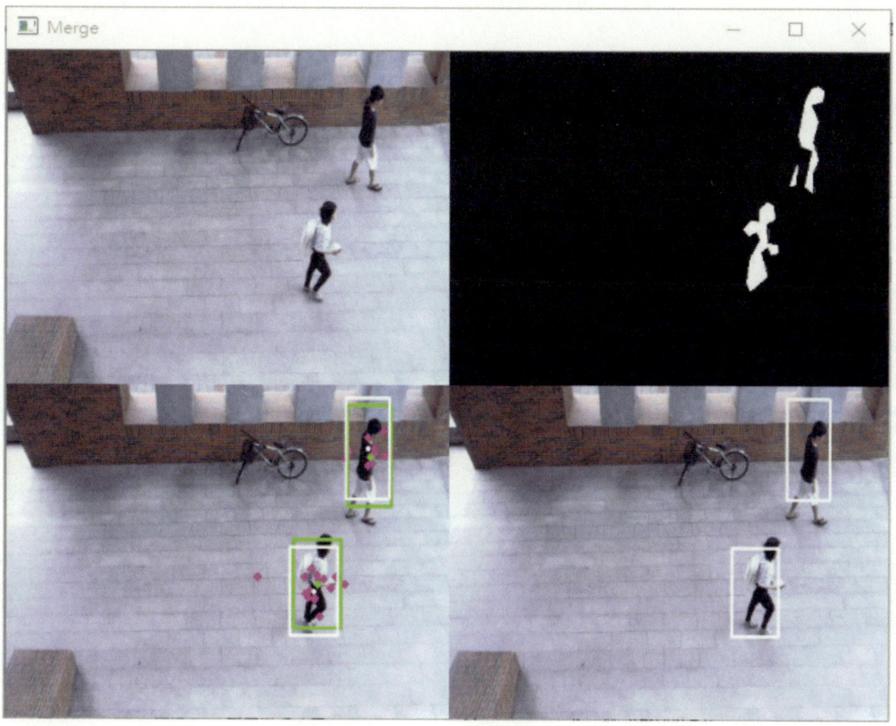

Figure 8. Illustration of the IVS operation process.

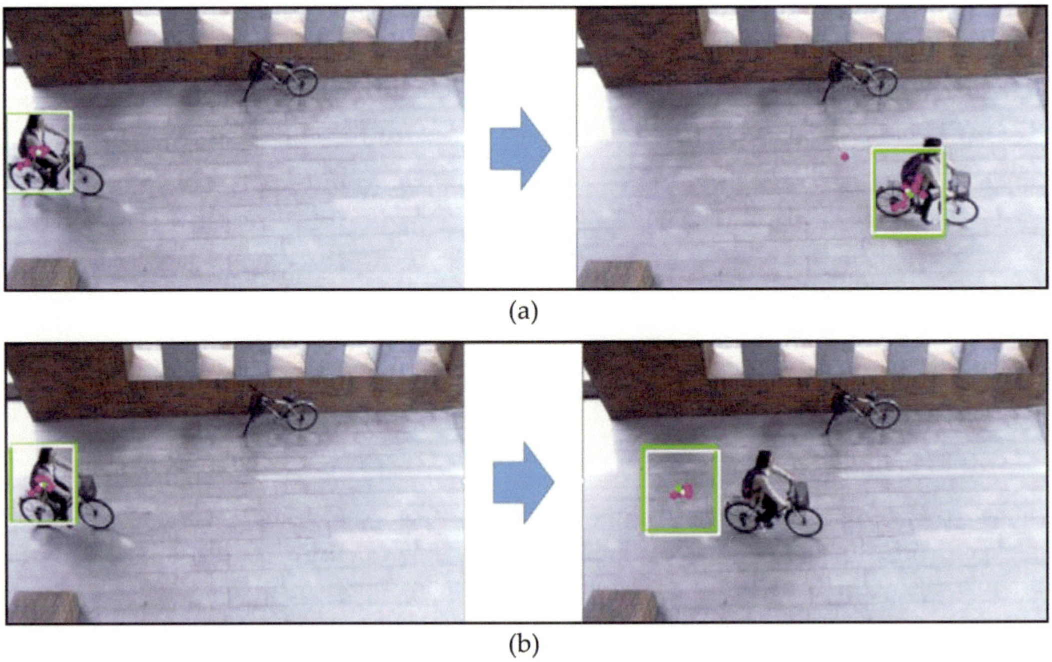

Figure 9. A fast-moving bicycle tracked by the particle filter (a) with Eq. (24) and (b) without Eq. (24).

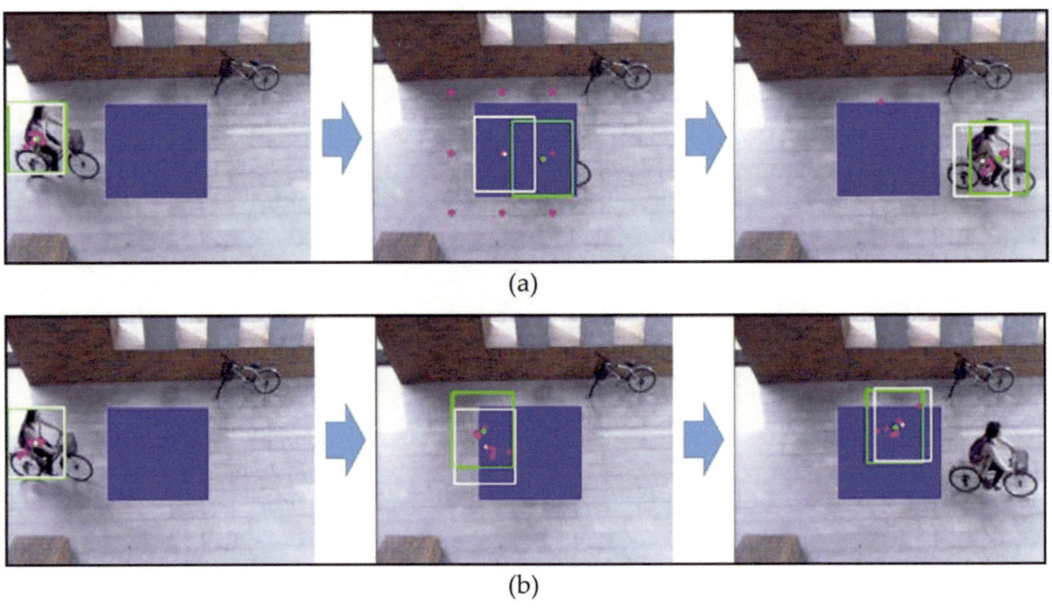

Figure 10. (a) Applying Kalman filter to estimate the position of the occluded object and (b) without applying Kalman filter to estimate the position of the occluded object.

utility of adding the estimating speeds of the Kalman filter to the position of each sample of the particle filter, i.e., to show the utility of Eq. (24). It can be seen that a fast-moving bicycle can be tracked by the particle filter with Eq. (24) as shown in **Figure 9(a)**. However, the fast-moving bicycle cannot be tracked by the particle filter without Eq. (24) as shown in **Figure 9(b)**. **Figure 10** makes a comparison to show the utility of applying Kalman filter to estimate the position of the occluded object. It can be seen that the particle filter can retrieve tracking after occlusion with applying Kalman filter to estimate the position of the occluded object as shown in **Figure 10(a)**. However, it can be seen that the particle filter cannot retrieve tracking after occlusion without applying Kalman filter to estimate the position of the occluded object as shown in **Figure 10(b)**. Moreover, it can also be seen in **Figure 10(a)** that all samples of the particle filter are uniformly distributed around the estimating position such that the particle filter can retrieve tracking after the object recovering from occluded.

5. Conclusion

Based on the particle filter, an IVS system has been designed in this study. Utilizing the Gaussian mixture background model, the moving objects appearing in the margin of the video frame can be detected and considered as a new person. Then, a new particle filter is established and designated to track the new considered person. Moreover, the Kalman filter is applied to correct the tracking result and estimate the position when the tracked person is occluded. By analyzing the tracking paths, the information of the number of persons in the area, the number of persons having been in the area, and hot spots can be obtained. Finally, the information is fed back to the user through the user interface.

Author details

Ying-Jen Chen

Address all correspondence to: yjcheng@mail.ntpu.edu.tw

Department of Electrical Engineering, National Taipei University, New Taipei City, Taiwan

References

[1] Li SR, Tsai HC, Wang YK, Sun TH, Chen YJ. Particle-filter-based intelligent video surveillance system. In: Proceedings of the International Conference on System Science and Engineering (ICSSE'16); 7-9 July. 2016. pp. 1-4

[2] Collins RT, Lipton AJ, Kanade T. A system for video surveillance and monitoring. In: Proceedings of American Nuclear Society (ANS) Eighth International Topical Meeting on Robotic and Remote Systems; April 1999

[3] Nam Y, Rho S, Park JH. Intelligent video surveillance system: 3-tier context-aware surveillance system with metadata. Multimedia Tools and Applications. 2012;**57**:315-334. DOI: 10.1007/s11042-010-0677-x

[4] Stauffer C, Grimson WEL. Adaptive background mixture models for real-time tracking. Computer Vision and Pattern Recognition. 1999;**2**:252-258

[5] KaewTraKulPong P, Bowden R. An improved adaptive background mixture model for real-time tracking with shadow detection. In: Proceedings of the 2nd European Workshop on Advanced Video Based Surveillance Systems (AVBS'01); September. 2001. pp. 1-5

[6] Zhai Y, Yeary M. An intelligent video surveillance system based on multiple model particle filtering. In: Proceedings of the IEEE Instrumentation and Measurement Technology Conference Proceedings (IMTC'08); 12-15 May 2008; Victoria, BC, Canada

[7] Li SR, Tsai HC, Wang YK, Sun TH, Chen YJ. Particle-filter-based intelligent video surveillance system. In: Proceedings of the International Conference on System Science and Engineering (ICSSE'16); 7-9 July 2016; Puli, Taiwan. pp. 1-4

[8] Gaddigoudar PK, Balihalli TR, Ijantkar SS, Iyer NC. Pedestrian detection and tracking using particle filtering. In: Proceedings of the International Conference on Computing, Communication and Automation (ICCCA'17); 5–6 May 2017; Greater Noida, India. pp. 110-115

[9] Amor N, Chebbi S. Performance comparison of particle swarm optimization and extended Kalman filter methods for tracking in non-linear dynamic systems. In: Proceedings of the International Conference on Control, Automation and Diagnosis (ICCAD'17); 19–21 Jan. 2017; Hammamet, Tunisia. pp. 116-119

[10] Cheng HY, Hsu SH. Intelligent highway traffic surveillance with self-diagnosis abilities. IEEE Transactions on Intelligent Transportation Systems. 2011;**12**:1462-1472. DOI: 10.1109/TITS.2011.2160171

[11] Banu VC, Costea IM, Nemtanu FC, Bădescu I. Intelligent video surveillance system. In: Proceedings of the IEEE 23rd International Symposium for Design and Technology in Electronic Packaging (SIITME'17); 26–29 October 2017; Constanta, Romania. pp. 208-212

[12] Wahyono, Filonenko A, Kurnianggoro L, Jo KH. A fuzzy model-based integration framework for vision-based intelligent surveillance systems. In: Proceedings of the IEEE International Conference on Mechatronics (ICM'17); 13-15 February 2017; Churchill, VIC, Australia. pp. 358-361

[13] Chung YC, Lai YK. A shape-perceived object tracking algorithm for intelligent surveillance systems. In: Proceedings of the IEEE International Conference on Consumer Electronics-Taiwan (ICCE-TW'15); 6-8 June 2015; Taipei, Taiwan. pp. 394-395

[14] Filonenko A, Hernández DC, Shahbaz A, Jo KH. Unified smoke and flame detection for intelligent surveillance system. In: Proceedings of the IEEE 25th International Symposium on Industrial Electronics (ISIE'16); 8–10 June 2016; Santa Clara, CA, USA. pp. 953-957

[15] Yang JH, Hung JW. A preliminary study of emotion recognition employing adaptive Gaussian mixture models with the maximum a posteriori principle. In: Proceedings of the 2014 International Conference on Information Science, Electronics and Electrical Engineering (ISEEE'14); 26–28 April 2014; Sapporo, Japan. pp. 1576-1579

[16] Davis B, Blair WD. Adaptive Gaussian mixture modeling for tracking of long range targets. In: Proceedings of the 2016 IEEE Aerospace Conference; 5-12 March 2016; Big Sky, MT, USA. pp. 1-9

[17] Huh J, Lee B, Lee DD. Adaptive motion planning with high-dimensional mixture models. In: Proceedings of the 2017 IEEE International Conference on Robotics and Automation (ICRA'17); 29 May-3 June 2017; Singapore, Singapore. pp. 3740-3747

[18] Nummiaro K, Koller-Meier E, Van Gool L. Object tracking with an adaptive color-based particle filter. In: Van Gool L, editor. Pattern Recognition. DAGM 2002. Lecture Notes in Computer Science, vol 2449. Berlin, Heidelberg: Springer; 2002. pp. 353-360. DOI: 10.1007/3–540-45783-6_43

[19] Yang S, Hao K, Ding Y, Liu J. Adaptively self-driving tracking algorithm based on particle filter. In: Proceedings of the 4th International Conference on Smart and Sustainable City (ICSSC'17); 5-6 June 2017; Shanghai, China

[20] Sans-Muntadas A, Brekke E, Pettersen KY. Vehicle guidance with control action computed by a rao-blackwellized particle filter. In: Proceedings of the 11th Asian Control Conference (ASCC'17); 17-20 December 2017; Gold Coast, QLD, Australia. pp. 2855-2860

[21] Xiao Y, Ou Y, Feng W. Localization of indoor robot based on particle filter with EKF proposal distribution. In: Proceedings of the 2017 IEEE International Conference on Cybernetics and Intelligent Systems and IEEE Conference on Robotics, Automation and Mechatronics; 19–21 November 2017; Ningbo, China. pp. 568-571

[22] Welch G, Bishop G. An Introduction to the Kalman Filter. Tech. Rep. TR95041. Chapel Hill: Dept. Comput. Sci., Univ. North Carolina; July 2006

[23] Si F, Zhao Y, Zhang X. Memory fading unscented Kalman filter and its application in navigation by stellar refraction. In: Proceedings of the 2017 IEEE Aerospace Conference; 4-11 March 2017; Big Sky, MT, USA. pp. 1-8

[24] Zhang T, Gao J, Ye F. Anti-spoofing algorithm based on adaptive Kalman filter for high dynamic positioning. In: Proceedings of the 2017 Progress in Electromagnetics Research Symposium-Fall (PIERS-FALL'17); 19–22 November 2017; Singapore, Singapore. pp. 838-845

[25] Li K, Zhang K. Building occupancy estimation with robust Kalman filter. In: Proceedings of the 11th Asian Control Conference (ASCC'17); 17-20 December 2017; Gold Coast, QLD, Australia. pp. 1406-1410

[26] Ren X, Du S, Zheng Y. Parallel RCNN: A deep learning method for people detection using RGB-D images. In: Proceedings of the 10th International Congress on Image and Signal

Processing, BioMedical Engineering and Informatics (CISP-BMEI'17); 14–16 October 2017; Shanghai, China, China

[27] Andriluka M, Roth S, Schiele B. People-tracking-by-detection and people-detection-by-tracking. In: Proceedings of the IEEE Conference on Computer Vision and Pattern Recognition (CVPR'08); 23-28 June 2008; Anchorage, AK, USA

Chapter 2

Video Surveillance-Based Intelligent Traffic Management in Smart Cities

Fozia Mehboob, Muhammad Abbas, Abdul Rauf,
Shoab A. Khan and Richard Jiang

Additional information is available at the end of the chapter

http://dx.doi.org/10.5772/intechopen.76386

Abstract

Visualization of video is considered as important part of visual analytics. Several challenges arise from massive video contents that can be resolved by using data analytics and consequently gaining significance. Though rapid progression in digital technologies resulted in videos data explosion that incites the requirements to create visualization and computer graphics from videos, a state-of-the-art algorithm has been proposed in this chapter for 3D conversion of traffic video contents and displaying on Google Maps. Time stamped visualization based on glyph is employed efficiently in surveillance videos and utilized for event detection. This method of visualization can possibly decrease the complexity of data, having complete view of videos from video collection. The effectiveness of proposed system has shown by obtaining numerous unprocessed videos and algorithm is tested on these videos without concerning field conditions. The proposed visualization technique produces promising results and found effective in conveying meaningful information while alleviating the need of searching exhaustively colossal amount of video data.

Keywords: video visualization, traffic surveillance, smart cities, glyph-based visualization, Google Maps

1. Video visualization in smart cities

The quantity of surveillance video cameras increases at the public places results in increase in automated analysis of video contents and traffic video surveillance [43] considered as one of its application. These automated systems identify a number of traffic rule violations. Video features at object, pixel, and semantic level are extracted for analysis [53, 56, 59, 60]. The basic purposes of surveillance video-based systems are vehicle tracking, analyzing their patterns and behaviors, abnormal event prediction, and detecting anomalies before their occurrence. This research aims to develop a glyph-based system for the real-time video visualization covering a comprehensive set of traffic videos on complete length of highways.

Intelligent monitoring has rapidly progressed in last 10 years and intended to provide situational awareness and semantic information for understanding the environmental activity [14, 69]. VV illustrates the joint process of video analysis and subsequent derivation of representative presentation of essence of visual contents [2, 4, 19, 34, 45, 54, 57, 68]. The visualization of videos is gaining more attention because of addressing challenges of data analysis arisen from video camera contents [1, 15, 16]. Over the past decade, VV usefulness for traffic surveillance [17, 18] application has been effectively demonstrated by researchers [3, 75, 76].

VV offers spatio-temporal summary and overview of large collection of videos, and its abstract representation of meaningful information assists the users in video content [3, 35]. Conversely, conventional techniques [67] of visual representation such as time series plot have difficulties in conveying impressions from large video collection [3].

In addition, there is need to present visual contents of videos in compact forms such that user can quickly navigate through different segments of video sequence to locate segment of interest and zoom in to different detail levels [1]. Viewing videos is time-consuming process, consequently it is desirable to develop methods for highlighting and extraction interesting features in videos. There are numerous techniques designed for data analysis in images and a variety of statistical indicators for data processing. On the contrary, there is lack of effective techniques for conveying complex statistical information spontaneously to a layperson such as a security officer, apart from using line graphs to portray 1D signal levels [1]. Many researchers studied video processing in the context of video surveillance [16], monitoring vehicles, and monitoring crowds. However, main problem in automatic video processing is communication of results of

Figure 1. Video wall.

video processing to human operator. Since statistical results are not easily comprehensible, whereas sequences of difference images again need sequential viewing [1].

Conventional video surveillance systems heavily rely on human operators for activity monitoring and determining actions to be taken upon incident occurrence. There are several actionable incidents that miss-detect in such a manual system due to inherent limitations from deploying solely human operators eyeballing CCTV screens [58]. Hence, automatic VV [56] will prove very beneficial in improved traffic management. Miss-detections might be caused by monitoring excessive number of video screens to monitor as shown in **Figure 1** and tiredness due to prolonged monitoring. In fact, numerous studies have shown the limits of human-dependent surveillance. The United States Sandia National Laboratories conducted a study in which most people attention fell below an adequate level after only 20 minutes of video surveillance screen monitoring [67]. The video content analysis paradigm is shifting from a fully human operated model to an intelligent machine-assisted automated model [58].

2. State of the art

In the field of visualization, Borgo et al. [51] carried out a comprehensive survey on video visualization. Effectiveness of VV for conveying meaningful information enclosed in video sequences was demonstrated by Daniel et al. [1]. Andrienko et al. [47] also illustrated visual analytical technique to visualize huge amount of video data. Data were clustered and aggregated to display on map by using color arrows. Wang et al. [48] presented situational understanding approach by combining the video frame in 3D environment. Romero et al. [49] used visualization approach to analyze human behavior and explored the activity visualization in normal settings over time.

Hoummady proposed survey on sensory device shortcomings that are used for collection of traffic information real time [40], and video camera usage as data collection was also proposed for traffic management. This approach relies on computational device mainly for pedestrian recognition and vehicle, 2-wheel vehicles, etc.

For traffic visualization, commonly employed approach is coloring the areas demonstrating roads on the map [44]. Ang et al. [46] presented analytical approach for management of traffic from multiple cameras. Vehicle trajectory estimation and extraction of features was done. Subsequently, Jiang [62] demonstrated the analytical technique for visualizing the huge video data. Data were clustered and aggregated to display them on map by using color arrows. Afterward, Botchen [53] proposed technique for flow and volume signature visualization. It discovered that common people can recognize events on the basis of event signatures quite than viewing entire video contents.

End users and technology providers identify that manual process is inadequate to search comprehensively massive amount of video contents and screening timely. In order to lessen these issues of visualization, we try to project camera activity on Google Maps and have summarized and holistic view of video contents. Massive video data render ineffectual manual analysis of videos; however, present automatic analytic techniques of videos undergo better performance.

A state of art visualization technique for surveillance videos is presented and tested by using several traffic videos. It receives suitable visual representations to assist the process of decision making. One can perceive level and pattern of activities that are recorded from visualization of videos as it offers more spatial info than using statistical indicators. Semantic info is obtained from numerous surveillance videos which are connected to Google Maps in order to perform 3D association. In the same time, glyph [5, 20] is familiar and conveys multi-field video visualization [10]. Well-developed visualization approach based on glyph is proposed that enables efficient and effective information encoding and visual communication.

3. Glyph-based semantic information visualization

Proposed approach aims to visualize semantic information of traffic videos using time stamped glyph. Input video frames are processed continuously to detect change in visual information. The proposed approach consists of several steps for estimation of traffic flow.

3.1. Preprocessing

First step involves the segmentation of object from the surveillance video by using thresholding and subsequently converting it to binary image from grayscale image. Parts of road are thinned out, and holes are filled in video frames using morphological operations as shown in **Figure 2**.

Object segmentation considered to be a vital process in understanding of image in the preprocessing step. The purpose of object segmentation is to divide the image into region of interest, and objects are identified from the video frame using region growing method. The process of image segmentation results in binary image contains connected components which represents the multiple objects. Connected component analysis is performed to distinguish between the connected components. Features are extracted to track the moving objects in

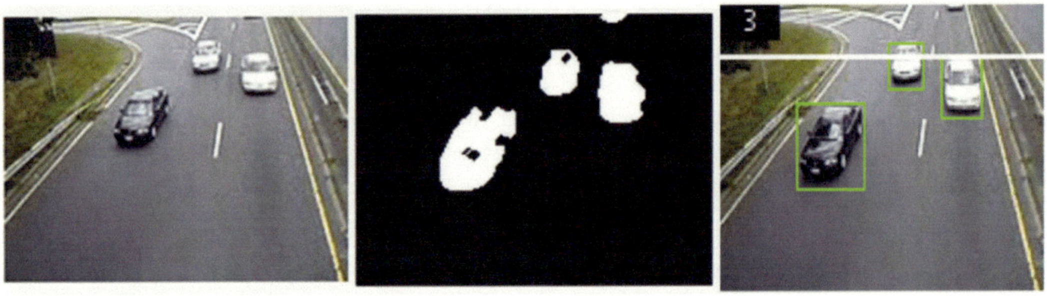

Figure 2. Vehicle segmentation from video space.

successive frames. Image is scanned pixel by pixel, and gray value of central pixel is compared with those of the top and left pixels. Surface or region grows, until it finds all the connected pixels. The values of the pixels are compared with the 3×3 neighboring pixels. If there is disconnect in the connected pixels and the gap is greater than threshold value, algorithm classifies the pixel to a new region. It is a user defined threshold whose value is chosen on the basis of distance between the pixels. All the pixels which are part of the object are set to value 1, and those which are not part of the object are set to value zero. In region growing method, 3×3 window finds all the neighboring pixels 1 and keep growing the region until pixel with zero value is found. Algorithm keeps finding the gap, and if the gap is greater than the threshold value, the algorithm classifies it as a new region. If there are only isolated pixels, they are marked as outliers. Proposed system is robust in handling problems such as occlusion and illumination variation encountered in surveillance videos. In case of sunny day, there are moving shadows of vehicles which can produce false alarms. But the proposed system estimates the vehicle size and is able to predict the shadow size. Based on the moving vehicles size, shadow can be removed. Proposed method is able to remove the extracted shadow of the vehicles. Proposed system is tested on several surveillance videos of different scenarios such as different weather conditions and densities. Proposed system is robust in handling problems such as occlusion and illumination variation encountered in surveillance videos. The data set contains a diverse set of scenarios in terms of traffic density and violations.

Traffic flow is assessed on each video frame, and the number of vehicles is counted in every frame. For every vehicle, mean speed is computed. The flow rate is found by dividing total vehicles by time. Top level flow diagram of the proposed approach is depicted in **Figure 3**.

Figure 3 represents the flow of proposed approach. Object tracking [7, 8] is part of the proposed system which collects temporal and spatial information about the object under consideration from the video sequence. Semantic information such as trajectories of detected objects is acquired by motion tracking that is given as input for mapping and 3D computation and revealing the outcomes on Google Maps. As Google space and video space coordinates are different, 3D mapping is performed amongst the two different spaces. Time-based glyph is created for representing semantic info on Google space and video.

Layout of table in order to store coordinates of vehicle is revealed in **Figure 4**. Blobs detected within frame signify the number of vehicles. It is illustrated in **Figure 4** that single vehicle exists in current video frame. Array is well-defined for storing vehicle coordinates. First two columns of array illustrate the y and x vehicle coordinates present in first frame, whereas the following y and x coordinates represents next frame coordinates of vehicle. Fifth column value demonstrates the number of frames consumed by vehicle in which vehicle becomes visible in field of view. Vanishing flag in last column defines the status of vehicle, for example, vehicle departure. Flag value remains zero till vehicles are in field of view and value will turn 1 when vehicles disappear. Last column is significant because values reshuffling in arrays change on the base of flag value.

Though, trajectories of vehicle are of different spans even vehicle travel on the same route since vehicle travel at different mean speeds [8, 12]. Motion vectors [77] are used for demonstrating information as motion information has strong relationship with semantic occurrence. Different

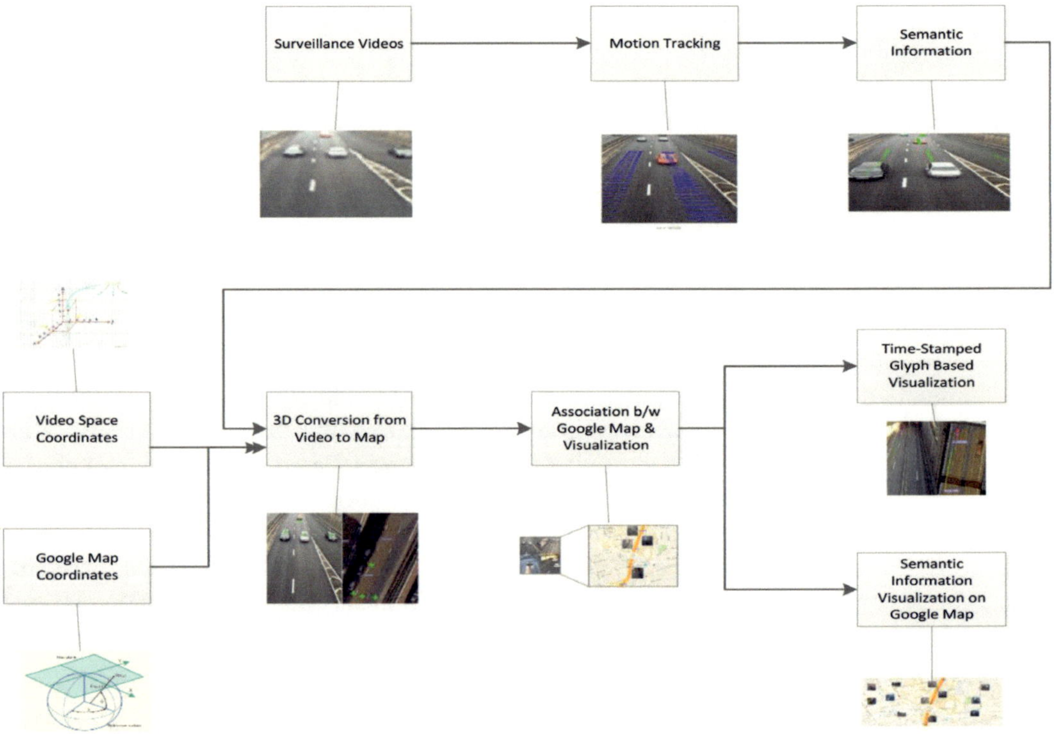

Figure 3. Top level diagram of proposed approach.

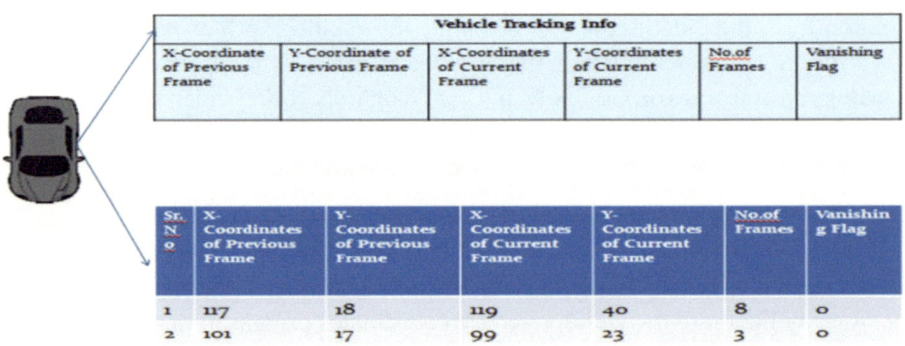

Vehicle Tracking Info					
X-Coordinate of Previous Frame	Y-Coordinate of Previous Frame	X-Coordinates of Current Frame	Y-Coordinates of Current Frame	No.of Frames	Vanishing Flag

Sr. No	X-Coordinates of Previous Frame	Y-Coordinates of Previous Frame	X-Coordinates of Current Frame	Y-Coordinates of Current Frame	No.of Frames	Vanishing Flag
1	117	18	119	40	8	0
2	101	17	99	23	3	0

Figure 4. Vehicle tracking information.

event identifications are done by analysis of motion features. Path demonstrates the vehicle movement and dynamical measurements that represent the raw vehicle trajectory. A common trajectory depiction is flow succession, for example,

$$F_T = \{f_1, f_2, \dots\dots\dots f_T\} \tag{1}$$

where the flow vectors

$$f_t = \left[x_t, y_t, v_x^t, v_y^t, a_x^t, a_y^t\right]^T \tag{2}$$

represent object velocity [v_x, v_y], position [x, y], and direction [a_x, a_y] at time t extracted by tracking the object.

3.2. Bezier fitting for glyph generation

Bezier curve mostly employed for modeling and smoothing the chaotic vehicle trajectories. Control points are used to define Bezier curve which have geometric modeling interpretation and can model trajectories inconsistency [61]. Curve is confined in control point's which are showed graphically and can be utilized for curve manipulation. By offering P_0 and P_0 points, Bezier curve is defined as straight line between two points such as,

$$\begin{aligned} B(t) &= P_0 + t(P_1 - P_0) = (I - t)P_0 + tP_1 \\ &0 \le t \le 1 \end{aligned} \tag{3}$$

That is equivalent to linear interpolation. Bezier curve is used to smooth the chaotic trajectories of vehicles obtained using motion tracking. As each car moves with different speeds, so the length of trajectories varies.

Figure 5(c) depicts the video taken from area around Northumbria University having frame rate 30fps and video resolution 1920 × 1080. Video consists of 25 frames. **Figure 5(a)** illustrates the chaotic trajectories of different vehicles that are smoothed using Bezier curve to visualize the traffic pattern as shown in **Figure 5(b)**. Time stamped semantic information is represented using glyph. Vehicle trajectory is tracked over time, and semantic info is delivered as presented in **Figure 5**. Outer circle of glyph denotes that vehicle changes lane although vehicle type was small which is signified by circle having red color. If vehicle is small and do not change the lane within field of view than outer circle of glyph is green.

Figure 5. (a) Chaotic vehicle trajectory, (b) smooth vehicle trajectory, and (c) time stamped glyph.

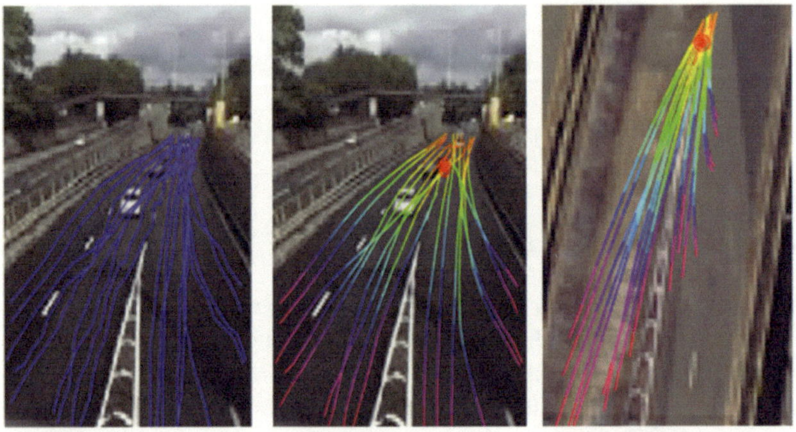

Figure 6. Proposed approach vehicle tracking.

3.3. Motion tracking and semantic event display

Motion tracking significance [9, 39, 64, 66, 71, 73] in surveillance videos is unquestionable; subsequently, it is valuable in countless applications. Semantic analysis [62, 63] of video is utilized for extraction of vital information particularly type of vehicle, speed and lane changing, and trajectory from the video [38, 41]. This semantic info is extracted automatically in order to represent indexing, high level descriptors, retrieving, and searching the video contents. Tracking of vehicle comprises of velocity, maintenance of appearance, and positioning of detected object over time. Vehicle detection is done by object linking to most alike object in consecutive video frames.

Flow vectors are used to symbolize the common trajectory representation which is basis of further analysis. **Figure 6(a)** characterizes the chaotic vehicle trajectories which are taken from different surveillance videos. Every trajectory of vehicle is attained by individual tracking of detected vehicle. **Figure 6(b)** displays the smoothed curves that are acquired by applying Bezier curve on the chaotic vehicle trajectories.

4. 3D conversion and perspective view from video space to Google Maps

To capture the real time, info is considered as main challenge in dynamic VV [39]. 3D info recovery from surveillance video is essential to acquire some significant information from the videos. As frame of videos is the projection of 3D space, abstraction of vital information is difficult task. In proposed approach, 3D transformation on Google Maps from surveillance video is processed by using homographic transformation. In homographic transformation, plane mapping to image space is performed by projective transformation that maps the point from one plane to second one. Homography amongst image space and video space is estimated requires four-point correspondence [42]. Calibration of image is acquired through transformation H, in which pixels pf image mapping on ground plane matches to latitude and longitude coordinates of maps.

Individual location of vehicle in each video frame sequence is signified by plus symbol in **Figure 7** that is computed by homography matrix in order to calculate map and of video space coordinates. In perspective projection, location or points are alike in two dissimilar spaces, however, not equivalent because of universal scale uncertainty. The homography [6, 11, 45, 72, 79] in camera-based view geometry attains a particular interpretation $H = KE$, where E represents Euclidean transformation matrix which defines camera pose while viewing, and K characterizes the matrix of camera perspective recognized as intrinsic measures. Consider a pair of correspondence points, for example, $\mathrm{p} = (\mathrm{x}_1, y_1, z_1)^T$ and $\mathrm{u} = (\mathrm{x}_2, y_2, z_2)^T$ is related by homography H:

$$\begin{bmatrix} \mathrm{x}_2 \\ y_2 \\ z_2 \end{bmatrix} \sim \begin{bmatrix} \mathrm{h}_{11}\ \mathrm{h}_{12}\ \mathrm{h}_{13}\ \mathrm{h}_{14} \\ \mathrm{h}_{21}\ \mathrm{h}_{22}\ \mathrm{h}_{23}\ \mathrm{h}_{24} \\ \mathrm{h}_{31}\ \mathrm{h}_{32}\ \mathrm{h}_{33}\ \mathrm{h}_{34} \end{bmatrix} \begin{bmatrix} x_1 \\ y_1 \\ z_1 \end{bmatrix} \tag{4}$$

Thus, each correspondence $p \leftrightarrows u$ results in two linear equations in the unknowns $\mathrm{h} = (\mathrm{h}_{11}, h_{12,\ldots\ldots\ldots\ldots, h_{34}})^T$. With manifold correspondences, numerous pairs of linear constraints need to be stored for obtaining coefficient matrix A. Least square h solution is acquired by solving the

$$(\mathrm{A}^T A)h = 0 \tag{5}$$

The h solution is acquired as eigenvector which corresponds to $AT\,A$ smallest value. Corner points of video after the H computation are projected on Google Maps correspondence points. Each position of pixel in dimension space is estimated on map by the use of H matrix, and

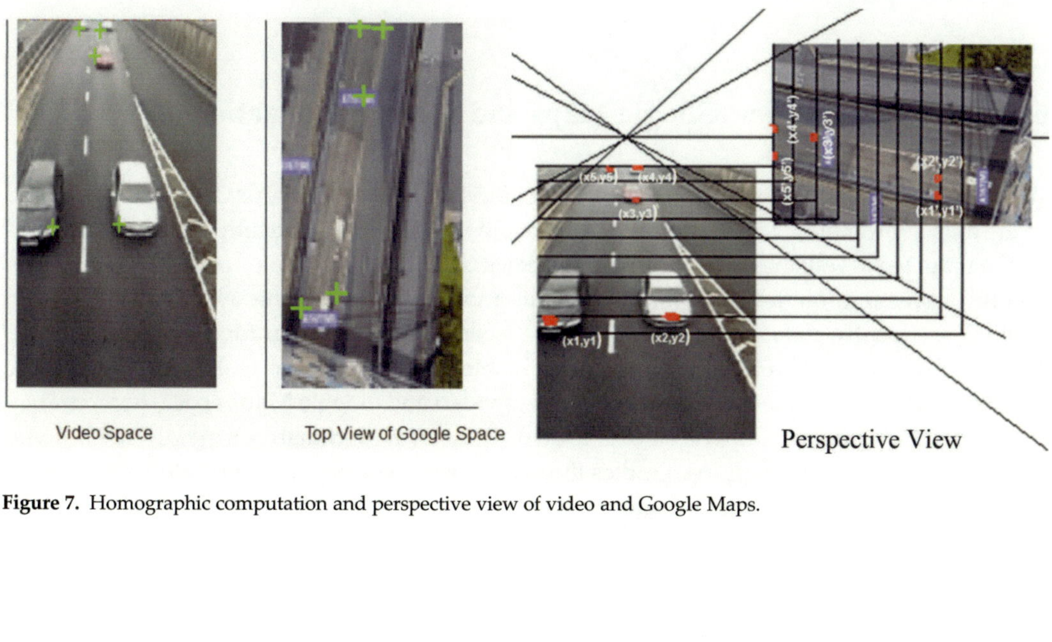

Figure 7. Homographic computation and perspective view of video and Google Maps.

resultant longitude and latitude coordinates are stored. Inverse of H is also computed to map the space coordinates on video.

5. Time stamped semantic glyph representation

Visualization based on glyph is considered as common procedure of visual scheme in which group of graphic objects is employed for representing data set known as glyph [35]. Glyph method is utilized for visualizing motion vectors that are over laid on video stream frame. Our main concern is to collect visual info that seems in all frames of video till the object remains within the view. Time stamped glyph is also generated in order to signify the type of car, speed with distinctive colors, and event information such as lane change information. The proposed system accurately determines the lane change of vehicle at a specific time due to precise localization. In the proposed system, an abnormal event detection is performed by specifically giving vehicle trajectories [52]. Trajectory analysis and interaction with scene feature allows recognizing interesting events. A time stamped glyph is generated to represent speed and lane change information of vehicle. For any image point, the position of corresponding scene point in every video frame is determined until the vehicle leaves the field of view.

There is variation in vehicle speed even in obstacles' absence because of curves and turns. Experimental data authenticate the common insight of speed which is considered most significant factors of safe driving. Variation in vehicle speed considered to be one of likely factors of congestions and accidents [37, 51, 94]. Therefore, proposed algorithm determines the speed variation of vehicles in each frame on the basis of trajectory analysis. Trajectories with different speeds are identified and represented using glyph. At each time frame, if vehicle speed is lower than the threshold, then the same color is assigned; however, if vehicle speed changes abruptly then at each instance of time, it is assigned a different color. With this time stamped identification method, precise instance of speed variation is identified in the video frame that causes a disruption in flow of the traffic movement.

6. Association between Google Maps and video visualization

To properly visualize analysis of results on Google Maps, the output must be properly aligned to the map coordinates [13]. Rectification of camera image is automatically done and mapped on the map. In surveillance video, activity is detected in each frame, and location of vehicle on ground is gained through correspondence points and trajectory learning which are mapped on map. Consequently, video inspection of several road cameras is upgraded by projecting the activity of outdoor surveillance camera on Google Maps. In order to localize the vehicle coordinates on the Google Maps or association of video and Google Maps space, homography is computed, and its perspective view is drawn. Transformation matrix provides the association information and its mapping. And as the events occur, correspondence video is visualized on the Google Maps as shown in **Figure 8**.

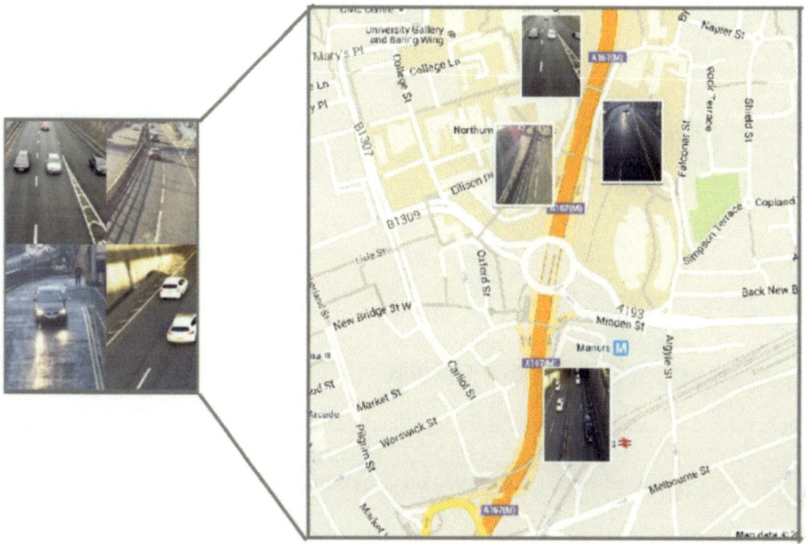

Figure 8. Holistic view of videos on Google Maps.

7. Holistic view of video using Google Maps

A surveillance video naturally takes the perspective view of the visual scene which is recognized as quasi-3D. Significant information is gathered from the different videos and is viewed to represent unusual events in videos as depicted in **Figure 8**.

In video surveillance-based system, identification of unusual events is considered to be most significant task. Anomalous behavior can be drastic and subtle [36, 58, 63]. Changing of lanes on highways is traumatic. The proposed system precisely identifies the vehicle lane change at specific time because of precise localization. Anomalous detection of events [40] can be performed by giving the trajectory [62]. Subsequently, now the vehicle trajectory specifies the frightening behavior by performing trajectory analysis. Different glyph colors during the video visualization portray the type, vehicle position, and event information within video frame.

7.1. Small scale

The proposed technique has been tested on the small scale, for example, area across Northumbria University City Campus, Newcastle Upon Tyne, UK. Detected object trajectories are shown in outcome till the objects remain in the scene using semantic glyph as shown in **Figure 9**.

There is possibility of future work in the area of visualization. Proposed visualization approach can be utilized for traffic management system at city level and have precise view of bigger cite. Spatio-temporal view of collection of videos can be acquired by mapping the trajectory on Google Maps as shown in **Figure 10**.

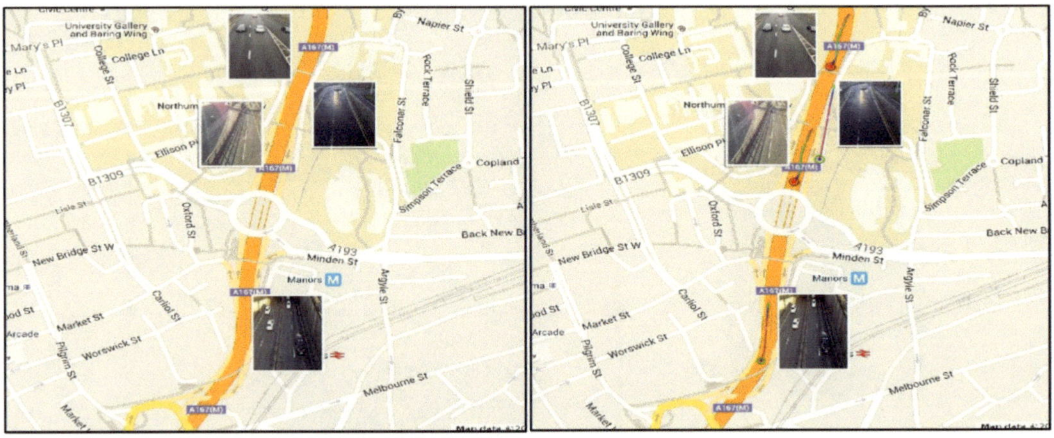

Figure 9. Time stamped glyph-based video visualization on Google Maps.

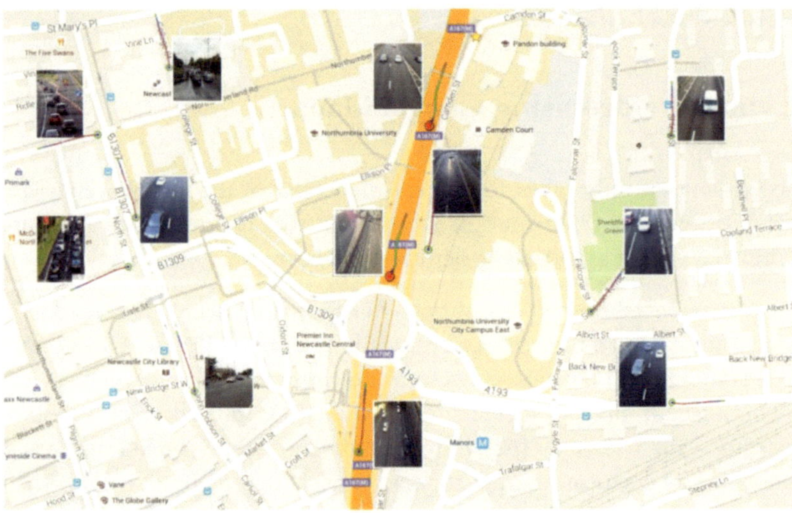

Figure 10. Multiple video visualization on large scale.

To interpret the data in real time system, visualization of video data offers instinctive information that can be expended for acquiring trends and patterns. Conversely, gathering statistics automatically from video data are computationally costly. Subsequently, Walton et al. [39] visualized the traffic video data on Google Maps to display traffic info. Though, displaying numerous traffic videos instantaneously was challenging because of heavy transmission load. Human intellect was used to gather semantic features from surveillance videos in graphic mapping scheme. Lately, Hsieh and Wang [50] proposed a traffic system for visualizing traffic information by inferring vehicle data and constitute a video in the database. Flow of traffic was assessed from surveillance videos and Google mapping was created amongst vehicle detector data and videos. While visualizing the traffic information, approach was ineffective in simulating all types of kinematics and dynamics because of driving behavior in various regions.

8. Conclusion

The concern of VV is with visual illustration of input surveillance video for see-through vital features and events in surveillance video. It is envisioned for providing assistance in intellectual reasoning whereas easing the load of observing videos. A novel visualization approach based on glyph has been proposed that can be efficiently utilized for road surveillance videos. A visual analysis is done on the basis of motion tracking to monitor live road traffic on the highways. The proposed approach has been verified on numerous video frame rates and resolution for visualizing the traffic flows. Experimental outcomes illustrate that approach can be employed in field conditions and permit better utilization of previous systems of traffic management.

Author details

Fozia Mehboob[1,3]*, Muhammad Abbas[1], Abdul Rauf[2], Shoab A. Khan[1] and Richard Jiang[3]

*Address all correspondence to: fouzia.malik10@hotmail.com

1 National University of Sciences and Technology, Islamabad, Pakistan

2 Imam Mohammed ibn Saud Islamic University (IMSIU), Riyadh, Saudi Arabia

3 Northumbria University of Digital Science and Technology, Newcastle Upon Tyne, UK

References

[1] Daniel G, Chen M. Video visualization. Proceedings of the 14th IEEE Visualization. IEEE; 2003

[2] Höferlin M et al. Evaluation of fast-forward video visualization. IEEE Transactions on Visualization and Computer Graphics; 2012. pp. 2095-2103

[3] Duffy B et al. Glyph-based video visualization for semen analysis. IEEE Transactions on Visualization and Computer Graphics; 2015. pp. 980-993

[4] Morris BT et al. Real-time video-based traffic measurement and visualization system for energy/emissions. IEEE Transactions on Intelligent Transportation Systems; 2012. pp. 1667-1678

[5] Fuchs J et al. Evaluation of alternative glyph designs for time series data in a small multiple setting. In: Proceedings of the SIGCHI Conference on Human Factors in Computing Systems; ACM; 2013

[6] Ranganathan P, Olson E. Locally-weighted homographies for calibration of imaging systems. IEEE/RSJ International Conference on Intelligent Robots and Systems; IEEE; 2014

[7] Chincholkar AA. Moving object tracking and detection in videos using MATLAB: A review. International Journal of Advent Research in Computer and Electronics (IJARCE). 2014;**1**(5):2348-5523

[8] Morris BT, Mohan MT. Learning, modeling, and classification of vehicle track patterns from live video. IEEE Transactions on Intelligent Transportation Systems; 2008; pp. 425-437

[9] Kappe CP et al. Reconstruction and visualization of coordinated 3D cell migration based on optical flow. IEEE Transactions on Visualization and Computer Graphics; 2016; pp. 995-1004

[10] Borgo R, Kehrer J, Chung DH, Maguire E, Laramee RS, Hauser H et al. Glyph-based visualization: Foundations, design guidelines, techniques and applications. Eurographics State of the Art Reports; 2013. pp. 39-63

[11] Dubrofsky E. Homography estimation [Doctoral dissertation]. University of British Columbia (Vancouver); 2009

[12] Morris BT, Mohan MT. A survey of vision-based trajectory learning and analysis for surveillance. San Diego: IEEE Transactions on Circuits and Systems for Video Technology; 2008. pp. 1114-1127

[13] Morris B, Trivedi MM. Contextual Activity Visualization from Long-Term Video Observations. San Diego: University of California Transportation Center; 2010

[14] Dee HM, Velastin SA. How close are we to solving the problem of automated visual surveillance? Machine Vision and Applications. 2008;**19**(5):329-343

[15] Cavallaro A, Ebrahimi T. Change detection based on color edges. In: IEEE International Symposium on Circuits and Systems (No. 2, pp. 141-144) (2001, May); IEEE; 1999

[16] Collins RT, Lipton AJ, Kanade T, Fujiyoshi H, Duggins D, Tsin Y et al. A system for video surveillance and monitoring (pp. 1-6). Technical Report CMU-RI-TR-00-12; Robotics Institute, Carnegie Mellon University; 2000

[17] Dollár P, Rabaud V, Cottrell G, Belongie S. Behavior recognition via sparse spatio-temporal features. In: IEEE International Workshop on Visual Surveillance and Performance Evaluation of Tracking and Surveillance; IEEE. pp. 65-72

[18] Girgensohn A, Kimber D, Vaughan J, Yang T, Shipman F, Turner T et al. DOTS: Support for effective video surveillance. In: Proceedings of the 15th ACM international conference on Multimedia; ACM; 2007. pp. 423-432

[19] Ward MO. Multivariate data glyphs: Principles and practice. In: Handbook of data visualization. Berlin Heidelberg: Springer; 2008. pp. 179-198

[20] Ward MO. A taxonomy of glyph placement strategies for multidimensional data visualization. Information Visualization. 2002;**1**(3/4):194-210

[21] Bertin J. Semiology of Graphics: Diagrams, Networks, Maps; Madison, Wis.; London: University of Wisconsin Press; 1983

[22] Maguire E, Rocca-Serra P, Sansone S-A, Davies J, Chen M. Taxonomy-based glyph design —With a case study on visualizing workflows of biological experiments. IEEE Transactions on Visualization and Computer Graphics. 2012;**18**(12):2603-2612

[23] Post F, Vrolijk B, Hauser H, Laramee R, Doleisch H. The state of the art in flow visualisation: Feature extraction and tracking. Computer Graphics Forum. 2003;**22**(4):775-792

[24] Wong PC, Foote H, Kao DL, Leung R, Thomas J. Multivariate visualization with data fusion. Information Visualization. 2002;**1**(3/4):182-193

[25] Hlawitschka M, Scheuermann G, Hamann B. Interactive glyph placement for tensor fields. In: International Symposium on Visual Computing. Berlin Heidelberg: Springer; 2007. pp. 331-340

[26] Fuchs R, Hauser H. Visualization of multi-variate scientific data. Computer Graphics Forum. 2009;**28**(6):1670-1690

[27] Pearlman J, Rheingans P. Visualizing network security events using compound glyphs from a service-oriented perspective. In: VizSEC 2007. Berlin Heidelberg: Springer; 2008. pp. 131-146

[28] Aigner W, Miksch S, Schumann H, Tominski C. Visualization of Time-Oriented Data. Berlin, Springer-Verlag; 2011

[29] Hlawatsch M, Leube P, Nowak W, Weiskopf D. Flow radar glyphs—Static visualization of unsteady flow with uncertainty. IEEE Transactions on Visualization and Computer Graphics. 2011;**17**(12):1949-1958

[30] Peng Z, Grundy E, Laramee R, Chen G, Croft N. Mesh-driven vector field clustering and visualization: An image-based approach. IEEE Transactions on Visualization and Computer Graphics. 2012;**18**(5):283-298

[31] Ropinski T, Preim B. Taxonomy and usage guidelines for glyph-based medical visualization. In: SimVis; 2008. pp. 121-138

[32] Ropinski T, Oeltze S, Preim B. Survey of glyph-based visualization techniques for spatial multivariate medical data. Computers & Graphics. 2011;**35**(2):392-401

[33] Chung DH, Legg PA, Parry ML, Bown R, Griffiths IW, Laramee RS, et al. Glyph sorting: Interactive visualization for multi-dimensional data. Information Visualization. 2015; **14**(1):76-90

[34] Botchen RP, Bachthaler S, Schick F, Chen M, Mori G, Weiskopf D, et al. Action-based multifield video visualization. IEEE Transactions on Visualization and Computer Graphics. 2008;**14**(4):885-899

[35] Parry ML, Legg PA, Chung DHS, Grif-Fiths IW, Chen M. Hierarchical event selection for video storyboards with a case study on snooker video visualization. IEEE Transactions on Visualization and Computer Graphics. 2011;**17**:1747-1756

[36] Venugopal KR, Patnaik LM. Moving vehicle identification using background registration technique for traffic surveillance. In: Proceedings of the International MultiConference of Engineers and Computer Scientists (Vol. 1); 2008

[37] Johnson C, Sanderson A. A next step: Visualizing errors and uncertainty. IEEE Computer Graphics and Applications. 2003;**23**(5):6-10

[38] Liu S, Yi H, Chia LT, Rajan D, Chan S. Semantic analysis of basketball video using motion information. In: Pacific-Rim Conference on Multimedia. Berlin Heidelberg: Springer; 2004. pp. 65-72

[39] Min Chen, Walton S, Chen M, Ebert D. LiveLayer: Real-time Traffic Video Visualisation on Geo-graphical Maps

[40] Hoummady B. U.S. Patent No. 6,366,219. Washington, DC: U.S. Patent and Trademark Office; 2002

[41] Beymer D, McLauchlan P, Coifman B, Malik J. A real-time computer vision system for measuring traffic parameters. In: Proceedings of the IEEE Computer Society Conference on Computer Vision and Pattern Recognition; IEEE; 1997. pp. 495-501

[42] Arrospide J, Salgado L, Nieto M, Mohedano R. Homography-based ground plane detection using a single on-board camera. IET Intelligent Transport Systems. 2010;**4**(2):149-160

[43] Kumar P, Ranganath S, Weimin H, Sengupta K. Framework for real-time behavior interpretation from traffic video. IEEE Transactions on Intelligent Transportation Systems. 2005;**6**(1):43-53

[44] Shekhar S, Lu CT, Liu R, Zhou C. CubeView: A system for traffic data visualization. In: Proceedings of the IEEE 5th International Conference on Intelligent Transportation Systems; IEEE; 2002. pp. 674-678

[45] Lu CT, Boedihardjo AP, Zheng J. Aitvs: Advanced interactive traffic visualization system. In: 22nd International Conference on Data Engineering (ICDE'06); IEEE; 2006. pp. 167-167

[46] Ang D, Shen Y, Duraisamy P. Video analytics for multi-camera traffic surveillance. In: Proceedings of the Second International Workshop on Computational Transportation Science; ACM; 2009. pp. 25-30

[47] Andrienko G, Andrienko N. A visual analytics approach to exploration of large amounts of movement data. In: International Conference on Advances in Visual Information Systems. Berlin Heidelberg: Springer; 2008. pp. 1-4

[48] Wang Y, Krum DM, Coelho EM, Bowman DA. Contextualized videos: Combining videos with environment models to support situational understanding. IEEE Transactions on Visualization and Computer Graphics. 2007;**13**(6):1568-1575

[49] Romero M, Summet J, Stasko J, Abowd G. Viz-A-Vis: Toward visualizing video through computer vision. IEEE Transactions on Visualization and Computer Graphics. 2008;**14**(6): 1261-1268

[50] Hsieh C-Y, Wang Y-S. Traffic situation visualization based on video composition. Computers & Graphics. 2016;**54**:1-7

[51] Borgo R, Chen M, Daubney B, Grundy E, Janicke H, Heidemann G et al.. A survey on video-based graphics and video visualization. In Proceedings of the EuroGraphics conference, State of the Art Report; 2011. pp. 1-23

[52] Denman H. Video visualization. In: Proceedings of IEEE Visualization; Seattle, WA; 2003. pp. 409-416

[53] Botchen R, Hashim R, Weiskopf D, Ertl T, Thornton IM. Visual signatures in video visualization. IEEE Transactions on Visualization and Computer Graphics. 2006;**12**(5):1093-1100

[54] Heidi Lam. Visualization and Computer Graphics. IEEE Transactions on. 2008;**14**(6):1261-1268

[55] Chen W. Automatic animation for time-varying data visualization. Computer Graphics Forum. 2010;**29**(7):2271-2280

[56] Robinson JA. Techniques for automated reverse storyboarding. IEE Proceedings - Vision, Image and Signal Processing. 2005;**152**(4):425-436

[57] Yeung MM, Yeo B-L. Video visualization for compact presentation and fast browsing of pictorial content. IEEE Transactions on Circuits and Systems for Video Technology. 1997; **7**(5):771-785

[58] Loy CC. Activity understanding and unusual event detection in surveillance videos [Doctoral dissertation]; 2010

[59] Cavallaro A, Steiger O, Ebrahimi T. Semantic video analysis for adaptive content delivery and automatic description. IEEE Transactions on Circuits and Systems for Video Technology. 2005;**15**(10):1200-1209

[60] Papadopoulos GT et al. Statistical motion information extraction and representation for semantic video analysis. IEEE Transactions on Circuits and Systems for Video Technology. 2009;**19**(10):1513-1528

[61] Faraway JJ, Reed MP, Wang J. Modelling three-dimensional trajectories by using Bézier curves with application to hand motion. Journal of the Royal Statistical Society: Series C: Applied Statistics. 2007;**56**(5):571-585

[62] Jiang F, Wu Y, Katsaggelos AK. Abnormal event detection from surveillance video by dynamic hierarchical clustering. In: IEEE International Conference on Image Processing (Vol. 5, pp. V-145); IEEE; 2007

[63] Medioni G et al. Event detection and analysis from video streams. IEEE Transactions on Pattern Analysis and Machine Intelligence. 2001;**23**(8):873-889

[64] Buch N, Velastin S, Orwell J. A review of computer vision techniques for the analysis of urban traffic. IEEE Transactions on Intelligent Transportation Systems. 2011;**12**(3): 920-939

[65] Zhu F, Li L. An optimized video-based traffic congestion monitoring system. In: Third International Conference on Knowledge Discovery and Data Mining. WKDD'10. IEEE; 2010. pp. 150-153

[66] Cheung S-CS, Kamath C. Robust background subtraction with foreground validation for urban traffic video. EURASIP Journal on Advances in Signal Processing. 2005;**2005**:2330-2340

[67] Goldgof DB, Sapper D, Candamo J, Shreve M. Evaluation of Smart Video for Transit Event Detection (No. Report No. 2117-7807-00); 2009

[68] Matthew F, Rehg JM. Video-based crowd synthesis. IEEE Transactions on Visualization and Computer Graphics. 2013;**19**(11):1935-1947

[69] Qianwen C, Shen J, Jin X. Video-based personalized traffic learning. Graphical Models. 2013;**75**(6):305-317

[70] BKP H, Schunck BG. Determining optical flow. Artificial Intelligence. 1981;**17**(1–3):185-203

[71] Hans-Hellmut N. On the estimation of optical flow: Relations between different approaches and some new results. Artificial Intelligence. 1987;**33**(3):299-324

[72] Xu C, Liu J, Benjamin K. Motion segmentation by learning homography matrices from motor signals. In: Canadian Conference on Computer and Robot Vision (CRV); IEEE; 2011

[73] Aslani S. Optical flow based moving object detection and tracking for traffic surveillance, World Academy of Science, Engineering And Technology. International Journal of Electrical, Computer, Energetic, Electronic and Communication Engineering. 2013;**7**(9)

Chapter 3

Advance Intelligent Video Surveillance System (AIVSS): A Future Aspect

Mritunjay Rai, Agha Asim Husain,
Tanmoy Maity and Ravindra Kumar Yadav

Additional information is available at the end of the chapter

http://dx.doi.org/10.5772/intechopen.76444

Abstract

Over the last few decades, remarkable infrastructure growths have been noticed in security-related issues throughout the world. So, with increased demand for Security, Video-based Surveillance has become an important area for the research. An Intelligent Video Surveillance system basically censored the performance, happenings, or changing information usually in terms of human beings, vehicles or any other objects from a distance by means of some electronic equipment (usually digital camera). The scopes like prevention, detection, and intervention which have led to the development of real and consistent video surveillance systems are capable of intelligent video processing competencies. In broad terms, advanced video-based surveillance could be described as an intelligent video processing technique designed to assist security personnel's by providing reliable real-time alerts and to support efficient video analysis for forensic investigations. This chapter deals with the various requirements for designing a robust and reliable video surveillance system. Also, it is discussed the different types of cameras required in different environmental conditions such as indoor and outdoor surveillance. Different modeling schemes are required for designing of efficient surveillance system under various illumination conditions.

Keywords: surveillance system, AIVSS, digital camera, types of camera, background model, illumination

1. Introduction

In recent times, surveillance systems are gaining a lot of popularity. The government, various organizations, residential societies, etc., are using these systems to keep a check on various activities for safety and security purposes. Earlier surveillance systems had a lot of dependence on human operators, it is lately that automated systems are being preferred because of their better efficiencies and reliability [1]. It has been seen that surveillance with full human operators' involvement has certain inadequacies like the high cost of labor, variations in long-duration capturing and limited ability for multi-screen monitoring [2]. Traditional surveillance systems are being complemented and even replaced by the advanced intelligent surveillance systems (AISS), as the latter is used in identifying abnormal behavior and patterns in videos by developing artificial intelligence technologies, pattern recognition, and computer vision. This enables high accuracy monitoring of more scenarios by a few observers. In the last few years, the video surveillance market has seen a major transformation into third generation video surveillance systems, moving to IP video from traditional analog video causing better processing power and improved compression algorithm [3]. These Intelligent video surveillance systems are not just confined to laboratories but have hit the marketplace as well. With this generation, the era of Intelligent Video Surveillance began, not only in research labs but also in the marketplace. With the start of 2010, many research labs, such as Kiwi Security Labs, started to broadcast the "Advanced Intelligent Video Surveillance Systems" (AIVSS). With this production, a new category of features is presented, which are expected to have a big impact on the marketplace security and a sensor control. The **Figure 1**, shows an Intelligent Video Surveillance System. All the components of the system are interconnected using many cameras for critical sites, by means of IP mega pixel cameras. Selective ID protection feature has been provided in this architecture of AIVS.

Here, the disseminated keen design of the AIVS was used to execute the component Selective ID Protection. Appropriately, the system could respect the current security law necessities in a few nations, notwithstanding the prerequisites of governments and knowledge specialists to ensure the character of their operators.

Apart from the hardware (H/W) and software (S/W) which are considered as performance improvisers and the architecture of inter-operational processing, the performance of the

Figure 1. The distributed architecture of the advanced intelligent video surveillance system.

system depends upon the privacy of the system. Moreover, in many countries, privacy issues are becoming more crucial and are considered as a performance decelerator. On one side, the performance of the network depends upon the performance of each of Network Element (NE), access performance, transmission performance, etc., which are also considered as performance decelerator and on the other side, the network's performance depends much upon the Security Management Process [4] of the advanced IVS system. Protection assumes again a noteworthy part of security execution and in security administration forms and accordingly on the system execution as an execution decelerator. From the perspective of the Security Management Process, the suggestive development of process science was the driving potential to build up an elite propelled IVS, which uses a keen Security Management Process, which is controlling the system execution, i.e., system accessibility, secrecy and trustworthiness, bringing about a substantial scale vital answer for security specialists and governments [3, 4], **Figure 2** demonstrates the execution effect of the progress smart video surveillance system [5].

The remaining structure of the article is organized as the Section 2 deals with the basic requirements for designing of video surveillance system including different types of cameras and video management systems using surveillance display. Section 3 discusses the surveillance system for both indoor and outdoor environmental especially with illumination conditions. Section 4 discusses the different modeling schemes used for surveillance systems. Lastly, Section 5 holds the conclusion and the future aspects.

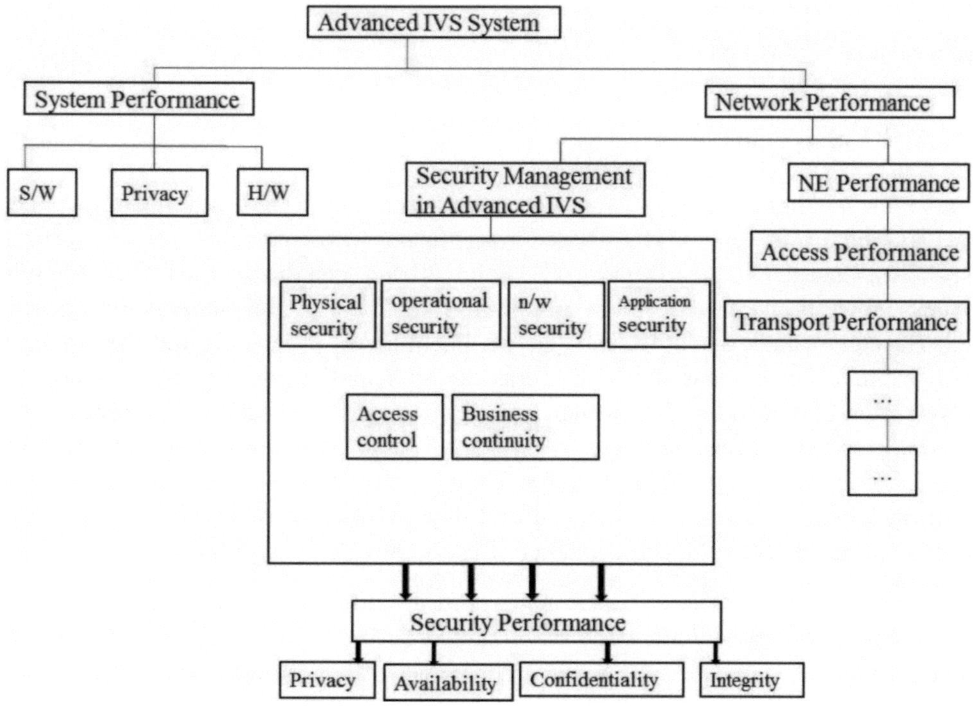

Figure 2. Performance impact on the distributed architecture of the advanced intelligent video surveillance system.

2. Video surveillance system design requirements

This section provides the details of decisions taken while designing the video surveillance system. The design of a video surveillance system requires decisions that need familiarity with the basic options and the basis behind the selection of any available choice in the market [11]. So, designing a system requires better remote access, further remarkable mix with different systems, enhanced picture quality and additionally that requires flexibility with others system [12, 13]. In any case, for end clients to take the full preferred standpoint of the advantages, the outline and execution of the arrangement should be precisely arranged and executed. This will guarantee the system is adaptable and future-sealed and is proper for a client's need. These six stages cover guidance about choosing the correct hardware, an assessment of the accessible innovation and help with the decisions that should be made. The following decisions are to be made for designing of video surveillance system are as follows:

1. Camera and its type.
2. Video management system.
3. Types of video management system.
4. Storage type.
5. Types of video analytics.
6. Surveillance video display.

2.1. Camera and its type

In late 1990s, the digital cameras came into the market, they were built on Complementary Metal Oxide Semiconductor (CMOS) based image sensor whose performance is better and are cheaper than Charge-Coupled Devices (CCD). It has been seen during the last decade that on an average there is an annual growth rate of around 12% of digital cameras throughout the world. The credit can be attributed built-in intelligent image processing and pattern recognition algorithms. These smart digital cameras can spot motion, detect objects, read vehicle number plates, and even identify human behaviors. They have become an essential component to build active and automated control systems for many applications and will continue to play a significant role in our daily life in the future [7]. Smart cameras are generally intended to perform specific, repetitive, high-speed and high-accuracy jobs. The typical applications of these smart cameras are Machine vision or intelligent video surveillance systems (IVSS).

Video surveillance technology is functionally used in traffic cameras [9], which are used for traffic footage recording and are many times shown during traffic reports on TV news. They are placed over the traffic signals, along with the busy roads, and at busy junctures of the

http://dx.doi.org/10.5772/intechopen.76444

highway. Whether they record the movement of traffic for future study or to monitor traffic and issue challans/tickets for any traffic rule violations, they are an extremely popular form of video surveillance. They are commonly used in the monitoring & management of traffic, computerized parking garages, driver support and control access systems, etc. License Plate Recognition (LPR) is the most well-known and widely used application in the category of traffic management and monitoring. Yet, due to increasing demand other categories of vehicle classification have been added recently. Make and Model Recognition (MMR) & Color Recognition (CR) of cars is a major and comparatively new functionality which helps in detecting the model of the car, along with the vehicle types for, e.g., Light Motor Vehicle, Heavy Motor Vehicle, etc. Installation of Camera plays an important role in the advance intelligent video surveillance system.

Cameras are the key contributors to the video surveillance system. The camera position and the type of cameras used under various conditions are important factors in video surveillance. These two parameters are briefly explained below:

i. **Positions for camera installation:** Cameras should be placed in appropriate areas to record relevant video. The appropriate areas for proper placement of cameras can be entrances, hallways, driveways, T- Points, highway intersection points, exits, etc., and in areas where there is a high density of people or vehicles. Moreover, cameras can be placed in areas that require security such as parking spots, VIP areas, schools, restaurants & hotels, bank locker rooms, hospitals, etc. Planting cameras at crucial and suitable points is a cost-effective way to monitor and document people and vehicles arriving and departing certain facility.

ii. **Type of cameras to be used:** There are many types of camera available on the market. The suitability of the camera depends upon the situation in hand. Fixed camera can be used for recording only one specific view while a PTZ camera is generally used to cover wider fields of views. Mostly fixed cameras are used in video surveillance as they are five to eight times less costly than PTZ cameras. Color cameras are preferred during day time and in highly illuminated areas. However, during night time and in poorly lit areas infrared or thermal cameras are used that gives black and white images. Thermal cameras can also be used under settings of complete darkness, where they produce only contours of objects. Cameras can be standard definition or high definition cameras that provide a resolution of up to 16 MP.

IP cameras digitize the recordings within the camera while analog cameras' recordings (which are used as surveillance cameras) are digitized on the computer. Video surveillance systems usually make use of a combination of different type of cameras. Some of the camera types are discussed briefly as under:

a. **PTZ camera:** One of the commonly used camera for security purpose is PTZ camera; where P stands for Pan, T for Tilt and Z for Zoom. Pan, Tilt, and Zoom are the main features of this camera which is controlled by a software or via joystick. This security camera has an ability to rotate 360 degrees so that it can cover a wide area and can zoom into detail. The other features that attract toward this security camera are Weatherproof, Night Vision, Multiple Alarms, Auto Focus, and Tamper Resistant.

b. **Box camera:** Box Style security camera is an outdoor camera where customization of the lens is possible. The lens can be variable or fixed. Box surveillance camera is an ultra-high-resolution CCTV camera made with the new image sensor processor which is capable of capturing video at 700 TV lines of resolution in color and black & white, 960H CCTV resolution. This box camera includes a 6-60 mm variable focal auto-iris lens which gives security installers a lot of flexibility to adjust the camera angle of view and zoom level.

c. **Dome camera:** It is a combination of lens, camera and ceiling mount packaged in a dome shape. This is well suited for surroundings that tend to get dirty, like kitchens and storerooms, etc., the best part of it is compact in size and artistically very attractive too.

d. **IP camera:** An Internet Protocol camera generally transmits a digital signal using Internet Protocol over a network. The main features of these security cameras are its high resolution and scalability. Right now, up to 30 Mega pixels are available in the market.

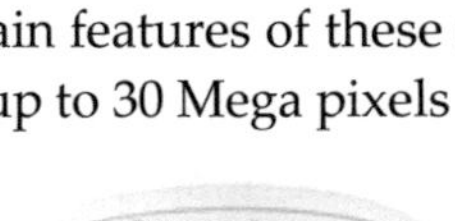

e. **Wireless IP camera:** As its name suggests that this type of camera is completely wireless, installation is easy and reduces the rate of network cabling. The camera also has the feature of tilting and revolving which helps in maximum viewing with clarity and even in low light conditions.

f. **Bullet camera:** This security camera shaped like a bullet which is a combination of camera, lens and packaged in a bullet style. This camera is good for dim light situations and can be easily mounted to ceilings or walls because most of them use a tri-axis type of base. Bullet cameras come in all sizes (small, medium & large). Infrared bullet cameras generally are larger in diameter to put up the extra space that their infrared Light Emitting Diodes require.

g. **Day and night camera:** This security camera is used for both indoor and outdoor environments with low or dim illumination conditions. A day and night camera has distinctive lenses that permit infrared emission formed by infrared LEDs and imitated from objects to go through and reach to a Charge Coupled Device or Complementary MOSFET chip inside the camera. As a result, the end user can see the picture in total darkness at the distance of infrared emission produced by LEDs. A day and night camera can have infrared LEDs mounted on its housing or can accept the emission, produced by an infrared steeple. A Day and night cameras over and over again have changes in their digital signal processor that pays for the alteration in illumination between day and night methods.

h. Thermal camera (FLIR): The first commercial thermal imaging camera was used in 1965 for high voltage power line inspections. Since then the utility of thermal imaging cameras for industrial applications has become a pivotal market segment for FLIR (Forward-looking IR) systems, a later name for high voltage power lines. The thermal imaging technology has drastically evolved since then, and thermal imaging cameras have evolved to become compact in size and look like a digital photo camera, they are now easy to use and produce real-time crisp high-resolution images making them a widely important tool for industrial applications [8]. They can detect anomalies that are generally invisible to the naked human eye, thus taking corrective preventing costly systems going for a total breakdown. Thermal imaging cameras are used to determine the maintenance requirements for electrical and mechanical installations as they tend to generate unusual heat before they fail. Preventive actions can be taken by discovering these hot-spots. A thermal imaging camera is a non-invasive instrument which scans and visualizes the temperature distribution of surfaces of a machine quickly and accurately, thus reducing cost and saving time across the world.

2.2. Video management system

Video management system is the recording and management of access to the video, which is captured by a camera and is then transferred to the module of the video surveillance system [4]. There are two types of connections through which the captured video is transferred:

i. Videos can be transmitted over the computer network IP or they can be sent as analog videos. Videos from both IP cameras and analog cameras can be transferred over the computer network whereas unlike analog cameras, IP cameras can connect directly to an IP network. In case of analog cameras, an encoder must be installed to transmit analog video over IP. The input from an analog camera is encoded and output a digital stream for transmission over an IP network.

ii. Depending upon whether IP camera or analog video camera is used, the captured video can be transmitted over cables or through the air. Cables are generally considered inexpensive and the most reliable method of transferring video but, wireless is an important alternative for transmitting videos as setting wires can be expensive for certain applications such as parking lots, fence lines, remote buildings, etc.

2.3. Types of video management system

In a Video management system, videos taken by the cameras are stored, managed and are transmitted to various viewers. The video management systems usually used in video surveillance systems are:

a. In a digital video recorder (DVR), videos are recorded from a surveillance camera on a hard disk. It is a security system device in which the rate of the frame can be converted from real-time to time lapse to save the disk space. They are more flexible as compared to earlier analog VHS tape systems and allow easier transmission of video over a computer network. Digital Video Recorders accepts only analog camera feeds as inputs and supports remote viewing over the Internet. DVR is a combination of software, hardware, and video storage.

b. Hybrid digital video recorders (HDVRs) support IP cameras. They can perform all the functions of a digital video recorder mentioned above and adds support for IP and megapixel cameras.

c. Network video recorder (NVR) supports IP cameras only, however, to support analog cameras it requires an encoder. NVR can record videos from a no. of digital CCTV cameras that are transmitted over the network.

d. IP video surveillance software is a product application that does not accompany any equipment or capacity. The client must load and set up the PC/server for the product which gives considerably more prominent opportunity and possibly bring down cost yet in the meantime it accompanies noteworthy greater many-sided quality and time important to set up and advance the system. IP video surveillance software is the most regular decision for video systems that contain extensive camera tallies like at least hundreds.

2.4. Storage type

In a video surveillance system, storage of the surveillance video is very vital. This video is used for later retrieval and review. Cost of storage and security related fears specific to the application of the video surveillance system determines the duration for which the video should be stored [11]. For example, in supermarkets and restaurants video recordings are kept for a relatively shorter duration as compared to the bank where there is a greater need to hold videos for a longer duration (60–90 days) as there is a major threat of fraudulent investigations that are often reported after many days of the incident. The digital data is stored permanently in the Storage, till it is purposely deleted. Even without power, this source holds its content. Storage generally means magnetic disks, solid-state disks, and USB drives and may also refer to magnetic tapes and optical discs like CDs, DVDs, etc. Although storage prices are falling, the demand for the surveillance system and for the amount of storage is rising. Several techniques have been developed to optimize the use of storage because of its high cost. There are three main types of storage:

i. Hard drives that are built inside a digital video recorder, network video recorder or server represents the internal storage. It is the most reasonably priced but may be less reliable and scalable. Most frequently it is used in video surveillance systems and can provide a storage of 2 TB to 4 TB.

ii. Directly attached storage are the hard drives that are located outside of the digital video recorder, network video recorder or server. It is more expensive as compared to internal storage but has greater scalability, flexibility, and redundancy.

iii. Capacity clusters are IP based capacity places had some expertise in putting away video gushing from an expansive number of cameras. They give proficient, adaptable and versatile capacity.

2.5. Video analytics type

Video analytics encompasses the below-mentioned tasks:

i. **Storage optimization:** Storage optimization is realized based on the motion detection. The video management systems decide to store the video when any motion/ moving object [10] is spotted in the observed scene or else the video is either not stored or is stored at a lower frame rate or a lower resolution to save storage space. Cameras may capture long durations of inactivity when placed in buildings when they are locked, staircases, etc. This application helps in reducing the consumption of storage by 60–80% as compared to continuous recording.

ii. **Identify threatening events:** Video analytics can also be used to identify threatening events to pro-actively identify any lapse in security incidents, be alert, and to stop them; for example, license plate recognition, perimeter violation, abandoned objects detection, and people counting.

2.6. Display of surveillance video

Videos captured by a surveillance system are eventually viewed by human beings and is usually used for past investigations. Some surveillance videos are watched online continuously, e.g., in educational institutions to keep a check on student actions, in shops to keep an eye on shoplifters and in public areas to identify criminal threats. Some surveillance videos are viewed online infrequently by the owner of the apartment. Videos can be viewed in 4 different ways:

i. **Local:** It is viewed directly from the digital video recorder. Small facilities like Banks, retail outlets, and small businesses ideally use the network video recorder to monitor their sites.

ii. **Remote:** It is viewed through standard remote PCs for viewing live and recorded videos through an installed application, a web browser, or a powerful web viewing.

iii. **Mobile:** This kind of viewing allows an instant check of the captured video. It holds great importance in video surveillance systems. Mobile clients exist in the market for the last few years, but there are challenges related to its implementation on PDAs/phones. However, a few latest technology phones have renewed interest in mobile viewing.

iv. **Video:** Big security operation centers where a lot of cameras must be examined or scrutinized, video wall viewing is generally preferred. Video walls offer a very big screen so that many people can watch the captured videos from a number of cameras at the same time. They can change between numerous video streams and could automatically show videos from points where alarms have been triggered.

http://dx.doi.org/10.5772/intechopen.76444

3. Surveillance system and its types

The word Surveillance has been derived from the French word "sur" means "from above" and "veiller" means "to watch." Surveillance means to monitor behaviors, movements, activities, and information for controlling, managing, and protecting people. It can include observing from assistance through an electronic device like CCTV cameras (Closed-circuit television) or by keeping a track on electronically transmitted information like on phone calls & internet traffic. It may also include a number of or relatively lesser technology means such as intelligence agents, detectives, etc. Surveillance systems are readily being used by governments for crime prevention and investigation, in intelligence gathering, and to protect people, objects, processes, etc. For many, surveillance may be a violation of one's privacy and has often been criticized by many civil liberty activists. Laws in many countries have restricted their domestic government & the private use of surveillance, generally restraining it to situations where public safety is in jeopardy.

Dictator government at times have any residential confinements, and universal secret activities are normal among a wide range of nations. While observation systems have been exceptionally ordinary for business properties, it took a while for them to wind up plainly mainstream for private homes too. One reason is that wrongdoing insights demonstrate that the further developed and cutting edge a security and observation system is, the more culprits will maintain a strategic distance from them through and through. Also, the cost of camera gear for home utilization has altogether dropped as of late. The best sorts of observation system have certain traits that you should give careful consideration to remember the ultimate objective to ensure that you totally secure your property. One fundamental thing is that the system must be effortlessly expandable to guarantee that as and when required you can cover more indoor and outdoor regions with cameras.

More established systems can be extremely restricted once introduced and will likewise just permit a specific constrained measure of identification gadgets, including cameras, vibration, and movement locators. This can turn out to be expensive if a system must be supplanted because of extending business or private premises. Here are two or three signs on what to pay uncommon identity to while exploring diverse sorts of security systems that will expand insurance.

3.1. Outdoor video surveillance

Outdoor video cameras play a very important role in law enforcement by not only capturing video of potential criminals but also by preventing crimes. Past statistics on crimes show that the more noticeable and better technology the camera systems are, the more it helps in preventing criminal activities in business or residential buildings [6]. Factors that are necessary for an outdoor camera are: they should be weather- resistant, and should include night vision even in well-lit locations. This helps in ensuring that switching off the light may not affect the camera captures. Cameras should be installed at a point capturing a wider angle & that is not easily accessible from the ground.

3.2. Indoor video surveillance

There is no necessity for Indoor cameras to be weatherproof, that means they are easier to install, are smaller with lesser restrictions. For indoor locations as shown in **Table 1**, a camera that provides a very wide angle of view is needed so as reduce the requirement of the no of cameras and to reduce the dark spots. Night vision and quality of the video captured are also essential for Indoor video surveillance.

3.3. Illumination and artificial lighting

Amid no light conditions, it is not conceivable to see anything, yet to security cameras, they are barely exceptional, some high fragile security cameras can get clear monochrome images

Intruder detection • Intrusion detection • Object tracking • Detection of an object in uncrowded scenes	
Counting • Statistical analysis • Marketing • Traffic flow analysis and reporting • High accuracy	
Nonmotion detection • Detects static changes to a scene • Handle crowded and busy environment • Can detect tiny objects • Can detect invisible object in low contrast	
Crowd management • Crowd management • Traffic management • Queue management	

Table 1. Different application areas of video surveillance system.

in starlight lighting up condition, they in like manner can see the object in whole darkness while using additional infrared lighting. In this section, we offer the essential finding out about the general lighting up, and the wide grouping of fake lighting. Lux is a prevented unit in see from claiming lumen, and the lumen is a precluded unit in light from securing candela. The lumen (structure: lm) is the SI unit of luminous change, a measure of the vitality of light obvious by the human eye and the candela is the SI base unit of luminous intensity. One lux is equal to one lumen for each square meter, where 4n lumens is the total luminous change of a light wellspring of one candela of luminous intensity.While picking a proper surveillance camera to present, make a point to consider the illumination condition in the environment. Lux, it is the illumination level unit used to address the allocated domain illumination. In incredible illumination region, the customer can use a general execution security camera. In any case, the shading system for environmental illumination is under 2.0 Lux, a monochrome illumination system for under 0.2 Lux environment use the higher execution security camera (i.e., starlight security camera), which is extremely fundamental. Using Lux meter can evaluate illumination level. If we do not have a lux meter, we can follow the general illumination data table.

Utilizing infrared LEDs to transmit vague (to human) infrared lights. The infrared light wave length is 850 nm, which empowers camera to get monochrome images. While using the IR illumination, the camera will encounter infrared-submersion issue because the photo setback purposes of enthusiasm for objects arranged in central and short division watching an area. Remembering the true objective to handle this issue, IR sharp development was brought into various security cameras. The Infrared splendid limit can modify camera's Infrared intensity as demonstrated by the watching objects, keep up a vital separation from IR-drenching issue. Starting at as of late, the IR illumination can cover 0–200 meters independent. Using white light LEDs to illuminate the area under observation. The white light LED wavelength is 450 nm, which has a place with noticeable light.

The white light illumination can empower camera catch shading images in low illumination or zero illumination environments. Compared with infrared illumination, white light illumination can work in particular application, for example, acknowledgment of vehicle number plate. Moreover, the white light illumination can be utilized to stop interlopers/crooks. Sony double light IP camera can naturally turn on white light illumination when individuals stroll into observing territory. The white light has substantially shorter illumination separate than infrared, its range is 0–50 m. Frequently, laser maker is set up into PTZ camera which offers 30× optical zoom limit. The bigger piece of laser maker utilizes 808 nm wavelength diodes, laser maker has various purposes of intrigue; long detachment illumination, adaptability, acclimate to the environment, long life expectancy. Laser illumination can help the camera to get clear images with high clearness. Besides, it enables the camera to get pictures inside 1 kilometer or even 3 km long partitioned.

In indoor surveillance, the cutting edge highlights liberal change revelation and following estimation. Indoor conditions are passed on utilizing unmistakable truly little spaces that are pulled back with dividers and give each other through passages and sections. In this condition, it is crucial to relate the district of a specific individual in various parts of the building structure. It is less pivotal to track continually the difference in a man as this movement will no vulnerabilities or conceivably buts break reliably because of building's geology. In outside surveillance, the cutting edge moreover merges veritable change request and following tallies. The limit is that these figures are normally stunningly besides made than the relating indoor checks on account of the distinctive quality presented by exceedingly factor lighting.

The topology of outside conditions is correspondingly completely not exactly the same as that of indoor conditions. Moving things are people and what more vehicles is in like manner, going at all around higher speed. Snappier moving things require faster sorting out paces, yet the figuring is liberally more computationally than those related to indoor surveillance conditions. These repudiating necessities on a to a great degree basic level mean the specific difficulties of a pushed outside security system. Utilizing Lux meter can check light level. If you do not have a lux meter, you can propose **Tables 2** and **3** to the running with general illumination information.

At the point when security camera works in entire darkness environment (i.e., 0 Lux), the camera picture sensor would not have the capacity to catch images. In this condition, the cameras have an artificial lighting system, for example, infrared LEDs, white light LEDs, and

S. No.	Places	Luminance intensity (in Lux)
1.	Warehouse	20—75
2.	Emergency passway	30—75
3.	Corridor	75—200
4.	Shop	75—300
5.	Office	300—500
6.	Bank	200—1000
7.	Meeting room	300—1000

Table 2. Various indoor illumination conditions at different places.

S. No.	Places	Luminance intensity (in Lux)
1.	Sunny	10,000—1,000,000
2.	Cloudy	100—10,000
3.	Dawn Twilight	1—10
4.	Full moon over head	0.1—1
5.	Quarter moon	0.01—0.1
6.	Sunny Starlight	0.001—0.01
7.	Cloudy Starlight	0.0001—0.001

Table 3. Various outdoor illumination conditions at different places.

also laser producers. These counterfeit lighting systems can help the camera to catch clear monochrome or shading images in low illumination or zero illumination environments. As of late, Hikvision and Sony propelled day and night security cameras which use double lighting system.

4. Different strategies for smart video observation

The present security system could be outlined as takes after: (a) security system act locally and they do not participate in compelling way (b) high esteem resources are ensured deficiently by obsolete innovation system. (c) Reliance on escalated human focus to identify and survey dangers. Various strategies and calculations have been created and actualized, basically in programming, for question following, identification, and acknowledgment. A couple of endeavors have been made to execute a portion of the calculations in equipment. Be that as it may, those endeavors have not yielded ideal outcomes as far as exactness, power and memory necessities. The decision of the ideal calculation can upgrade the execution and help in settling these difficulties. Many question discovery calculations are by all accounts fantastic applicants (e.g., difference-of-Gaussians (DoG), maximally stable extremal regions (MSER), fully affine invariant feature detector (FIAF), scale invariant feature transform (SIFT), speeded up robust features (SURF), background subtraction, and so on.), contrasting in their capacities and prerequisites.

a. Background subtraction

Foundation subtraction is generally utilized for recognizing moving articles from static cameras. By evaluating the foundation, it would then be able to subtract it from the info outline, by applying some limit esteem, to get the frontal area, i.e., the question. Diverse procedures could be utilized to gauge the foundation, the easiest expect the foundation to be the past casing, and another probability is to apply a mean/middle channel for the keep going N outlines, and accepting the foundation to be the outcome. This calculation is versatile to dynamic foundation changes, simple to actualize and quick and pertinent for constant usage. Be that as it may, the disadvantages are its reliance on the question speed, outline rate, colossal memory, and above all, the edge utilized is neither worldwide nor time-invariant. A vigorous foundation subtraction calculation ought to have the capacity to deal with lighting changes, monotonous movements from the mess and long-haul scene changes [14, 15]. The accompanying examinations influence utilization of the capacity of $V(x,y,t)$ as a video to succession where t is the time measurement, x and y are the pixel area factors. For example, $V(1,2,3)$ is the pixel power at (1,2) pixel area of the picture at $t = 3$ in the video grouping. A portion of the foundation subtraction techniques are examined underneath:

1. Using frame differencing

A movement identification calculation starts with the division part where the frontal area or moving items are sectioned from the foundation. The easiest method to execute this is to take a picture as foundation and take the casings got at the time t, indicated by I (t) to contrast and the foundation picture meant by B. Here utilizing basic number-crunching computations, we can portion out the articles basically by utilizing picture subtraction method of PC vision importance for every pixel in I(t), take the pixel esteem indicated by P[I(t)] and subtract it with the comparing pixels at a similar position on the foundation picture meant as P[B].

In a mathematical equation, it is written as:

$$P[F(t)] = P[I(t)] - P[B]$$

The background is assumed to be the frame at time t. This difference image would only show some intensity for the pixel locations which have changed in the two frames. Though we have seemingly removed the background, this approach will only work for cases where all foreground pixels are moving and all background pixels are static. A threshold "Threshold" is put on this difference image to improve the subtraction (see Image thresholding).

$$|P[F(t)] - P[F(t+1)]| > \text{Threshold}$$

This implies the distinction picture's pixels' intensity is "thresholded" or sifted based on the estimation of Threshold. The precision of this approach is reliant on speed of development in the scene. Quicker developments may require higher edges

2. Mean filter

For figuring the picture containing just the foundation, a progression of going before pictures arrive at the midpoint of. For figuring the foundation picture now t,

$$B(x, y, t) = \frac{1}{N}\sum_{i=1}^{N} V(x, y, t-i)$$

where N is the quantity of going before pictures taken for averaging. This averaging alludes to averaging comparing pixels in the given pictures. N would rely on the video speed (number of pictures every second in the video) and the measure of development in the video. In the wake of figuring the foundation B(x, y, t) we would then be able to subtract it from the picture V(x, y, t) at time t = t and limit it. In this manner the closer view is given as:

$$|V(x, y, t) - B(x, y, t)| > \{Th\}$$

where Th is a threshold. Similarly, we can also use median instead of mean in the above calculation of B(x, y, t).

a. Maximally stable extremal regions (MSER)

The MSER calculation is an intrigue area identifier initially utilized as a part of wide-standard stereo coordinating. MSER works on the information picture straightforwardly with no smoothing, which brings about the location of both fine and coarse structures [16]. MSER performs all around contrasted with other nearby finders. The principle favorable circumstances of the MSER recognition are that it is the speediest relative invariant area locator. To the best of our insight, the main downside of the MSER is that its execution debases with obscured pictures, which can be settled utilizing keen establishment of the camera topology.

b. Speeded up robust features

SURF is a scale-and pivot invariant intrigue point indicator and descriptor. The calculation extricates striking focuses on the picture and registers descriptors of their surroundings that are invariant to scale, turn and brightening changes. Nonetheless, identification and extraction are computationally requesting and consequently cannot be utilized as a part of systems with restricted computational power [17].

5. Discussion and conclusion

The principal points of Advance Intelligent video surveillance system (AIVSS) are to build up an observation system which can function as an indoor/open-air observation system. As Advance Intelligent Video Surveillance System has a more extensive degree to take a shot at. As nowadays security and protection assume an essential part of the survival of the individual. The perfect observation engineering will have the accompanying attributes: elite, adaptability, simple upgradability, low advancement cost, and a movement way to bring down cost as the application develops and volume inclines. Also, the step by step expanding innovations restricted the working of the Surveillance system, therefore the level of security must be expanded with a specific end goal to stop the obstruction of interlopers. At present, the video surveillance industry utilizes simple CCTV cameras and interfaces as the premise of observation systems. These system parts are not effortlessly expandable and have low video determination with practically zero flag preparing. Nonetheless, the up and coming age of video surveillance systems will supplant these segments with more current computerized LAN cameras, complex picture handling, and video-over-IP steering. They will never again be essentially surveillance camera systems yet in addition video correspondence systems.

The internet protocol (IP) based structure of the new surveillance systems takes into consideration versatility, adaptability, and digital security. Different encoding and translating gauges transport the video stream (MPEG4 CODEC is the standard utilized today). Other than the CODEC work, picture pre-and post-handling improves the photo quality progressively with low dormancy. Programmable rationale with inserted DSP squares, recollections, interfaces, and off-the-rack IP arrangements enables a planner to meet the new system requirements. Security surveillance systems can be generally isolated into a few components, for example, cameras, interchanges, stockpiling, picture preparing, and administration and back-end. Beginning with the camera, the present observation cameras are pushing toward the top-quality period. Regardless of whether it is an IP camera that has turned out to be generally acknowledged or HD-SDI cameras broadcasting in superior quality, they both can give up to full 1080p HD determination surveillance pictures. Giving completely clear pictures is the main role of shrewd surveillance, so top quality picture catch is fundamental, so the data gave by the camera can be handled precisely. In this way, top notch cameras have turned into a key part of observation system merchants. Be that as it may, cameras are only one a player in the general surveillance system, and regardless of whether an ever-increasing number of cameras and video encoders are incorporated, progressed and complex picture examination is still performed on the backend, regularly using cloud-based preparing administrations.

Author details

Mritunjay Rai[1]*, Agha Asim Husain[1], Tanmoy Maity[1] and Ravindra Kumar Yadav[2]

*Address all correspondence to: er.mritunjayrai@gmail.com

1 Department of MME, IIT(ISM), Dhanbad, India

2 Department of ECE, SIET, Greater Noida, India

References

[1] Aldasouqi I, Hassan M. Human face detection system using HSV. In: Proceedings Ninth WSEAS Int. Conf. On Circuits, Systems, Electronics, Control & Signal Processing. Stevens Point, Wisconsin, USA: World Scientific and Engineering Academy and Society (WSEAS); 2010. pp. 13-16

[2] Salahat E, Saleh H, Mohammad B, Al-Qutayri M, Sluzek A, Ismail M. Automated real-time video surveillance algorithms for SoC implementation: A survey. IEEE International Conference on Electronics Circuits and Systems. December 2013

[3] Hae-Min Moon. Implementation of the Privacy Protection in Video Surveillance System. Proceedings of the Third IEEE International Conference; 2010

[4] Kraus K. Security management process for video surveillance system. Proceedings in Advanced Intelligent Video Surveillance, Proceedings of IFIP Wireless Days, 6th IFIP Network Control Conference; November 2008

[5] Kraus K. High performance security management processing in advanced intelligent video surveillance. Informatics and Systems (INFOS), The 7th International Conference. March 2010:28-30

[6] Foresti LG. A real-time system for video surveillance of unattended outdoor environments. IEEE Transactions on Circuits and Systems for Video Technology. 1998;**8**(6):697-704

[7] Foresti LG, Regazzoni CS. A change detection method for multiple object localization in real scenes. In Proceedings of IEEE Conference. 1994:984-987

[8] Rai M, Maity T, Yadav RK. Thermal imaging system and its real time applications: A survey. Journal of Engineering Technology. July 2017;**6**(2):290-303. (ISSN: 0747-9964)

[9] Inigo RM. Application of machine vision to traffic monitoring and control. IEEE Transactions on Vehicular Technology. 1989;**38**(3):112-122

[10] Mecocci A. Moving object recognition and classification in external environments. Signal Processing. 1989;**18**(2):183-194

[11] Lingkang GU, Mingzheng Z. Intelligent surveillance system used one new method of image recognition. International Conference on E-Business and E-Government (ICEE). May 2011:6-8

[12] Wang X. Intelligent multi-camera video surveillance: A review. Pattern Recognition Letters. 2013;**34**(1)

[13] Venetianer PL, Deng HL. Performance evaluation of an intelligent video surveillance system—A case study. Computer Vision andImage Understanding. 2010;**114**(11):1292-1302

[14] McIvor A. Background subtraction techniques. In: Proc. of Image and Vision Computing, New Zealand; November 2000

[15] Piccardi M. Background subtraction techniques: A review. Proceedings of the IEEE International Conference on Systems, Man, and Cybernetics. October 2004;**4**:3099-3104

[16] Matas J, Chum O, Urban M, Pajdla T. Robust Wide Baseline Stereo from Maximally Stable Extremal Regions. Proc. 13th British Machine Vision Conf. pp. 384-393; 2002

[17] Bay H, Tuytelaars T, Van Gool LJ. SURF: Speeded Up Robust Features. In ECCV. 2006. pp. 404-417

Section 2

Human Activity Recognition

Chapter 4

Real-Time Action Recognition Using Multi-level Action Descriptor and DNN

Cheng-Bin Jin, Trung Dung Do, Mingjie Liu and
Hakil Kim

Additional information is available at the end of the chapter

http://dx.doi.org/10.5772/intechopen.76086

Abstract

This work presents a novel approach to the problem of real-time human action recognition in intelligent video surveillance. For more efficient and precise labeling of an action, this work proposes a multilevel action descriptor, which delivers complete information of human actions. The action descriptor consists of three levels: posture, locomotion, and gesture level; each of which corresponds to a different group of subactions describing a single human action, for example, smoking while walking. The proposed action recognition method is able to localize and recognize simultaneously the actions of multiple individuals using appearance-based temporal features with multiple convolutional neural networks (CNN). Although appearance cues have been successfully exploited for visual recognition problems, appearance, motion history, and their combined cues with multi-CNNs have not yet been explored. Additionally, the first systematic estimation of several hyperparameters for shape and motion history cues is investigated. The proposed approach achieves a mean average precision (mAP) of 73.2% in the frame-based evaluation over the newly collected large-scale ICVL video dataset. The action recognition model can run at around 25 frames per second, which is suitable for real-time surveillance applications.

Keywords: multilevel action descriptor, action recognition, video surveillance, deep neural networks

1. Introduction

Visual action recognition—the detection and classification of spatiotemporal patterns of human motion from videos—is a challenging task, which finds applications in a variety of domains including intelligent surveillance system [1], pedestrian intention recognition for advanced driver assistance system (ADAS) [2], and video-guided human behavior research [3]. For delivering complete description about human actions, this work proposes a multilevel action descriptor (**Figure 1**) to solve the existing representation problem of an action. For instance, traditional methods give the action representation of *phoning* for one person who is *phoning while running* and the same action descriptor for another person who is *phoning while sitting*. The action semantics for these two cases should be substantially different. The first difference is posture: one person is *standing*, and the other is *sitting*. The second difference is locomotion: one person is *running*, and the other is *stationary*. The proposed multilevel action descriptor consists of three levels: posture, locomotion, and gesture, which describe different categories of human subactions in a single action to address the above problem. Each level of subaction can be recognized by a corresponding convolutional neural network (CNN)-based classifier, which captures different appearance-based temporal features to represent a human subaction.

Most of the existing works [4, 5] have focused on video-based action recognition (*"Is there a certain action in the video?"*) trying to classify the video clip as a whole via globally pooled features. This global feature pooling method works well, however, fails to consider the difference in the actions of multiple individuals that are present at the same time. For instance, one person in the video is *texting* and, besides him, another person is *smoking*. In our work, the problem of action detection in video surveillance is addressed as: *"is there a certain action in the video, and where is it spatially and temporally?"* The rationale behind the action detection strategy is partly inspired by the technique used in a recent paper [6], where the regions of

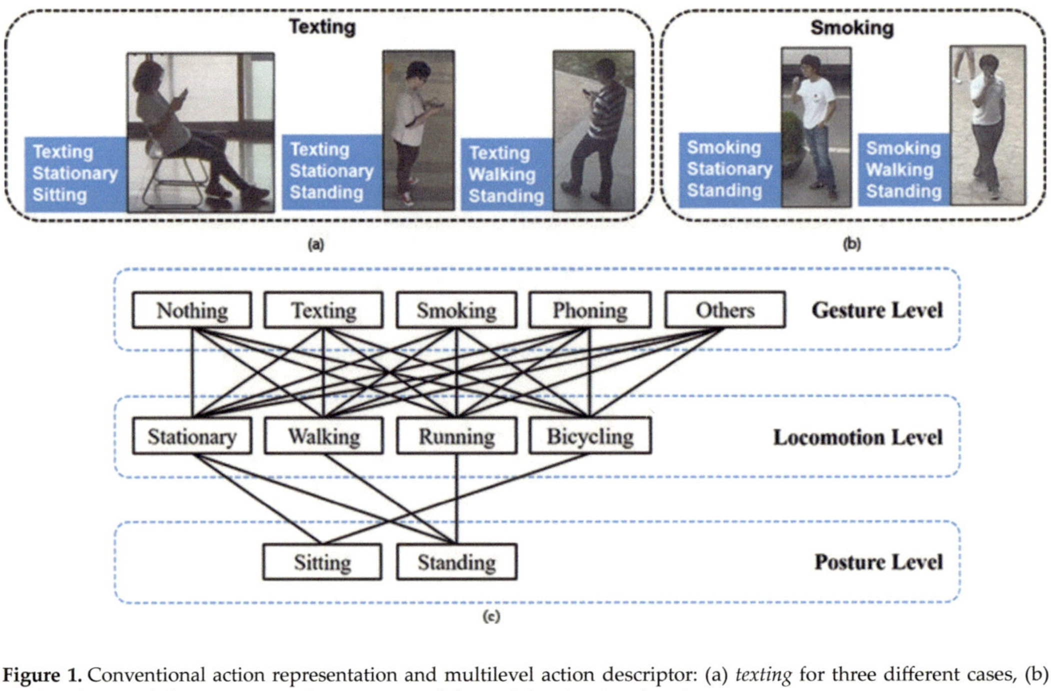

Figure 1. Conventional action representation and multilevel action descriptor: (a) *texting* for three different cases, (b) *smoking* for two different cases, and (c) structure of the multilevel action descriptor.

action are located and then classified to improve the representational power and classification accuracy.

This work aims to develop a real-time action recognition system with localizing and recognizing actions for multiple persons at the same time. Many works have been studied to estimate human pose [7–10] and analyze motion information [11] in real time. However, to the best of our knowledge, the real-time multilevel action descriptor was first introduced by the authors in [12] and this work is the extended version by adding two new actions, *bicycling* and *phoning*, and the evaluation of the processing time.

Figure 2 shows the overall scheme of the proposed real-time action recognition model. Through background modeling, motion-detection, human-detection, and multiple-object tracking, the appearance-based temporal features of the regions of interest (ROIs) are fed into the three CNNs, which make predictions using the shape, the motion history, and their combined cues. In the training phase, the ROIs and the multilevel action annotations are acquired manually in each frame of the training videos, and three appearance-based temporal features, namely—binary difference image (BDI), motion history image (MHI), and weighted average image (WAI)—are computed from the ROIs. Every level of the subaction has its own CNN classifier denoted as PostureNet, LocomotionNet, and GestureNet, respectively.

In the testing phase, the prediction of each CNN in the multi-CNN model corresponds to the decision in one subaction level. A motion saliency region is generated using a Gaussian mixture model (GMM) to eliminate regions that are not likely to contain the motion. This

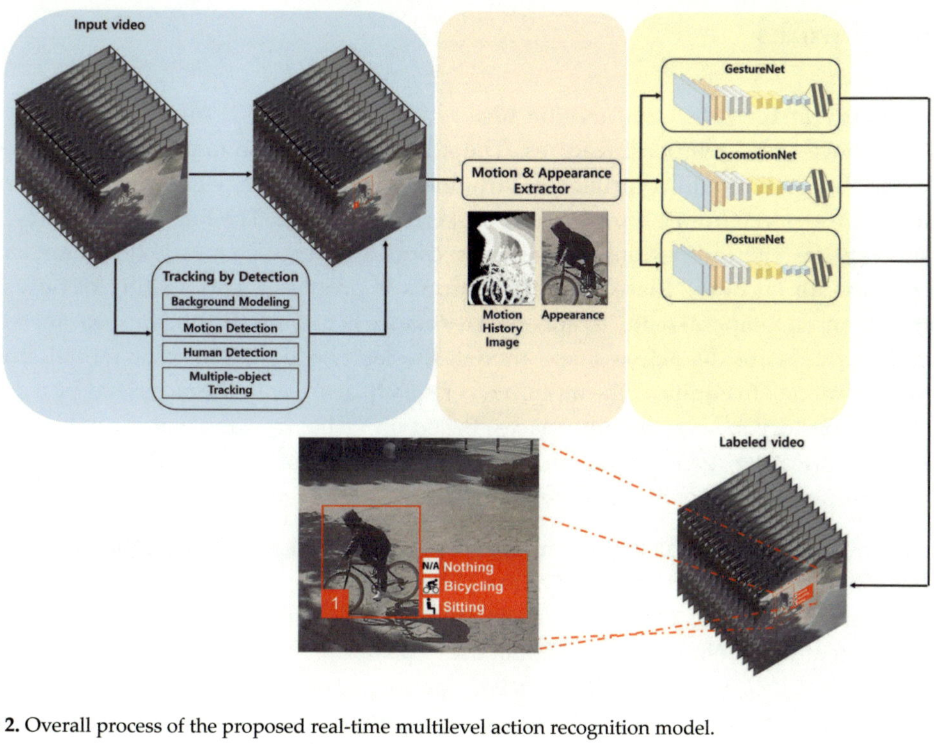

Figure 2. Overall process of the proposed real-time multilevel action recognition model.

leads to a big reduction in the number of regions to be processed. The conventional sliding window-based scheme is used on the motion saliency region as a mask. In the sliding window, a human-detection histogram of oriented gradient (HOG) descriptor [13] with a latent support vector machine (SVM) [14] is used to detect an initial human action in the ROIs. Then, the regions undergo Kalman filtering-based refinement of the locations in the image plane. Given the refined action in the ROI, the shape, the motion history, and their combined cues are used with the aid of the CNNs to predict three subaction categories. Finally, the postprocessing stage checks for any conflicts in the structure of the subaction descriptor and applies temporal smoothing according to the previous action history of each individual for the purpose of noise reduction.

The main contributions of this work can be summarized as follows:

- The multilevel action descriptor is presented for the real-time action recognition. The multilevel action descriptor consists of three levels. The combination of subaction from three levels can describe many different types of actions precisely. Furthermore, new subactions or action-levels can be easily incorporated into the multilevel action descriptor.
- A real-time action recognition model is developed on the basis of appearance-based temporal features with a multi-CNN classifier. Presented in this study is a model for action recognition that simultaneously localizes and recognizes multiple actions of individuals with both low computational cost and high accuracy.

2. Related works

Motion energy image (MEI) and motion history image (MHI) [15, 16] are the most pervasive appearance-based temporal features. The advantage of these methods is that they are simple, fast, and efficient in controlled environments, for instance, when the background of the surveillance video (from a top-view camera) is always static. The fatal flaw in MHI is that it cannot capture interior motions—it can only capture human shapes [12]. In our work, a novel method for encoding these temporal features is proposed, and a study of how many appearance-based temporal features affect performance is provided. Other appearance-based temporal methods are the active shape model, the learned dynamic prior model, and the motion prior model. In addition, the motion is consistent and easily characterized by a definite space-time trajectory in some feature spaces. Based on visual tracking, some approaches use motion trajectories (e.g., generic and parametric optical flow) of predefined human regions or body interest points to recognize actions [17, 18].

Over the past few years, local spatiotemporal feature-based algorithms are the most popular ones for recognizing human actions. Laptev [19] proposed space-time interest point (STIP) by extending the 2D Harris corner to a 3D spatiotemporal domain. Kim et al. [20] introduced a multiway feature pooling approach that uses unsupervised clustering of segment-level HoG3D [21] features. Li et al. [22] extracted spatiotemporal features that are a subset of improved dense trajectory (IDT) features [5, 23], namely, histogram of flow (HoF), motion

http://dx.doi.org/10.5772/intechopen.76086

boundary histogram (MBH), MBH_x, and MBH_y, by removing camera motion to recognize egocentric actions. However, the disadvantage of the local spatiotemporal algorithms is that it is computationally expensive.

Some alternative methods for action recognition have been proposed. Vahdat et al. [23] developed a temporal model consisting of key poses for recognizing higher level activities. Lan et al. [24] introduced a structure for a latent variable framework that encodes contextual information. Jiang et al. [6] proposed a unified tree-based framework for action localization and recognition based on an HoF descriptor and a defined initial action segmentation mask. Lan et al. [25] introduced a multiskip feature-stacking method for enhancing the learnability of action representations. In addition, hidden Markov models (HMMs), dynamic Bayesian networks (DBNs), and dynamic time warping (DTP) are well-studied methods for speed variation in actions. However, actions cannot be reliably estimated in real-world environments using these methods.

Computing handcrafted features from raw video frames and learning classifiers on the basis of the obtained features are a basic two-step approach used in most of the existing methods. In real-world applications, the design of the feature and the choice of the feature are the most difficult and highly problem-dependent issues. Especially for human action recognition, different action categories may look dramatically different according to their appearances and motion patterns. Deep CNNs make some impressive results for the task of action classification [26, 27]. Karpathy et al. [28] trained a deep CNN using 1 million videos for action classification. Gkioxari and Malik [29] built action detection models that select candidate regions using CNNs and then classify them using SVM. Using two-stream deep CNNs with optical flow, Simonyan and Zisserman [30] achieved a result that is comparable to IDT [5]. Ji et al. [31] built a 3D CNN model that extracts appearance and motion features from both spatial and temporal dimensions in multiple adjacent frames.

3. Proposed model for human action recognition

3.1. Multilevel action descriptor

Intraclass variation in the action category is ambiguous, as shown in **Figure 1(a)** and **(b)**. Although the actions of the three persons are *texting* in **Figure 1(a)**, they can be distinguished from a deeper aspect: the first is *texting while sitting*, the second *texting while standing* and is *stationary*, and the third is *texting while walking*. Assigning the same action label (*texting*) is insufficient in video surveillance because they are of different states either in posture or in locomotion for the same action. This is the same problem for the action of *smoking* in **Figure 1(b)**.

The proposed multilevel action descriptor is depicted in **Figure 1(c)**, where the subactions shown in each level are just examples that have been studied in this work and can be easily expanded by adding new subactions. Each of the three action levels, posture, locomotion, and gesture, has a corresponding CNN, and the total three CNNs work simultaneously. The first network, PostureNet, operates on a static cue and captures the shape of the subject of the motion. The second network, LocomotionNet, operates on a motion cue and captures the history of the motion of the subject. And, the third network, GestureNet, operates on a combination of static and motion cues and captures the patterns of a subtle action by the subject. In this descriptor, three levels can be combined to represent many different types of actions with a large degree of freedom.

3.2. Tracking by detection

For real-time applications, a processing time of 20–30 ms for each frame, a stable bounding box for the human action region, and a low false detection rate are the important factors for human detection and tracking. Therefore, we adapt existing methods to provide a stable human action region for subsequent action recognition.

The sliding window is the bottleneck in the processing time of the object detection because many windows, in general, contain no object. To this end, motion detection is performed before object detection to discard regions that are void of motion. The size of the mini motion map is computed with the following equation:

$$\text{size}_{\text{mni-map}} = \frac{\text{size}_{\text{original}} - \text{size}_{\text{detection}}}{\text{stride}}. \tag{1}$$

The default value of $\mathbf{size}_{\text{detection}}$ is (64, 128) and that of **stride** is (8, 8) in HOG [12]. **Figure 3** shows the mini motion map. For instance, if the size of the original image is 640 × 360, then the size of the mini motion map is 77 × 34.

In object tracking, three cases exist in the data association problem: (1) adding a new track, (2) updating an existing track, and (3) deleting a track [32]. The procedure for handling multiple detections and tracks is shown in **Figure 4**. When a new track is added, it starts to count the number of frames that the track has updated without detection. If the number is larger than the threshold n_{skip}, the track is considered being disappeared and is therefore deleted.

Figure 3. Mini motion map for reducing the unnecessary computation in the HOG-based human detector: (a) original image with a size of 640 × 360 and (b) mini motion map with a size of 77 × 34, which was calculated from the GMM-based motion detection.

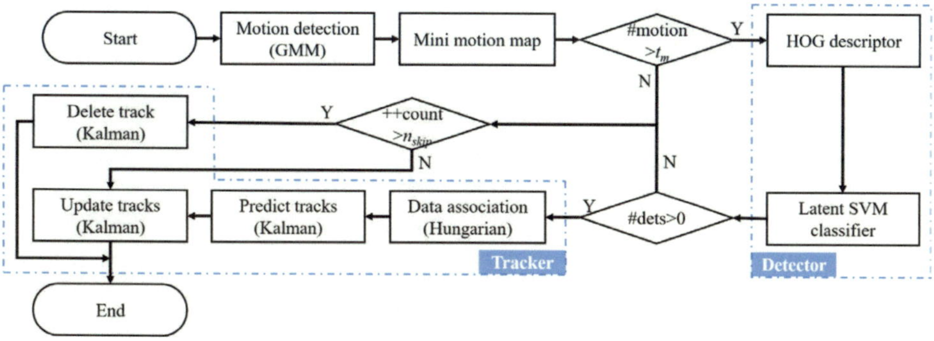

Figure 4. Procedure for multiple detections and tracks.

3.3. Appearance-based temporal features

Appearance-based temporal features are very simple, fast, and work effectively in controlled environments, such as in surveillance systems where the cameras are installed on rooftops or high poles. Therefore, the view angles of the cameras are toward dominant ground planes. A video F is just a real function of three variables:

$$F = f(x, y, t). \tag{2}$$

The frame coordinate (x, y) and t is the index of the video frame. In a multilevel action descriptor, each level has one independent CNN that obtains different appearance-based temporal features. The BDI encodes the static shape information of the subject, denoted as $b(x, y, t)$, and is given by Eq. (3):

$$b(x, y, t) = \begin{cases} 255, & if f(x, y, t) - f(x, y, t_0) > \xi_{thr} \\ 0, & otherwise \end{cases}, \tag{3}$$

It calculates the difference between the current frame $f(x, y, t)$ and the background frame $f(x, y, t_0)$ and compares with a threshold ξ_{thr}. Examples are given in **Figure 5** where BDIs are utilized for the posture level of the subaction descriptor, for example, *sitting* and *standing*.

In a motion history image, pixel intensity is a function of the temporal history of motion at that point. MHI captures the motion history patterns of the actor, denoted as $h(x, y, t)$, and is defined using a simple replacement and a decay operator in Eqs. (4)–(6) [14].

$$d(x, y, t) = \begin{cases} 255, & if f(x, y, t) - f(x, y, t-1) > \xi_{thr} \\ 0, & otherwise \end{cases} \tag{4}$$

$$h(x, y, t) = \begin{cases} \tau_{max}, & if d(x, y, t) = 255 \\ max(0, h(x, y, t-1) - \Delta\tau) & otherwise \end{cases} \tag{5}$$

Figure 5. Examples of BDI for different subactions.

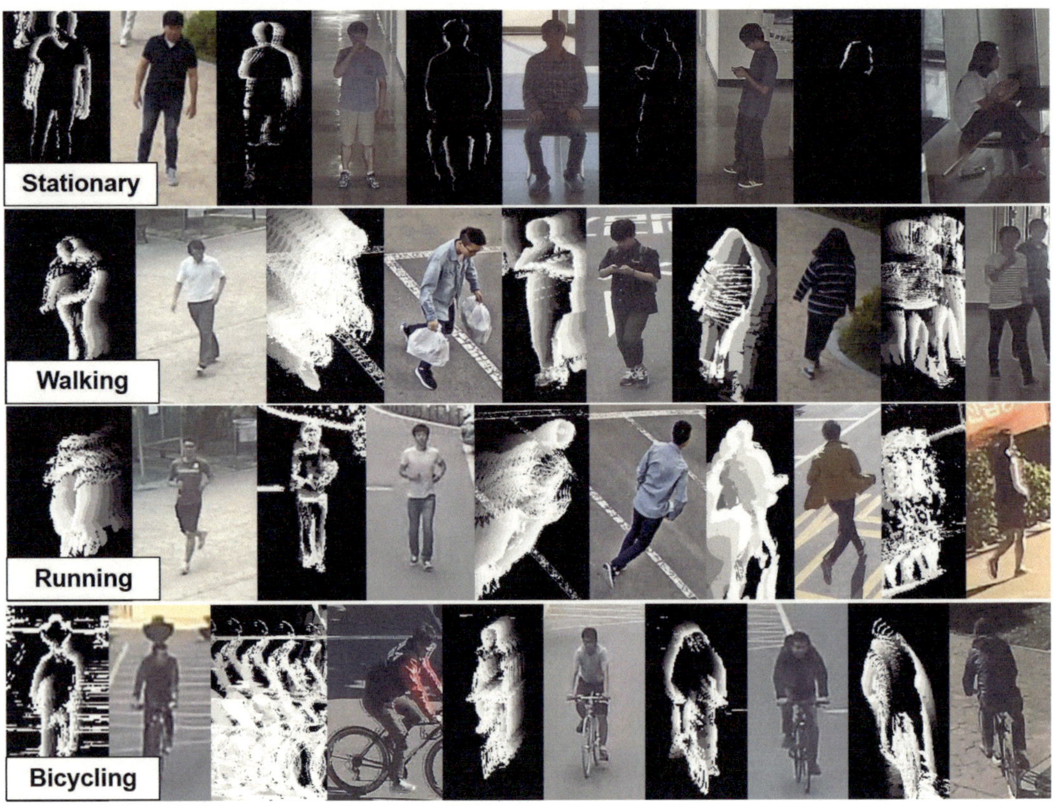

Figure 6. Examples of MHI for different subactions.

$$\Delta\tau = \frac{\tau_{max} - \tau_{min}}{n}. \qquad (6)$$

MHI is calculated from the difference between the current frame $f(x, y, t)$ and the previous frame $f(x, y, t\text{-}1)$ in Eq. (4). MHI is a vector image of motion, where more recently moving regions are brighter (see **Figure 6**). MHIs are used for the locomotion level of the multilevel action descriptor, which comprises *stationary*, *walking*, *running*, and *bicycling*. MHI captures the motion history cue of the subject, where more recently moving pixel regions are brighter. In Eq. (6), hyperparameter n is critical in defining the temporal range of an action. An MHI with a large n covers a long range of action history; however, it is insensitive to current actions. Similarly, MHI with a small n puts the focus on the recent actions and ignores past actions. Hence, choosing a good n can be fairly difficult.

Weighted average images (WAIs) are applied at the gesture level of the multilevel action descriptor, which comprises *nothing*, *texting*, *smoking*, *phoning*, and *others*. For recognizing

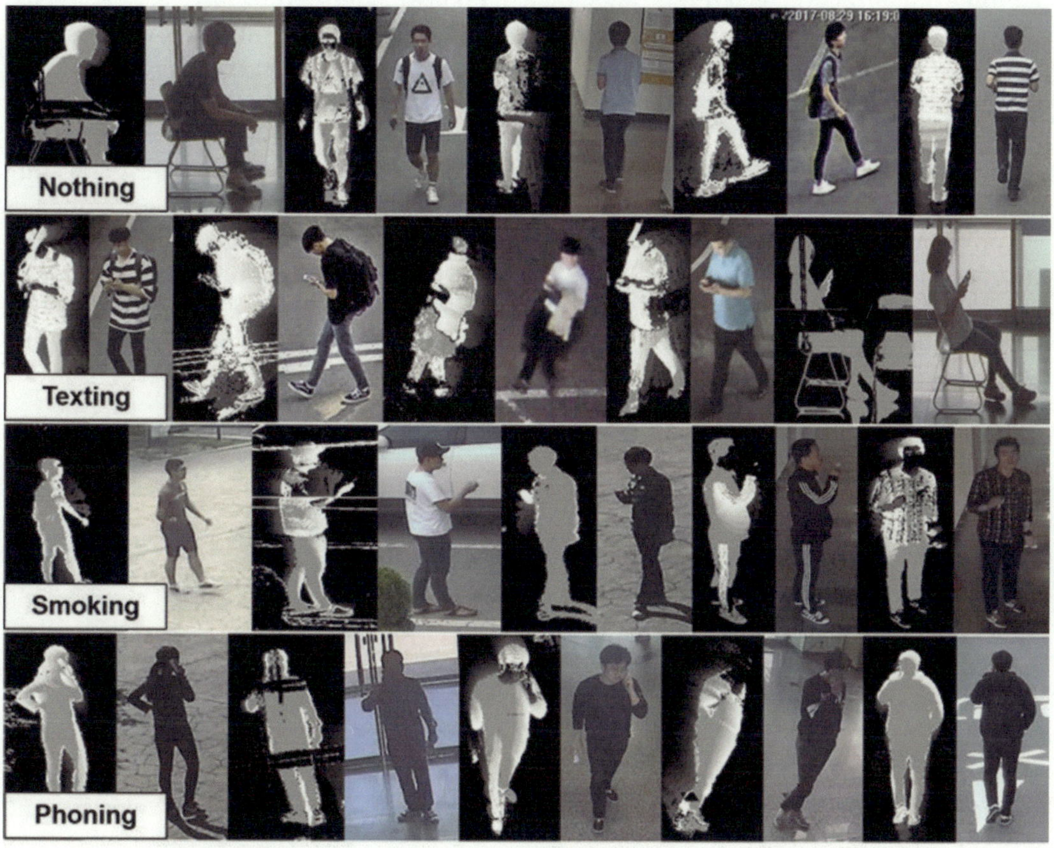

Figure 7. Examples of WAI for different subactions.

subtle actions, the easiest way would be to use the shape or motion history of the actor. It is constructed as a linear combination of BDI and MHI, which is given by Eq. (7):

$$s(x, y, t) = w_1 \cdot b(x, y, t) + w_2 \cdot h(x, y, t), \quad \text{s.t. } w_1 + w_2 = 1. \tag{7}$$

Here, $\mathbf{w} = \{w_1, w_2\}^T$ is another hyperparameter. **Figure 7** shows some examples of WAI for different subactions. WAIs were applied at the gesture level of the subaction descriptor, which comprises *nothing, texting, smoking, phoning,* and *others*. WAI obtained the combined cues of the shape and the motion history. *Texting* (frequently moving fingers) and *smoking* (repeated hand-to-mouth motion) were captured in WAIs.

3.4. Multi-CNN action classifier

In order to reduce the computation time, a lightweight CNN architecture is devised for real-time human action recognition, as shown in **Figure 8**. The architectures of PostureNet, LocomotionNet, and GestureNet are identical with two convolutional layers, two subsampling layers, two fully connected layers, and one softmax regression layer. However, they need to be trained based on the different training data of multilevel action descriptor. The architecture of the network is as follows: Input-Convolution-ReLUs-Max pooling-Convolution-ReLUs-Max pooling-Fully connection-Dropout-Fully connection-Dropout-Fully connection-Softmax regression. The output layer consists of the same number of units as the number of subactions at the corresponding level of the descriptor. If the computational efficiency is not critical, one could use more complicated architectures [33, 34]. In our study, Adam optimizer [35] is used with a learning rate of 1e−3 and $\beta_1 = 0.5$ with a batch size of 256 examples and a weight decay of 5e−4. The networks are trained for 1K iterations [36].

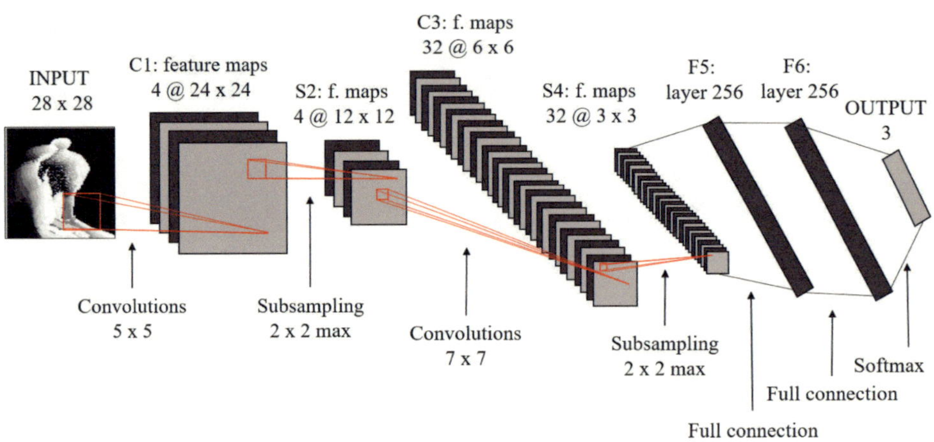

Figure 8. Architecture of a CNN.

4. Experimental results

In this section, an ablation study of the appearance temporal features with the CNN-based approach is presented, and the results of the action recognition are shown with the ICVL dataset. The average processing time was computed based on the ICVL test videos. The experimental results showed that appearance-based temporal features with a multi-CNN classifier effectively recognize actions in surveillance videos.

4.1. Evaluation metrics

To quantify the results, we use the average precision at the frame-based *frame-AP*. The *frame-AP* was used in other approaches at the frame-based evaluation. Frame-AP: recognition is correct if the intersection-over-union (IOU) with the ground truth and detection area at that frame is greater than $\sigma(\sigma = 0.5)$, and the action label is correctly predicted.

4.2. Action recognition on ICVL dataset

LocomotionNet encodes sequential frames as memory capacity to represent actions. However, deciding the number of frames n in Eq. (6) is a highly action-dependent issue. In this work, the number of frames in the MHI was defined by performing a grid search from 5 to 50 frames with an interval of 5. **Figure 9** plots the classification accuracy (mAP) at the frame-based measurement for the subactions at the locomotion level of the multilevel action descriptor. The gray circles are drawn while training LocomotionNet from 100 to 1K iterations with an interval of 100. The circles lie over a 1.96 standard error of the mean and standard deviation in white. The baseline accuracy at $n = 10$ is given by encoding the temporal features. With n equal to 25 frames, LocomotionNet was able to get a performance boost from 1 to 2% of the mAP. This evidence indicates that correctly recognizing one action would need approximately 2 s (15 fps in the ICVL videos).

Table 1 shows the results of each temporal feature with CNN. An ablation study of the proposed approach at the gesture level is presented by evaluating the performance of the two appearance-based temporal features, BDI and MHI, and their combination. Frame-AP is reported for PostureNet, LocomotionNet, and GestureNet. The leading scores of each label are displayed in bold font. As in Eq. (7), WAI is the weighted average of BDI and MHI. GestureNet performed significantly better than PostureNet and LocomotionNet, showing the significance of the combined cues for the task of gesture-level subaction recognition. The GestureNet combines the static and motion history cues to capture specific patterns of the action.

Figure 10 shows the mAP across subactions at the gesture level of the multilevel action descriptor at the frame-based measurement with regard to varying weights on WAI and training iterations of the GestureNet. In the experiment, $w_1 = 0.6$ and $w_2 = 0.4$ show a significant improvement beyond $w_1 = 0.5$ and $w_2 = 0.5$. This implies that the shape cue is more important than the motion history cue in WAI and is quite different from the results in **Table 1**. One possible explanation for this finding is that the motion history cue is more informative than the

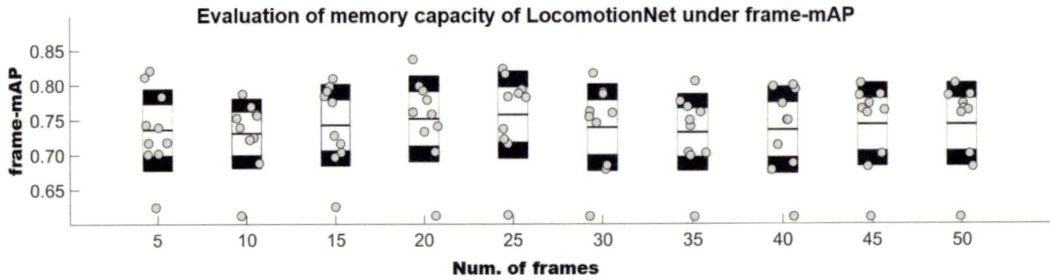

Figure 9. Memory capacity in MHI for the locomotion level of the multilevel action descriptor.

Frame-AP (%)	Nothing	Texting	Smoking	Phoning	mAP
PostureNet	51.3	42.0	11.2	37.9	35.6
LocomotionNet	**62.4**	53.5	14.7	49.2	45.0
GestureNet	53.4	**83.3**	**26.7**	**57.9**	**55.3**

Table 1. Results of the ablation study on the gesture level of ICVL dataset.

shape cue if they are used individually. For the remainder of the experimental results, $w_1 = 0.6$ and $w_2 = 0.4$ were used in WAI.

To evaluate the effectiveness of the action-recognition model, we included the full confusion matrixes as a source of additional insight. **Figure 11** shows that the proposed approach achieved an mAP of 73.2% at the frame-based measurement. The horizontal rows are the ground truth, and the vertical columns are the predictions. Each row was normalized to a sum of 1. The proposed method was able to get most of the subaction categories correct, except for *smoking*. The results of the experiment show that a multilevel action descriptor can eliminate many misclassifications by dividing one action into many subactions that are not at the same levels.

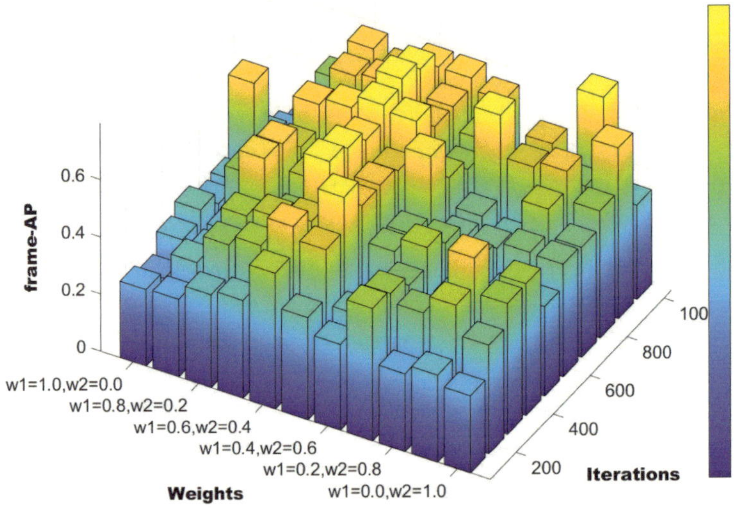

Figure 10. Recognition results with regard to varying weights of WAI and training iterations on GestureNet.

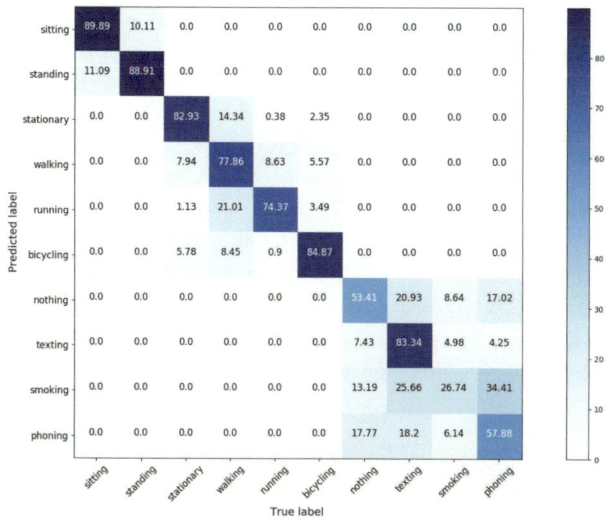

Figure 11. Confusion matrixes of the ICVL dataset at the frame-based measurement for the action-recognition task when using appearance-based temporal features with a multi-CNN classifier.

Figure 12. Examples of action localization and recognition results from the ICVL dataset.

Module	Motion	Detection	Tracking	BDI	MHI	WAI	CNNs	Others	Overall
Processing time (ms)	11.33	11.60	0.28	0.26	0.83	0.12	4.66	12.16	42.93

Table 2. Average processing time of the proposed action detection model.

Figure 12 shows qualitative localization and recognition results using the proposed approach on the test set of the ICVL dataset. Each block corresponds to a video from a different camera. Two frames are shown from each video. The test platform has a PC with an Intel Core i7-4770 CPU at 3.49 GHz with 32 GB memory. The input video was resized to 640 × 480, and the processing time was tested on 72 videos shown in **Table 2**.

5. Conclusions

This work introduced a new approach to real-time action recognition using multilevel action descriptor in video surveillance system. Experimental results demonstrated that a multilevel action descriptor delivers a complete set of information about human actions and significantly eliminates misclassifications by a large number of actions that are built by few independent subactions at different levels. An ablation study showed the effect of each temporal feature when considered separately. Shape and motion history cues are complementary, and the combination of both leads to a significant improvement in action recognition performance. In addition, the proposed action recognition model simultaneously localizes and recognizes the actions of multiple individuals at low computational cost with acceptable accuracy. The model ran at around 25 fps in 640 × 480 frame size, which is suitable for real-time surveillance applications. In future work, we will extend the approach to learn deep motion flow from original frame sequences and combine detecting and recognizing in one network for becoming an end-to-end human action detection framework.

Acknowledgements

This work was supported by the Industrial Technology Innovation Program, "10052982, Development of multiangle front camera system for intersection AEB," funded by the Ministry of Trade, Industry, & Energy (MOTIE, Korea).

Author details

Cheng-Bin Jin, Trung Dung Do, Mingjie Liu and Hakil Kim*

*Address all correspondence to: hikim@inha.ac.kr

Department of Information and Communication Engineering, Inha University, Incheon, South Korea

References

[1] Yamin H, Peng Z, Zhuo T, et al. Going deeper with two-stream ConvNets for action recognition in video surveillance. Pattern Recognition Letters. 2017 (available online). DOI: 10.1016/j.patrec.2017.08.015

[2] Andreas S, Rainer S. Pedestrian intention recognition using latent-dynamic conditional random fields. In: Intelligent Vehicles Symposium (IV). Seoul, South Korea: IEEE; June 28–July 01, 2015. pp. 622-627

[3] Michalis V, Christophoros N, Loannis K. A review of human activity recognition methods. Frontiers in Robotics and Artificial Intelligence. 2015;**2**(28):1-28. DOI: 10.3389/frobt.2015.00028

[4] Wang H, Klaser A, Schmid C, et al. Action recognition by dense trajectories. In: Proceedings of the IEEE Conference on Computer Vision and Pattern Recognition (CVPR '11). Colorado Springs, USA: IEEE; June 20-25, 2011. pp. 3169-3176

[5] Wang H, Schmid C. Action recognition with improved trajectories. In: Proceedings of the IEEE International Conference on Computer Vision (ICCV '13). Sydney, Australia: IEEE; December 3-6, 2013. pp. 3551-3558

[6] Jiang Z, Lin Z, Davis L. A unified tree-based framework for joint action localization, recognition and segmentation. Computer Vision and Image Understanding. 2013;**117**(10): 1345-1355. DOI: 1016/j.cviu.2012.09.008

[7] Shotton J, Girshick R, Fitzgibbon A, et al. Efficient human pose estimation from single depth images. IEEE Transitions on Pattern Analysis and Machine Intelligence. 2013;**35**(12):2821-2840. DOI: 10.1109/TPAMI.2012.241

[8] Siddiqui M, Medioni G. Human pose estimation from a single view point, real-time range sensor. In: Proceedings of the IEEE Conference on Computer Vision and Pattern Recognition (CVPR '11). San Francisco, USA: IEEE; June 13-18, 2011. pp. 1-8

[9] Plagemann C, Ganapathi V, Koller D, et al. Real-time identification and localization of body parts from depth images. In: Proceedings of the IEEE International Conference on Robotics and Automation (ICRA '10). Anchorage, USA: IEEE; May 3-7, 2010. pp. 3108-3113

[10] Cutler R, Davis L. Robust real-time periodic motion detection, analysis, and applications. IEEE Transitions on Pattern Analysis and Machine Intelligence. 2000;**22**(8):781-796. DOI: 10.1109/CVPR.1999.784652

[11] Zhang B, Wang L, Wang Z, et al. Real-time action recognition with enhanced motion vector CNNs. In: Proceedings of the IEEE Conference on Computer Vision and Pattern Recognition (CVPR '16). Las Vegas, USA: IEEE; June 26–July 1, 2016. pp. 2718-2726

[12] Jin C, Li S, Do T, et al. Real-time human action recognition using CNN over temporal images for static video surveillance cameras. Lecture Notes in Computer Science

(Including Subseries Lecture Notes in Artificial Intelligence and Lecture Notes in Bioinformatics). 2015;**9315**:330-339. DOI: 10.1007/978-3-319-24078-7_33

[13] Dalal N, Triggs B. Histograms of oriented gradients for human detection. In: Proceedings of the IEEE Conference on Computer Vision and Pattern Recognition (CVPR '05). San Diego, USA: IEEE; June 20-26, 2005. pp. 886-893

[14] Yu C, Joachims T. Learning structural SVMs with latent variables. In: Proceedings of the IEEE International Conference on Computer Vision (ICCV '09). Kyoto, Japan: IEEE; September 29–October 2, 2009. pp. 1169-1176

[15] Bobick AF, Davis JW. The recognition of human movement using temporal templates. IEEE Transitions on Pattern Analysis and Machine Intelligence. 2001;**23**(3):257-267. DOI: 10.1109/34.910878

[16] Davis JW, Bobick AF. The representation and recognition of human movement using temporal templates. In: Proceedings of the IEEE Conference on Computer Vision and Pattern Recognition (CVPR '97). San Juan, Puerto Rico: IEEE; June 17-19, 1997. pp. 928-934

[17] Ali S, Basharat A, Shah M. Chaotic invariants for human action recognition. In: Proceedings of the IEEE International Conference on Computer Vision (ICCV '07). Rio de Janeiro, Brazil: IEEE; October 14-20, 2007. pp. 1-8

[18] Fathi A, Mori G. Action recognition by learning mid-level motion feature. In: Proceedings of the IEEE Conference on Computer Vision and Pattern Recognition (CVPR '08). Anchorage, USA: IEEE; June 24-26, 2008. pp. 1-8

[19] Laptev I. On space-time interest points. International Journal of Computer Vision. 2005;**64**:107-123. DOI: 10.1007/s11263-005-1838-7

[20] Kim I, Oh S, Vahdat A, et al. Segmental multi-way local pooling for video recognition. In: Proceeding of the ACM International Conference on Multimedia (ICM '13). New York, USA: ACM; October 21-25, 2013. pp. 37-640

[21] Klaser A, Marszalek M, Schmid C. A spatio-temporal descriptor based on 3D-gradients. In: Proceedings of the British Machine Conference (BMC '08). Leeds, UK: Inria; September 3, 2008. pp. 275:1-10

[22] Li Y, Ye Z, Rehg JM. Delving into egocentric actions. In: Proceedings of the IEEE Conference on Computer Vision and Pattern Recognition (CVPR '15). Boston, USA: IEEE; June 7-10, 2015. pp. 287-295

[23] Vahdat A, Gao B, Ranjbar M, et al. A discriminative key pose sequence model for recognizing human interactions. In: Proceedings of the IEEE International Conference on Computer Vision (ICCV '11). Barcelona, Spain: IEEE; November 6-13, 2011. pp. 1729-1736

[24] Lan T, Wang Y, Yang W, et al. Discriminative latent models for recognizing contextual group activities. IEEE Transitions on Pattern Analysis and Machine Intelligence. 2012;**34**(8):1549-1562. DOI: 10.1109/TPAMI.2011.228

[25] Lan Z, Ming L, Xuanchong L, et al. Beyond Gaussian pyramid: Multi-skip feature stacking for action recognition. In: Proceedings of the IEEE Conference on Computer Vision and Pattern Recognition (CVPR '15). Boston, USA: IEEE; June 7-10, 2015. pp. 204-212

[26] Ni B, Yang X, Gao S. Progressively parsing interactional objects for fine grained action detection. In: Proceedings of the IEEE Conference on Computer Vision and Pattern Recognition (CVPR '16). Las Vegas, USA: IEEE; June 26–July 1, 2016. pp. 1020-1028

[27] Yeung S, Russakovsky O, Moi G, et al. End-to-end learning of action detection from frame glimpses in videos. In: Proceedings of the IEEE Conference on Computer Vision and Pattern Recognition (CVPR '16). Las Vegas, USA: IEEE; June 26–July 1, 2016. pp. 2678-2687

[28] Karpathy A, Toderici G, Shetty S, et al. Large-scale video classification with convolutional neural networks, In: Proceedings of the IEEE Conference on Computer Vision and Pattern Recognition (CVPR '14). Columbus, USA: IEEE; June 24-27, 2014. pp. 1725-1732

[29] Gkioxari G, Malik J. Finding action tubes. In: Proceedings of the IEEE Conference on Computer Vision and Pattern Recognition (CVPR '15). Boston, USA: IEEE; June 7-10, 2015. pp. 759-768

[30] Simonyan K, Zisserman A. Two-stream convolutional networks for action recognition in videos. In: Proceedings of the Advances in Neural Information Processing Systems (NIPS '14). Montreal, Canada: NIPS; December 08-13, 2014. pp. 568-576

[31] Ji S, Xu W, Yang M, et al. 3D convolutional neural networks for human action recognition. IEEE Transitions on Pattern Analysis and Machine Intelligence. 2013;**35**(1):221-331. DOI: 10.1109/TPAMI.2012.59

[32] Li S. Human re-identification using soft biometrics in video surveillance [thesis]. Incheon: Inha University; 2015

[33] Krizhevsky A, Sutskever I, Hinton GE. ImageNet classification with deep convolutional neural networks. In: Proceedings of the Advances in Neural Information Processing Systems (NIPS '12). Lake Tahoe, USA: NIPS; December 03-08, 2012. pp. 1-9

[34] Girshick R, Donahue J, Darrell T, et al. Rich feature hierarchies for accurate object detection and semantic segmentation. In: Proceedings of the IEEE Conference on Computer Vision and Pattern Recognition (CVPR '14). Columbus, USA: IEEE; June 24-27, 2014. pp. 580-587

[35] Kingma P, Ba J. Adam: A method for stochastic optimization. 2017. pp. 1-15. arXiv Preprint:1412.6980v9

[36] Jin C-B, Do T, Liu M, et al. Real-time action detection in video surveillance using a sub-action descriptor with multi-convolutional neural networks. Journal of Institute of Control, Robotics and Systems. 2018;**24**(3):298-308. DOI: 10.5302/J.ICROS.2018.17.0243

Chapter 5

Human Activity Recognition without Vision Tracking

Carlos Alberto Flores Vázquez, Joan Aranda,
Daniel Icaza, Santiago Pulla,
Marcelo Flores-Vázquez and
Nelson Federico Cordova

Additional information is available at the end of the chapter

http://dx.doi.org/10.5772/intechopen.82660

Abstract

This work describes the recognition of human activity based on the interaction between people and objects in domestic settings, specifically in a kitchen. The difference between this and other proposals is that considers a human activity in a process without vision tracking. Videos are a sequence of photographs. Taking this into account, if you analyze an orderly sequence of images it could be based on the objects present in each scene so that you can understand the possible activity performed. However, it is not enough to consider the objects present in the scene; it is necessary to determine if those objects are employed or not by the humans present. If they are used, it is evident that they are necessary to carry out the activity; if they are not used they would only provide noise to the recognized activity. Therefore, it is necessary to generate a conceptualization of objects in the scene with characteristics (definition of an object, motion detector, object recognition, object position, object action) that allows you to recognize them and to determine the degree of use (unchanged, added, removed, moved, and indeterminate) and influence the possible recognized activity.

Keywords: human activity, computer vision, human/computer interaction, human/robot interaction, feature extraction, behavior representation

1. Introduction

This study is part of a major research project called InHands [1, 2]. The approach specifically analyzes the recognition of human activity without using the traditional proposal that uses the follow-up of movements of hands and arms. A short version of this research is shown in [3] and this work presents several improvements to the initial proposal presented in [2].

To introduce the field of recognition of human activity is of interest in this research and the definition mentioned in [4] on human/object interactions is as follows:

"The most typical human-object interaction recognition approaches are the ones ignoring interplays between object recognition and motion estimation. In those works, objects are generally recognized first, and activities involving them are recognized by analyzing the objects' motion. They have made the object recognition and motion estimation independent or made it so that the motion estimation is strictly dependent on the object recognition" [2, 4].

In addition to the definition quoted here, this chapter defines the structure and classification of human activity recognition, from which we extract the following:

- Single-layered approaches are appropriate for gesture and action recognition by sequential characteristics [2, 4].
- Hierarchical approaches are human activity representations with a high level of abstraction. Within this topic we find a subclassification that is of interest to us [2, 4]:
    - Statistical: construct statistical state-based models concatenated hierarchically [2, 4].
    - Syntactic: use a grammar syntax such as stochastic context-free grammar to model sequential activities [2, 4].
    - Description-based: represent human activities by describing subevents of the activities and their temporal, spatial, and logical structures [2, 4].

This research applies the approach of human/object interactions, and included in these are more specific subtopics: syntactic and description-based.

In [5] a proposal for the recognition of activity based on description-based is presented. This methodology consists of motion detection and tracking complemented by event analysis, which is of interest for the detection of movement. On the basis of this the capture of images for our proposal is carried out. As in [5] we use a single camera for capture and for segmentation the background is extracted, but we use image difference.

Among the relevant works to establish an activity recognition procedure [6], each action event is assigned a symbol and then a sequence of actions corresponds to a string of symbols. In our proposal we will use words instead of symbols, and a set of words regardless of their order could form an activity.

A similar way to [6] is the proposal of [7]: a BOW (bag of words). A BOW considers that an image might be similar to a paragraph where repetition of one or more words would allow us to recognize the content or essence of the text. For us it is similar to considering the repetition of objects in the image, and to interact with them would give us indications of the activity that is developing.

For the InHands project, proactive assistance is very important, and with this premise in [8] they present a probabilistic prediction of the actions carried out, which is precisely what is intended to implement our proposal.

A similar work where the scenario is to employ a Kinect camera is [9]. However, to increase the reliability of this methodology of recognition radio-frequency identification tags are added, which will not be implemented in our proposal.

The first information this system considers is hand and object tracking, and later object and action recognition. Regarding the detail of the recognized actions, seven principals are defined: place; move; chop; mixing; pouring; spooning; and scooping [9].

An example of the results obtained is the preparation of a cake, for which seven objects, 17 actions, about 6000 frames, and approximately 200 seconds are used. For us the definition of actions is simpler. Therefore, our actions will be those explained in Section 2.1.5.

2. Methodology

In this research, we consider that the results of activity recognition would be useful to provide proactive assistance. Therefore, the recognition of the activity should be determined while the activity is being carried out and with the aim of facilitating the robotic assistance considered in later stages of the InHands project.

Recognition is approached with computer vision methods. In a specific way, it is based on the recognition of objects in the scene and the interaction with these objects based on their manipulation. However, it is necessary to detail that the interaction with the objects does not contemplate the tracking of the objects, arms, or hands of the person who intervenes in the action. The initial and final positions of the objects, their presence or not, are of importance in the recognition process.

2.1. Conceptualization of an object

In this proposal the conceptualization of an object is explained in five constitutive parts:

- Definition of an object
- Motion detector
- Object recognition
- Object position
- Object action

2.1.1. *Definition of an object*

Considering the relevance of the objects and interaction with these, it is necessary to develop a definition of the object with parameters that allow the differentiation between them. Therefore, the chosen parameters are:

1. *Identification number*: this allows us to have a unique number for each object despite having similar characteristics such as color.

2. *Color*: this is the main characteristic that allows us to recognize the type of object present in the scene.

3. *Position*: this is confirmed by the coordinates of the centroid for each object, taking as origin the lower left corner of the kitchen counter.

4. *Actions with objects*: four basic interactions have been defined with the objects by the user: add, remove, move, unchanged.

Figure 1(a) graphically shows the conception of an object in this proposal. **Figure 1(b)** shows the execution of the algorithm in parallel to generate the attributes of each object.

2.1.2. Motion detector

Motion detection is important so that we know that an activity is taking place in the scene. In addition, objects in the scene (OBJECT RECOGNITION) and their position (OBJECT POSITION) are acquired. Since we do not track, is important to recapture the objects in the scene after the movements made by the person present. By making this subsequent capture we avoid occlusions and we can determine an action (OBJECT ACTION) for each object when checking through their presence and position if they were moved, removed, added, or not used in the last action.

As demonstrated in the flow chart of **Figure 2**, one of the most important methods applied in this part of the system is image difference, specifically "the mixture of the Gaussian method" according to [10]. **Figure 2(a)** explains the flow chart for motion detection and **Figure 2(b)** shows the three results after executing the motion detection algorithm.

This image difference allows us to extract the objects from the background, which is dynamically updated while the system is working. The motion detection algorithm performs a continuous comparison of frames by setting a minimum threshold level to consider whether that variation between a frame at $t = 0$ and the following at $t + 1$, $t + 2$, and $t + 3$ implies an action performed or is only a visual noise.

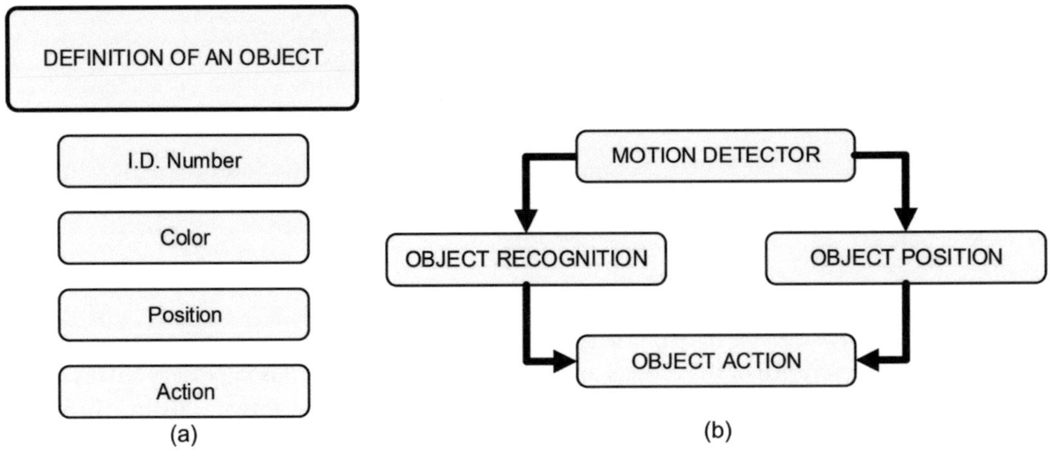

Figure 1. (a) Graphical model of our definition of an object. (b) General flow chart of the definition of an object.

http://dx.doi.org/10.5772/intechopen.82660

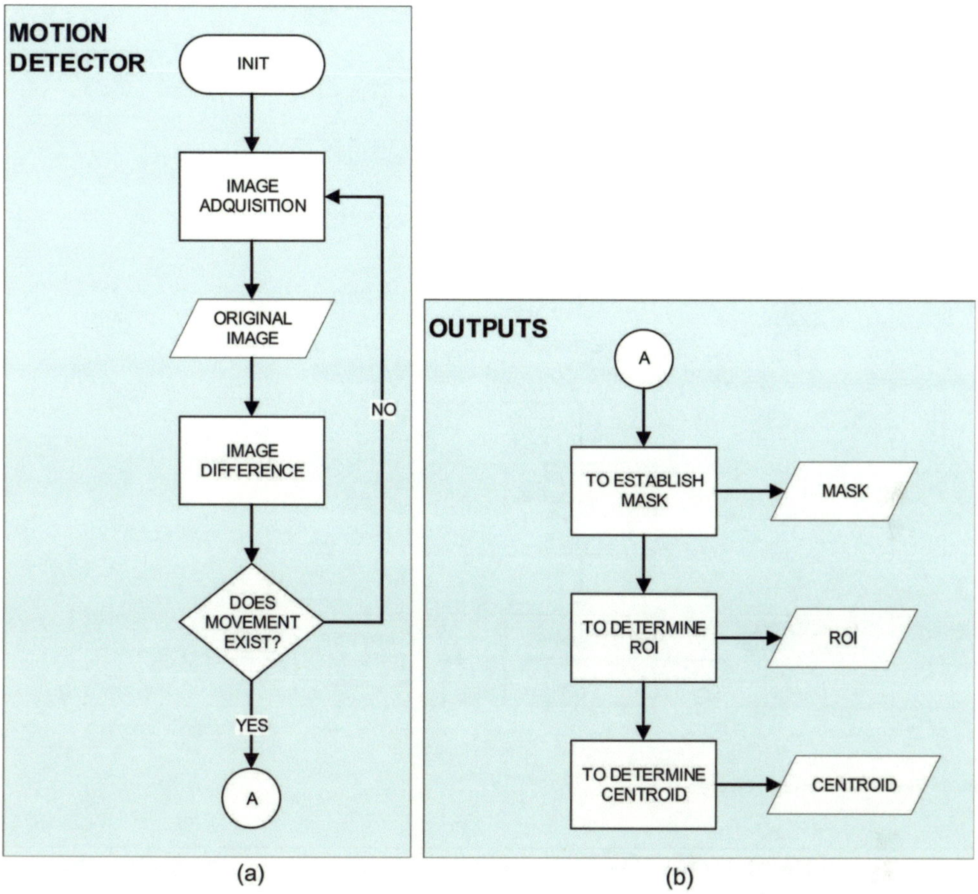

Figure 2. Flow charts: (a) motion detector, (b) outputs from motion detector.

2.1.3. Object recognition

The object recognition process is developed in **Figure 3**. The first step is to get the mask by difference of images and apply it to the original image. The result of the application of the mask is the region of interest (ROI).

From each ROI we obtain a histogram of 10 BINS RG chromaticity space (two-dimensional color space in which there is no color intensity information). Working with RG chromaticity allows us to avoid the problems of brightness, additionally normalized the images in RGB color space (a pixel is identified by the intensity of red, green and blue values) and was restricted by thresholds the colors black and white.

A comparison of the new histograms obtained from the ROI was made against our database. The selected comparison method was the Bhattacharyya distance. As evidenced in **Table 1** this method was selected considering the percentage of errors reduced and low amount of time.

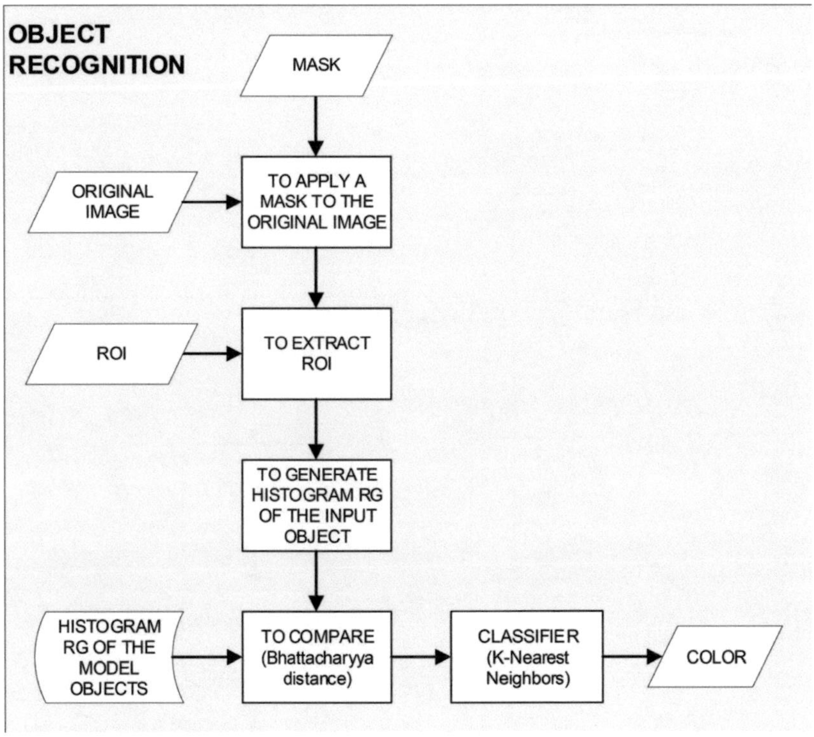

Figure 3. Flow chart for object recognition.

Method	Correlation	Chi-square	Intersection	Bhattacharyya distance
Samples	100	100	100	100
Error	8%	8%	2%	2%
Observations [5]	Quick	Moderately fast—more accurate matches	Quick—and—dirty matching	Moderately fast—more accurate matches
Range [exact … mismatch]	[1.0 …–1.0]	[0.0…2.0]	[1.0…0.0]	[0.0…1.0]

Table 1. Comparison of methods.

The database of the objects has five different perspectives for each one. As far as the classifier was concerned, K_{nn} (nearest neighbors) was chosen with $K = 1$.

Evaluation of the aforementioned classifier was performed in a similar way to the proposal in [11]. In detail, a confusion matrix is employed to measure the recognition of each of the objects. Forty images were used for validation and 30 for each test of a total of 1870 images. Some examples are shown in **Table 2**.

Probably a better alternative to reduce time in object recognition is [12]. The YOLO Detection System is a really fast detector that can process streaming video in real time with less than 25 ms

Coffee		Predicted label		Measure	Result
		Positive	Negative	Precision	91.67%
Known label	Positive	22	4	Recall/sensitivity	84.62%
	Negative	2	2	Specificity	50.00%
				Accuracy	84.62%
Glass		**Predicted label**		**Measure**	**Result**
		Positive	Negative	Precision	100.00%
Known label	Positive	24	5	Recall/sensitivity	82.76%
	Negative	0	1	Specificity	100.00%
				Accuracy	82.76%
Spoon		**Predicted label**		**Measure**	**Result**
		Positive	Negative	Precision	100.00%
Known label	Positive	23	2	Recall/sensitivity	92.00%
	Negative	0	5	Specificity	100.00%
				Accuracy	92.00%

Table 2. Confusion matrix and measurements: (a) coffee, (b) glass, (c) spoon.

of latency. However, the YOLO method is not convenient for localization errors, for example Fast R-CNN has 8.6% of localization errors versus 19% for the YOLO method. This is explained in Section 2.1.4; localization is an important part of this proposal for object definition.

Other alternatives taking to account reduced time can be [13, 14]. Tensor flow is a flexible system and can be used to express a wide variety of algorithms. For this proposal, the main advantage would be the capacity for distributing the process in many computational devices for object recognition.

2.1.4. Object position

In this proposal the position of the object is one of the essential characteristics; this allows us to define the actions resulting from the interaction with it. If the position does not change between images it means that the object was not used (UNCHANGED); if on the other hand it changes it means that the object is necessary in the developed activity (MOVE).

As for the technical details the centroid is a pixel in the image; this pixel is positioned in the coordinate system of the image. Taking into account that the InHands project requires obtaining world coordinates to assist with robots, then these coordinates must be referenced to the kitchen counter.

Homography matrix H is used according to [15]. It is necessary to apply matrix H; the intrinsic and extrinsic matrixes of the calibration of the camera are explained in [16]. The result of homography is expressed in millimeters and the final adjustment is made with rotation and translation matrixes (**Figure 4**).

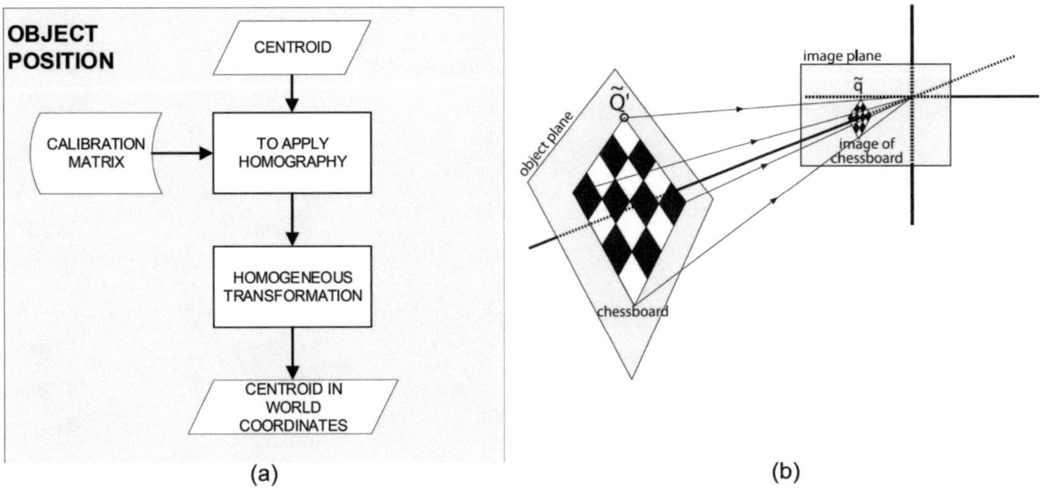

Figure 4. (a) Flow chart of object position. (b) View of a planar object as described by homography [15].

2.1.5. Object action

To build the object with the previously obtained characteristics (ID number, color, centroid), in "Action" we assign the state of "UNDETERMINED," see **Figure 5(a)**. The human/object interaction is defined in the feature of the object called Action. This can take four possible options:

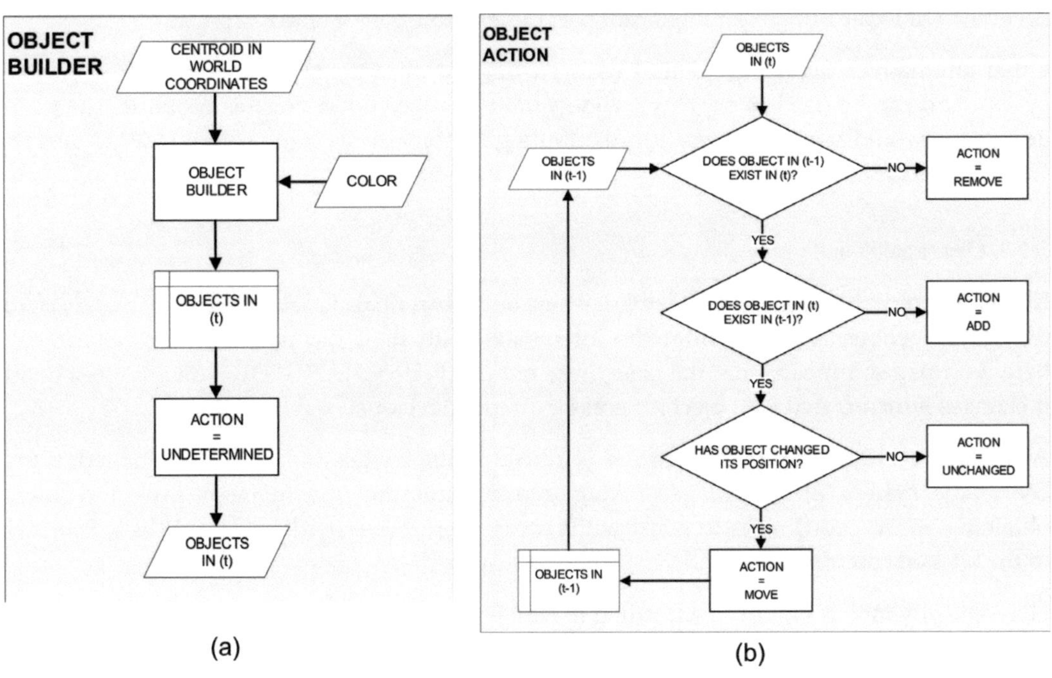

Figure 5. (a) Flow charts of object builder. (b) Flow charts of object action.

1. UNCHANGED: The object was present in the previous activity but it has not been moved, which implies that the object is present in the scene but it was not used in the activity.
2. MOVE: This indicates that the object was present in a previous scene and now changes position implying that it was used in the developing activity.
3. ADD: The object was not present in previous scene, and because it is now added to the scene it is assumed to be necessary for the developing activity.
4. REMOVE: An object present in previous scenes is no longer present. This induces the thought that it is now not necessary for the activity that is developing.

To avoid detecting false movements caused by occlusions or errors in the calculation of the centroid a tolerance range was established; only movements greater than 5 mm are recorded.

2.2. Human activity recognition

The taxonomy proposed in [4] allows us to illustrate an approximation to the approach that this research has. In detailed form it is typecast in hierarchical approaches and has many coincidences with the vision presented in syntactic and description-based. Specifically, the approach of human/object interactions uses a syntax to define human activity but it is not necessary to consider order, sequences, and logical structure (**Figure 6**).

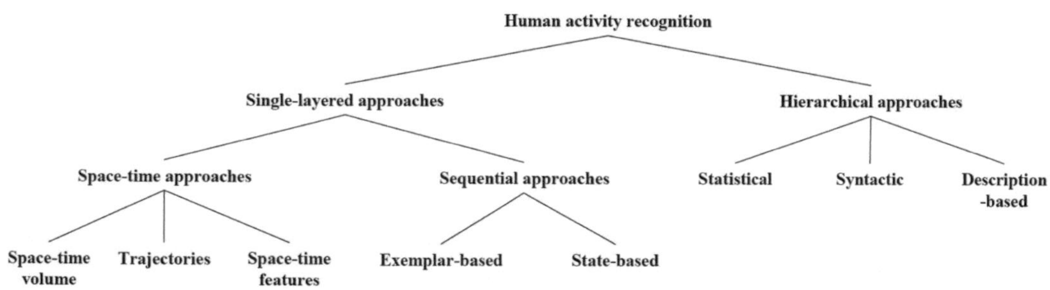

Figure 6. The hierarchical approach-based taxonomy [4].

An approach whereby it is important to make a comparison of the methodology used is [7]. BOW collects features by assigning the nearest word and the frequency of occurrence of this in the images. In our proposal, each object could be a word and the repetition of these words will be relevant to determine the activity, but unlike [7] it is not necessary to consider the sequence of occurrence of words.

2.2.1. *Definition of an activity*

How do you define an activity? This is one of the questions that arose during the project; in this case a recipe inspires it, so we will use ingredients, kitchen tools, and possible substitutes to define an activity, see **Figure 7(a)**.

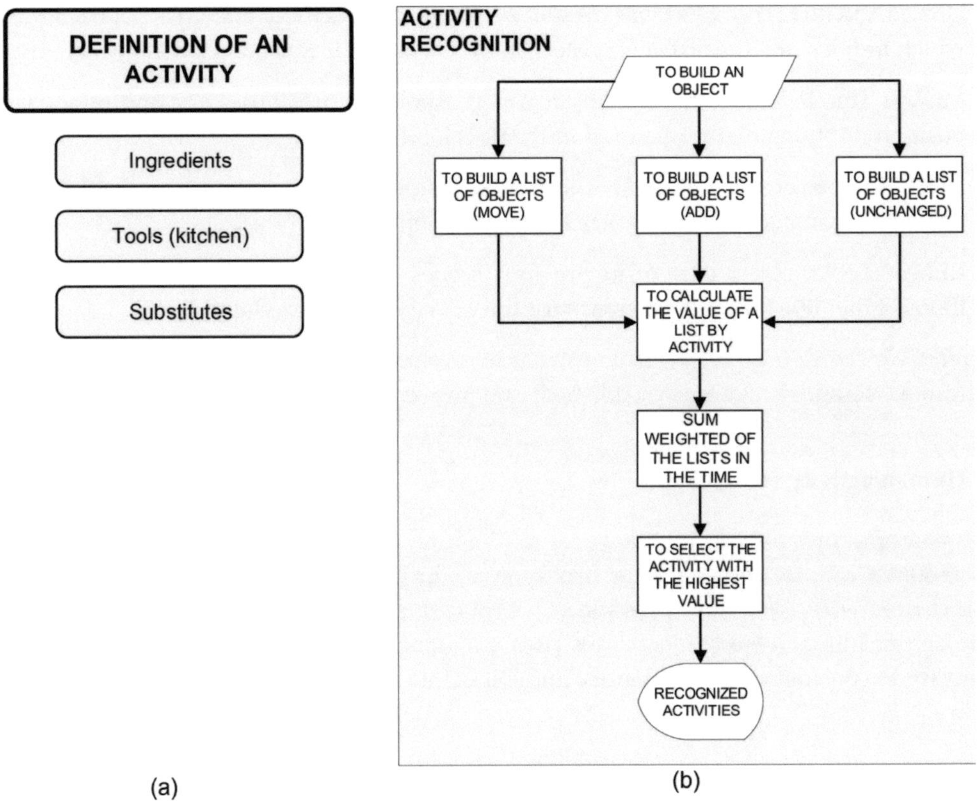

Figure 7. (a) Definition of an activity. (b) Flow chart of activity recognition.

- INGREDIENTS: This refers to objects considered as ingredients for the preparation of a recipe, e.g. for a cereal-activity (cereal, milk).
- TOOLS: This includes cooking utensils and cutlery necessary for the elaboration of the recipes-activities, e.g. cereal-activity (bowl, spoon).
- SUBSTITUTES: These are kitchen utensils that could be replaced by others that perform a similar function, e.g. a cup for a glass.

2.2.2. Evaluation function and activity recognition

To start the recognition of activity we made three groupings of objects according to their action, in other words a list for moved objects (MOVE), another one for objects added to the scene (ADD), and a list of objects present in the scene, but they do not have to be moved or withdrawn (UNCHANGED).

The first evaluation corresponds to calculating that the contribution of each ingredient, utensil, and substitute has undergone a movement, taking into account that the contribution of ingredients, utensils, and substitutes is being weighted by the constants a, b, and c, respectively. The result is the value that these objects provide for each of the probable activities carried out Eq. (1).

http://dx.doi.org/10.5772/intechopen.82660

The second evaluation corresponds to calculating the contribution of each ingredient, utensil, and substitute that has been added to the scene. Similar to the first evaluation, the contribution of ingredients, utensils, and substitutes is considered to be weighted by the constants a, b, and c, respectively. The result is the value that these objects provides for each of the probable activities carried out Eq. (2).

The third evaluation is exactly the same in its procedure as the two previously made, with the only difference being that the objects that intervene here are the ones that have remained in the scene without any change, i.e. they have not been moved, added, or removed (Eq. 3).

It is important to emphasize that an object could be a utensil or a substitute depending on the activity, for example a glass would be a utensil if the activity is to prepare juice (activity 1) but would be a substitute if the activity is to prepare coffee (activity N). where:

$$\begin{bmatrix} V_{Act\_1} \\ \vdots \\ V_{Act\_N} \end{bmatrix}_{[M]} = a \cdot \begin{bmatrix} I_{Act\_1} \\ \vdots \\ I_{Act\_N} \end{bmatrix}_{[M]} + b \cdot \begin{bmatrix} T_{Act\_1} \\ \vdots \\ T_{Act\_N} \end{bmatrix}_{[M]} + c \cdot \begin{bmatrix} S_{Act\_1} \\ \vdots \\ S_{Act\_N} \end{bmatrix}_{[M]} \tag{1}$$

$$\begin{bmatrix} V_{Act\_1} \\ \vdots \\ V_{Act\_N} \end{bmatrix}_{[A]} = a \cdot \begin{bmatrix} I_{Act\_1} \\ \vdots \\ I_{Act\_N} \end{bmatrix}_{[A]} + b \cdot \begin{bmatrix} T_{Act\_1} \\ \vdots \\ T_{Act\_N} \end{bmatrix}_{[A]} + c \cdot \begin{bmatrix} S_{Act\_1} \\ \vdots \\ S_{Act\_N} \end{bmatrix}_{[A]} \tag{2}$$

$$\begin{bmatrix} V_{Act\_1} \\ \vdots \\ V_{Act\_N} \end{bmatrix}_{[Un]} = a \cdot \begin{bmatrix} I_{Act\_1} \\ \vdots \\ I_{Act\_N} \end{bmatrix}_{[Un]} + b \cdot \begin{bmatrix} T_{Act\_1} \\ \vdots \\ T_{Act\_N} \end{bmatrix}_{[Un]} + c \cdot \begin{bmatrix} S_{Act\_1} \\ \vdots \\ S_{Act\_N} \end{bmatrix}_{[Un]} \tag{3}$$

- V_{Act} = Result for each activity from 1 to N.
- I_{Act} = Recognized objects that are considered ingredients for each activity.
- T_{Act} = Recognized objects that are considered utensils for each activity.
- S_{Act} = Recognized objects that are considered substitutes for each activity.
- $[M, A, Un]$ = MOVE, ADD, UNCHANGED.
- a, b, c = Constants for tuning contribution, $a = 0.5, b = 0.3, c = 0.2$ [2].

The fourth evaluation corresponds to the addition of the activity lists resulting from Eqs. (1)–(3). Explicitly the result of Eq. (4) (SUM WEIGHTED OF THE LISTS IN THE TIME) corresponds to adding the probable activities that result from moving, adding, or not changing objects in a scene (Eq. 4). This result would correspond to the probable instantaneous activity, i.e. in the last frames (1 to 4 frames).

$$\begin{bmatrix} \sum V_{Act\_1} \\ \vdots \\ \sum V_{Act\_N} \end{bmatrix} = \alpha \cdot \begin{bmatrix} V_{Act\_1} \\ \vdots \\ V_{Act\_N} \end{bmatrix}_{[M]} + \beta \cdot \begin{bmatrix} V_{Act\_1} \\ \vdots \\ V_{Act\_N} \end{bmatrix}_{[A]} + \gamma \cdot \begin{bmatrix} V_{Act\_1} \\ \vdots \\ V_{Act\_N} \end{bmatrix}_{[Un]} \tag{4}$$

where:

- $\sum V_{Act}$ = The summation of value by activity (the last 1 to 4 frames).
- α, β, γ = Variables changing on the time, $\alpha + \beta + \gamma \leq 1$.

$$\alpha = \frac{1}{3} + \left(\frac{1}{6} - \gamma\right) \tag{5}$$

$$\beta = \frac{1}{3} + \left(\frac{1}{6} - \gamma\right) \tag{6}$$

$$\gamma = \frac{1}{3} \bullet \left(\frac{ElapsedTime}{AverageTime}\right) \tag{7}$$

where:

- $ElapsedTime =$ The elapsed time from the start of an activity. Initial value is set to $AverageTime$, later decreased.
- $AverageTime =$ Average time for the execution of any predefined activity.

Factors α, β, γ serve to ponder the contribution of $[V_{Act}]_M$, $[V_{Act}]_A$, $[V_{Act}]_{Un}$. Note that activities resulting from actions such as moving (MOVE) or adding (ADD) objects to the scene are more relevant over time than the result of just keeping objects in the scene with no position changes (UNCHANGED).

The results of Eq. (4) represent activities recognized in the last four frames, so in no way would represent a global or final result of the activity recognized.

To obtain a more reliable result we must add a considerable group of results of Eq. (4), and by adding these results we obtain a statistically reliable result of the activity recognized activity, Eq. (8) being the maximum value of the activity recognized.

$$Activity\_Recognized = \max\left\{\sum_{1}^{Tsamples} \begin{bmatrix} \sum Act\_1 \\ \vdots \\ \sum Act\_N \end{bmatrix}\right\} \tag{8}$$

$Tsamples$ = Total samples of results of Eq. (4) during average time of activity recognized.

3. Results

The complete system that is obtained to perform our proposal of activity recognition is outlined in **Figure 8**; each of its constitutive parts was explained in the previous sections.

For experiments in a real domestic scenario, we count on the automated kitchen developed under the InHands project in **Figure 9(a)** [1].

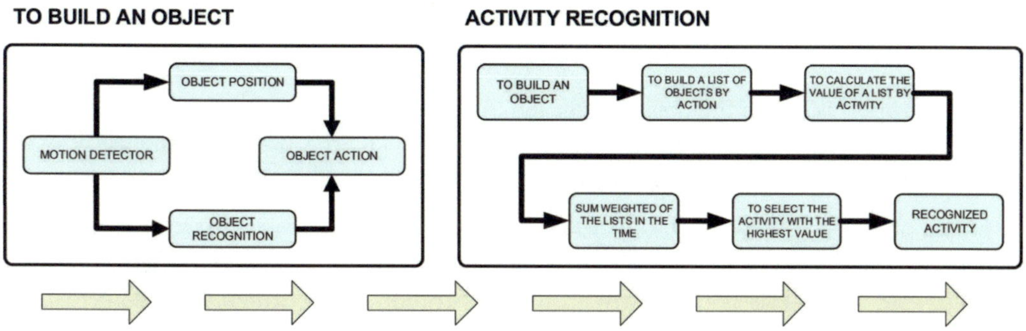

Figure 8. Complete implemented system.

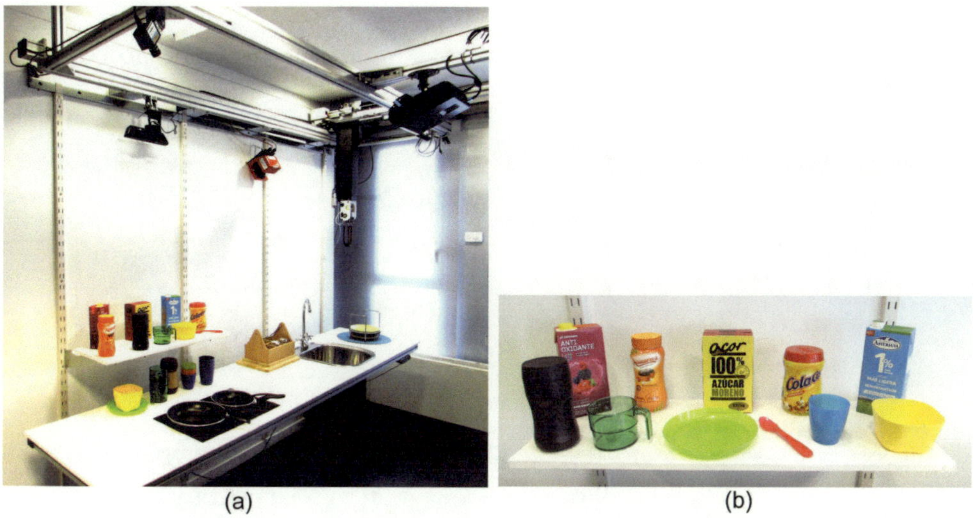

Figure 9. (a) InHands automated kitchen scenario. (b) Selected objects for the experiment.

In this research a color Kinect camera was employed; the depth of view was not used. People doing the cooking activities in **Figure 9(a)** did so randomly without any training or prepared script. The system was tested with four typical breakfast activities consisting of: brewing coffee, juice preparation, cereal preparation, and chocolate preparation.

The ingredients, cooking utensils, and substitutes are shown in **Figure 9(b)** as follows: coffee, sugar, chocolate, juice, cereal, milk, bowl, cup, glass, plate, and spoon.

The first tests of the system of recognition of the proposed activity used five videos for each of the four activities raised. The results were excellent and after 600 frames it could be clearly differentiated which was the activity being executed in **Figure 10(b)**. Partial results of Eq. (4) are illustrated in **Figure 10(a)**. It should be mentioned that the results of 1 to 4 frames illustrated in **Figure 10(a)** suffer from occlusions and changes in lighting that hinder a more accurate recognition of objects; however, thanks to the evaluation of Eq. (8) the erroneous partial results can be filtered to obtain a correct overall result.

Proactive support is one of the objectives of the InHands project, so our system should be able to recognize activities without having to be segmented, i.e. in a normal sequence of events recognize the different activities that are being developed.

As mentioned, the following test phase consisted of placing several activities without segmenting and checking whether the system was capable of recognizing them. **Figure 11** illustrates one of the tests performed with the preparation of unsegmented juice, cereal, and coffee without a preconfigured specific order. As evidenced in **Figure 11(a)** the instantaneous activity recognition system (1 to 4 frames) is unclear in showing the activity developed but after processing it with Eq. (8) the result is clear (**Figure 11(b)**). Therefore, the functioning of the systems in a continuous way without the need to segment activities is demonstrated. The

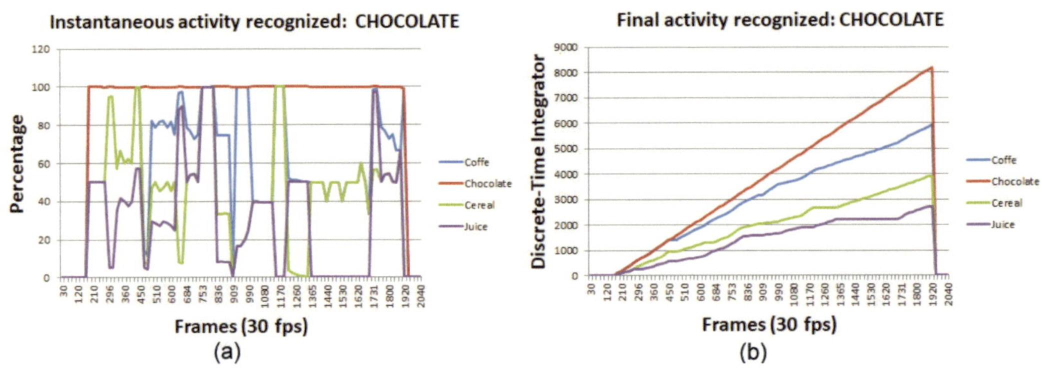

Figure 10. (a) Instantaneous activity recognized $(\sum V_{Act})$: CHOCOLATE. Vertical axis = percentage of similarity with the $(\sum V_{Act})$, horizontal axis = number of frames. (b) Final activity recognized $\left(\sum_{1}^{Tsamples}\right)$: CHOCOLATE.

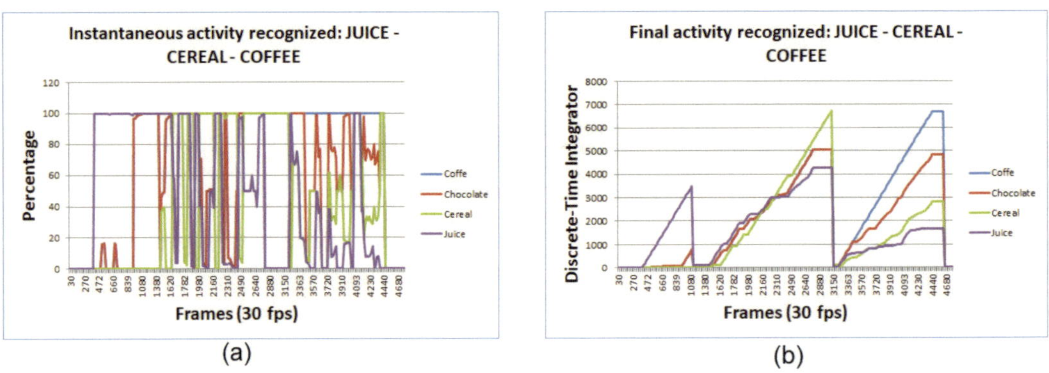

Figure 11. (a) Instantaneous activity recognized $(\sum V_{Act})$: JUICE—CEREAL—COFFEE. (b) Final activity recognized $\left(\sum_{1}^{Tsamples}\right)$: JUICE—CEREAL—COFFEE.

http://dx.doi.org/10.5772/intechopen.82660

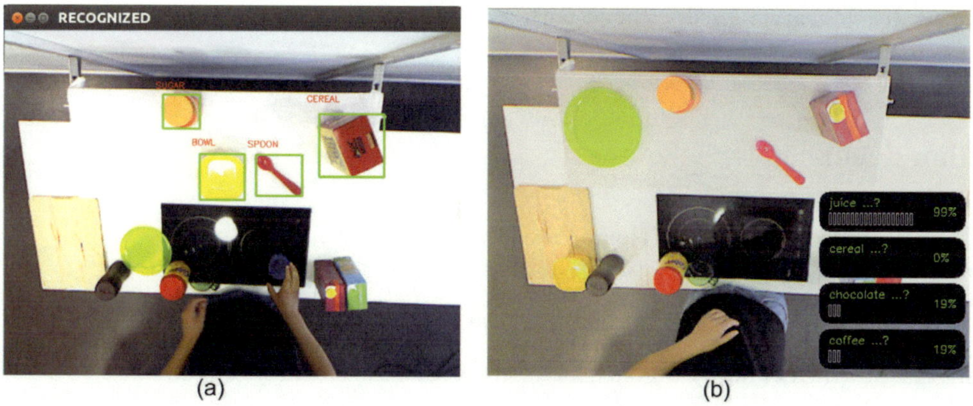

Figure 12. (a) Sample frame of a processed video sequence. (b) Sample frame of a processed video computer interface.

final activity is coffee preparation with satisfactory performance from the beginning. **Figure 12** shows a sample frame of our video process for the recognition of objects and activities [3].

4. Conclusions

This proposal for recognition of human activity is different from others based on tracking as shown in [17]. It is based on the preparation of cooking recipes, considering the interaction of the user with the objects present in the scene. In a detailed way, after the recognition of objects we classify them in categories (ingredients, utensils, and substitutes) and for the interaction we define four actions (add, remove, move, and unchanged) weighting the contribution of objects and interactions to determine possible activity.

Among its notable features are: it does not use intrusive methods with the user and requires an average time of 0.25 s for an instant recognition of activity [18–22]. It is also noted that in all the tests the recognitions were met by surpassing problems of brightness and occlusions to allow completely natural movements of the user.

The system is flexible and scalable by simply adding more activity definitions (recipes). The system works continuously with no default activity segmentation.

Future work would be to define with statistical methods the weighting constants here designated as a, b, c,α, β, γ.

Acknowledgements

This research was supported by the InHands project (Interactive robotics for Human Assistance in Domestic Scenarios), grant P6-L13-AL.INHAND founded by Fundaci La Caixa, inside the Recercaixa research program [3].

C. Flores and J. Aranda are associated with the Institute for Bioengineering of Catalunya and Universitat Politècnica de Catalunya, Barcelona-Tech, Spain [3].

Author details

Carlos Alberto Flores Vázquez[1]*, Joan Aranda[2], Daniel Icaza[1], Santiago Pulla[1], Marcelo Flores-Vázquez[3] and Nelson Federico Cordova[1]

*Address all correspondence to: cfloresv@ucacue.edu.ec

1 GIRVyP Research Group, Catholic University of Cuenca, Cuenca, Ecuador

2 IBEC Institute for Bioengineering of Catalonia, Polytechnic University of Catalonia, Barcelona–Tech, Barcelona, Spain

3 Salesian Polytechnic University, Cuenca, Ecuador

References

[1] Vinagre M, Aranda J, Casals A. An interactive robotic system for human assistance in domestic environments. In: International Conference on Computers for Handicapped Persons. Cham: Springer; 2014. pp. 152-155

[2] Flores Vázquez C. Human activity recognition from object interaction in domestic scenarios [MS thesis]. Universitat Politècnica de Catalunya; 2014. Available from: https://upcommons.upc.edu/bitstream/handle/2099.1/23706/TFM%20Carlos%20Flores%20Vazquez%2013062014.pdf?sequence=1&isAllowed=y [Accessed: 10-04-2018]

[3] Flores-Vázquez C, Aranda J. Human activity recognition from object interaction in domestic scenarios. In: Ecuador Technical Chapters Meeting (ETCM); IEEE. IEEE; 2016. pp. 1-6. Available from: https://upcommons.upc.edu/bitstream/handle/2117/100423/v2%2bHUMAN%2bACTIVITY%2bRECOGNITION.pdf?sequence=3&isAllowed=y [Accessed: 10-04-2018]

[4] Aggarwal J, Ryoo M. Human activity analysis: A review. ACM Computing Surveys. 2011; **43**(3):16

[5] Hongeng S, Nevatia R, Bremond F. Video-based event recognition: Activity representation and probabilistic recognition methods. Computer Vision and Image Understanding. 2004;**96**(2):129-162

[6] Moore D, Essa I. Recognizing multitasked activities from video using stochastic context-free grammar. In: Proceedings of 18th National Conference on Artificial Intelligence. 2002. pp. 770-776

[7] Liefeng B, Sminchisescu C. Efficient match kernel between sets of features for visual recognition. In: Advances in Neural Information Processing Systems (NIPS). 2009. pp. 135-143

[8] Ryoo M. Human activity prediction: Early recognition of ongoing activities from streaming videos. In: IEEE International Conference on Computer Vision (ICCV); IEEE; 2011. pp. 1036-1043

[9] Lei J, Ren X, Fox D. Fine-grained kitchen activity recognition using rgb-d. In: Proceedings of the 2012 ACM Conference on Ubiquitous Computing. Pittsburgh, Pennsylvania: ACM; 2012. pp. 208-211. http://dx.doi.org/10.1145/2370216.2370248

[10] Laganière R. OpenCV Computer Vision Application Programming Cookbook. 2nd ed. Birmingham, UK: Packt Publishing Ltd; 2014. pp. 272-277

[11] Sokolova M, Lapalme G. A systematic analysis of performance measures for classification tasks. In: Information Processing & Management. 2009. vol. 45, no. 4, pp. 427-437. https://doi.org/10.1016/j.ipm.2009.03.002

[12] Redmon J, Divvala S, Girshick R, Farhadi A. You only look once: unified, real-time object detection. In: Proceedings of the IEEE Conference on Computer Vision and Pattern Recognition; 2016. pp. 779-788

[13] Abadi M, Barham P, Chen J, Chen Z, Davis A, Dean J, Kudlur M. Tensorflow: A system for large-scale machine learning. In: OSDI. Vol. 16. 2016. pp. 265-283

[14] Szegedy C, Reed S, Erhan D, Anguelov D, Ioffe S. Scalable, high-quality object detection. arXiv preprint arXiv:1412.1441. 2014

[15] Bradski G, Kaehler A. Learning OpenCV: Computer Vision with the OpenCV Library. California, USA: O'Reilly Media, Inc.; 2008. pp. 201-204, 384-404

[16] Mordvintsev A, Abid K. OpenCV-Python Tutorials: Camera Calibration and 3D Reconstruction [Internet]. Available from: http://opencv-python-tutroals.readthedocs.io/en/latest/py_tutorials/py_calib3d/py_calibration/py_calibration.html#calibration [Accessed: 10-04-2018]

[17] Stauffer C, Grimson W. Adaptive background mixture models for real-time tracking. In: IEEE Computer Society Conference on Computer Vision and Pattern Recognition; IEEE; 1999. pp. 246-252

[18] Goebel R. ROS by Example. Vol. 2. Lulu.com; 2015

[19] Team OpenCV Dev. OpenCV 2.4.13.6 Documentation [Internet]. Available from: http://docs.opencv.org/2.4/modules/refman.html [Accessed: 10-04-2018]

[20] Creative Commons Attribution, Ros Tutorials [Internet]. Available from: http://wiki.ros.org/ROS/Tutorials [Accessed: 10-04-2018]

[21] Python Software Foundation. The Python Tutorial [Internet]. Available from: https://www.python.org/ [Accessed: 10-04-2018]

[22] Dennis D, Tin C, Marou R. Color Image Segmentation [Internet]. Available from: https://theiszm.wordpress.com/tag/color-segmentation/ [Accessed: 10-04-2018]

Chapter 6

Device-Free Localization for Human Activity Monitoring

Shaufikah Shukri, Latifah Munirah Kamarudin and
Mohd Hafiz Fazalul Rahiman

Additional information is available at the end of the chapter

http://dx.doi.org/10.5772/intechopen.79442

Abstract

Over the past few decades, human activity monitoring has grabbed considerable research attentions due to greater demand for human-centric applications in healthcare and assisted living. For instance, human activity monitoring can be adopted in smart building system to improve the building management as well as the quality of life, especially for the elderly people who are facing health deterioration due to aging factor, without neglecting the important aspects such as safety and energy consumption. The existing human monitoring technology requires additional sensors, such as GPS, PIR sensors, video camera, etc., which incur cost and have several drawbacks. There exist various solutions of using other technologies for human activity monitoring in a smartly controlled environment, either device-assisted or device-free. A radio frequency (RF)-based device-free indoor localization, known as device-free localization (DFL), has attracted a lot of research effort in recent years due its simplicity, low cost, and compatibility with the existing hardware equipped with RF interface. This chapter introduces the potential of RF signals, commonly adopted for wireless communications, as sensing tools for DFL system in human activity monitoring. DFL is based on the concept of radio irregularity where human existence in wireless communication field may interfere and change the wireless characteristics.

Keywords: device-free localization, indoor localization, human detection and tracking, human activity monitoring

1. Introduction

Human movement and behavior while performing their daily activities have inherent hierarchical structure. As enabling technology, real-time human activity monitoring plays an important role in many human-centric applications in different areas such as healthcare, security, surveillance, smart building, etc., particularly to protect elder people and children from some bad incidents. Due to the advanced development in medical, science and technology, the human average lifespan has increased rapidly where people are getting healthier and having longer lives, thus increased the aging population worldwide. The United States' medical research agency, known as National Institute of Health (NIH), reported that in 2012, 8.0% (or 562 million) of the 7 billion global human population are aged 65 and over, and the percentage has increased by 0.5% (or 55 million) in 2015 [1]. Based on the aging trends, NIH has projected that by 2050, the older population will grow substantially up to 17% (or 1.6 billion) throughout the world [1]. However, most of elderly people spend their extra lifespan in unhealthy manner, with often debilitating illness and disability due to the deterioration of physical or mental functions caused by age-related diseases. In fact, the increase in the older population has a slight impact on the increase in disability rates of world's population [2].

With the increasing of older and disabled population in most countries and regions across the world, human and activity monitoring has gained substantial attention from the research community for ambient assisted living or elderly care application. As reported in [3], majority of the elderly people are more comfortable to live independently at their own home and community. Nevertheless, in the modern society, the conventional ways of taking care of elders in the family are no longer effective. As a result, there is higher demand in the society for the assistive technologies such as an intelligent monitoring system that can record the elders' daily activities in which family can respectfully monitor their loved ones who live alone at home. Due to the lower income earner after retirement and higher standards of living, many of the elders cannot afford to pay their healthcare cost as well as the expensive healthcare system or private nursing home care services. Nonetheless, various human monitoring technologies have been developed that help elderly people to age in place.

Traditionally, the human activity monitoring technology is a vision-based [4], which requires the use of video camera to monitor the human activity. Although this vision-based is an effective security measure approach as it can retains the records with high resolution, it also has several drawbacks that involves cost-inefficiency for large-scale deployments, energy consumption, and serious user privacy concerns if it is used in inappropriate places such as lavatory or bathroom, bedroom, and even nursing room. However, in several applications like elderly care and assisted living, monitoring human activities in these privacy areas is very crucial and necessary. For instance, lavatory or bathroom is one of the potential places for falling due to its slippery condition, thus activity monitoring in this place is very important for elderly fall detection system in detecting the falling event [5]. Meanwhile, the activity monitoring in the bedroom is very important for patient sleep monitoring system in detecting unusual sleeping behavior. In fact, the video camera requires a good lighting area ineffective in the dark and has limited view angles.

In recent years, thousands of research study on human activity monitoring has been conducted involving the replacement of traditional vision-based approach with various technologies such as acoustic-based [6, 7], motion-based [8, 9], body-worn sensors [10, 11], gyroscope [12], as well as smartphone [13, 14]. While such approaches address the privacy concern issue, they are sensor-based or in other words impose the requirement that special sensors, that is to be attached to, carried or worn by the subject for an effective activity monitoring. This is inconvenient and inappropriate for human usage especially the elders or people with brain-related diseases (Alzheimer, amnesia, dementia, etc.) to remember each day to wear or to activate those sensors. Furthermore, the whole monitoring process is ineffective and futile if the subject forgets to carry the sensor. Besides, the acoustic-based approach is range limited and prone to false detections since it can only be used in a short range and can easily be influenced by other audio signals [15]. The motion-based sensor such as a single accelerometer is not able to provide sufficient information to the system if used alone, hence need to combine with other sensors for more efficient activity monitoring [16]. Nevertheless, both vision- and sensor-based approaches bear with huge costs due to expensive equipment, installation, and maintenance. All the advantages and disadvantages of above approaches are summarized in **Table 1**.

Recently, Radio Frequency (RF)-based approaches have received significant research attentions to be employed in the human presence detection and activity monitoring based on different wireless radio technologies such as RFID [17, 18], Wi-Fi [19, 20], ZigBee [21, 22], FM radio [23, 24], microwave [25], etc. According to studies on the impact of human presence and activity on the RF signal strength [26–28], it has been proven that the existence and movement of human body in wireless radio network environment will interfere the wireless signal profiles, either in

Category	**Sensor technology**	**(+) Advantages** **(−) Disadvantages**
Vision-based	Video camera	+ Effective security measure + Maintain records – Interfere with privacy – Ineffective in the dark – High computational cost
Motion-based	Accelerometer Gyroscopes PIR	+ No privacy issue + Lower cost (PIR) + High detection accuracy – Raise physical discomfort issue (accelerometer and gyroscopes) – No direct linear or angular position information – Low range and line-of-sight restriction (PIR) – Prone to false detection – Insensitive to very slow motions
Sound-based	Ultrasonic Acoustic Audio (microphone)	+ Very sensitive to motion + Objects and distances are typically determined precisely + Inexpensive (audio) – Work only directionally (ultrasonic) – Sensitive to temperature and angle of the target (ultrasonic) – Easily be influenced by other audio signals/noise – Prone to false detections – Range limited
Sensor-based	Body-worn sensors (Body sensor networks)	+ High detection accuracy + No privacy issue – Expensive devices (sensors) – Disturb or limit the activities of the users – Required sensors installation and calibration

Table 1. Advantages and disadvantages of existing sensor technologies.

constructive or destructive manners, in which will change the RF communication pattern between the wireless transceivers. This phenomenon is called radio irregularity, which often consider as a drawback in RF communication. In RF-based human detection and activity monitoring, researchers have seen the radio irregularity phenomenon as a benefit in which it can be exploited as sensing tools to locate the human presence in the indoor environment and discriminate human activities or gestures. Since RF-based human activity monitoring approaches only exploit the wireless communication features, there is no need for expensive physical sensing equipment and modules, which accordingly reduce the cost, ease the deployment, reduce the energy consumption, and protect user privacy [29].

The RF-based approaches can be classified into device-bound and device-free. Like the sensor-based, the device-bound RF-based approach requires the on-body wireless sensors or devices (such as RFID tags or cards, Bluetooth wristbands, smart watches, etc.) to be attached to the subject, which has been known as one of the drawbacks. Hence, the subject is required to actively participate in the activity recognition and monitoring process by always remembering to activate and carry the wearable wireless devices. This device-bound system is also known as active monitoring system and the subjects are usually willing to be monitored by the system. Therefore, we refer the subject in this active monitoring system as an active target. As an example, daily activities, such as walking, sitting, lying, falling, etc., of an active target wearing a simple RFID tag can be tracked using RFID readers [30, 31]. Another example is that an active target carrying mobile phone or other Wi-Fi-embedded devices can be easily tracked by Wi-Fi detectors or monitor [32, 33].

Although the on-body wireless sensors such as RFID tags and RFID cards are commercially available and relatively low cost compared to other wireless technologies, their placement on the target's body may cause physical discomfort [34], especially the elders under long-term monitoring. Recent research works introduce the placement of RFID in the environments and objects instead of target's body for activity monitoring [35, 36]. However, reading multiple RFID tags at once may cause malfunction due to signal collision, thus anticollision algorithms are required in which incur an extra cost [37]. On the contrary, device-free RF-based approach, known as device-free localization (DFL), is a passive monitoring system that can locate and monitor human position and activity without the subject's participation, where the subjects do not need to carry or wear any radio devices. They are usually unaware with the system's existence, and possibly want to avoid being monitored [21]. The subject in this passive monitoring case is referred as passive target.

In this chapter, we review the recent progress of DFL for indoor environment prioritizing on human activity monitoring with a particular focus on the monitoring systems targeting personal health and assisted living applications. Our aims are to provide a comprehensive review on the topic and to quickly update the researchers beyond this field the state of art, potential, opportunities, challenges, opens issues, and future directions of activity recognition using DFL technology. To the best of our knowledge, although there exist surveys on human activity monitoring and recognition using vision-based [4, 38], wearable sensors [10, 39, 40], mobile phones [41, 42], there are only few surveys published in this research field on human activity monitoring using device-free RF-based [29, 43–45], including a general architecture of existing work especially in the context of healthcare and assisted living applications. Surveys as in

Refs. [46, 47] are specifically on the Wi-Fi-based approaches. However, we do not focus on the classification approaches of human activity, as there exist several in-depth literatures on human activity classification methods [48–51].

The organization of the chapter is as follows: Section 2 "RF-based DFL Technology" briefly discusses the concept of DFL in the perspective of human activity monitoring as understood within this study and provide an extensive review on the existing works. We decompose the taxonomy of the existing RF-based DFL technologies for human activity monitoring into measurement-based categories, regardless the type of wireless radio technologies used. Section 3 "Opportunities and Potential" presents the potential applications based on the state-of-art of RF-based DFL technology. Based hereon, in the last Section 4 "Challenges, Open Issues and Future Directions," we outline the challenges and the possible solutions, discuss the open issues, and comment on the possible future research direction of activity recognition using DFL technology.

2. RF-based DFL technology

Historically, the DFL analogy was firstly introduced by Youssef et al. in 2009 as device-free passive (DfP) for location determination, in which the subject is not equipped with a radio device, or not required to actively participate in the localization system [52]. The concept of DFL relies on the fact that any changes on the radio network environment will fluctuate the received signal profiles, i.e., due to reflection, diffraction, absorption, or scattering phenomena. DFL exploits the potential of ubiquitous deployed Internet of Things (IoT) [53] devices for indoor localization by leveraging the RF fluctuations as an indicator of presence of obstruction, i.e., object or human body. In [54], we have briefly defined the concept of DFL technology in the context of human detection and counting, together with the comprehensive review on the publications related to DFL research.

In correspondence to the tremendous progresses on DFL research, Scholz et al. have expanded the area of DFL technology in the context of activity recognition by introducing the concept of device-free RF-based for human activity monitoring as device-free radio-based activity recognition (DFAR) [55]. Instead of utilizing radio signal analysis for object detection and tracking, it can also be utilized in the DFL technology to recognize specific human movement, and even their activities and gesture. For instance, the fluctuations of ambient and local continuous signals have been exploited in detecting human daily activities such as walking, lying, crawling, or standing [56]. To ease the reader's understanding, we defined the DFL and DFAM systems as:

DFL: device-free localization system: a system which detects the presence of a passive target and locates the target's position using radio signal information while the target is not equipped with a wireless device, nor required to actively participate in the localization system.

DFAM: device-free activity monitoring system: a system which monitors and recognizes the activity performed by a passive target using radio signal information while the target is not equipped with a wireless device, nor required to actively participate in the localization system.

We illustrate the overall conceptual framework of RF-based DFL technology for human activity monitoring as in **Figure 1**, including the three important modules: wireless radio sensor network (WRSN), human detection (HD), and human monitoring (HM). The WRSN is a self-configured wireless network consisting of radio devices connected wirelessly, acting as the sensors, for monitoring and recording of the physical or environmental conditions, and organizing the collected information to a predefined central location for processing. The WRSN module works by detecting the availability of radio-embedded devices (sensors) for human presence detection, localization, and activity monitoring, as well as the deployment of the radio sensor networks. WRSN can be deployed in the real-world environments using any radio devices that utilize the similar technology or IEEE standard. For instance, Wi-Fi-based sensor network can be deployed using any devices that utilized the IEEE802.11 wireless local area network (WLAN), while ZigBee-based sensor network can be deployed using devices that utilized the IEEE802.15.4 wireless personal area network (WPAN).

The sensors in WRSN collect the information of current environment and forward the information to be processed by the HD module. HD module consists of detection and localization algorithms which analyze the information and automatically discover the presence of target, the number of target, the location of the target, the body temperature of the target, the activities performed by the target, the humidity of the environment, etc. HM module consists of activity

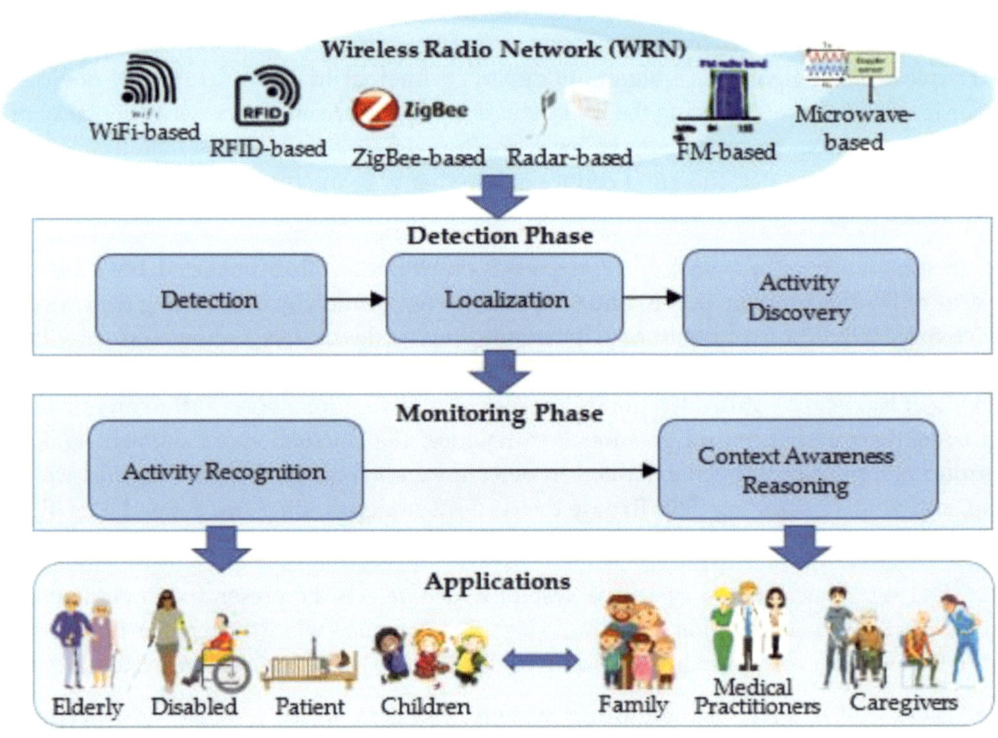

Figure 1. The overall conceptual framework of the RF-based DFL system.

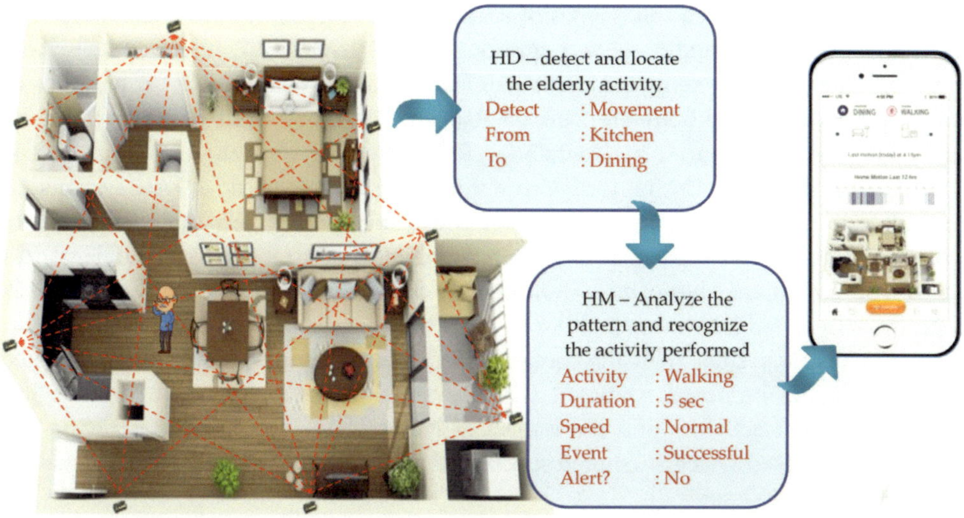

Figure 2. ZigBee-based sensor network deployed for elderly care application with the integration of mobile apps visualization.

classification algorithms connected with the designated context aware-based activity reasoning engines depending on the applications. Once an activity is detected, the HM module will observe, retrieve, and recognize the activities and alert the designated context aware-based activity reasoning engine to interpret ongoing events successfully or initiate actions as needed. For example, a ZigBee-based sensor network is deployed in a single bedroom apartment for elderly care application as depicted in **Figure 2**.

Following on the DFAM research in [55], many research works on human motion detection and activity monitoring have been presented utilizing different radio technologies such as RFID [35–37], WiFi [5, 19, 20], ZigBee [21, 22], FM radio [23, 24], microwave [25], etc., adopting different signal descriptors such as Receive Signal Strength (RSS) [57–61], Channel State Information (CSI) [5, 20, 62–64], Doppler effect [25, 65], and Packet Received Rate (PRR) [66], without neglecting the easy-of-use problem and physical discomfort issue. In the following subsection, we decompose the taxonomy of the existing RF-based DFL technologies for human activity monitoring into signal descriptor categories such as RSS-based, CSI-based, amplitude-based, Doppler-based, and PRR-based, regardless the type of wireless radio technologies used.

2.1. RSS-based

Similar to human presence detection, activity monitoring using RSSI-based DFL technology exploits the RF-signal fluctuation features, in which the components of the received signal are blocked, absorbed, and reflected by the human while performing an activity, inducing the RF signal in the vicinity of receivers into a specific characteristic pattern. Such pattern can be identified and classified for the corresponding activity by exploiting the changes on the RSS of the affected wireless links.

In [57], Sigg et al. introduced three types of RF-based DFAR systems: active continuous signal-based, active RSSI-based, and passive continuous signal-based DFAR; which exploit the fluctuation of RSS due to human movement and activities. Both active and passive continuous signal-based proposed are USRP Software Defined Radio (SDR)-based system, which are deployed using specialized SDR devices. Meanwhile the RSSI-based DFAR system utilized the 2.4 GHz INGA sensor nodes [57]. The performance accuracy of the proposed DFAR systems is then compared with the performance accuracy of the motion-based recognition system. In the motion-based recognition system, accelerometers are attached to the subjects while performing the activities. By implementing three well-known classifier algorithms that are Naive Bayes, Classification Tree, and k-nearest neighbor (k-NN), their proposed RF-based DFARs are able to achieve comparable results with the motion-based system. Furthermore, they evaluated the performance of the proposed RF-based DFAR system in the presence of multiple subjects performing different activities and the impact of increasing the number of receiving devices. However, the proposed systems required specialized SDR devices, where the hardware availability remains as an open issue [60].

Sigg et al. expanded their work by designing an RSS-based activity recognition system for the mobile phones [58, 59] based on the advantages of mobile phones as personal devices that often carried everywhere. The proposed system utilized the Wi-Fi-RSSI values of incoming packets at a mobile phone for the activities classification. Unlike other body-worn devices, the function of mobile phone in an RSS-based activity monitoring system remains feasible even when it is not carried by the user. By default, the firmware and operating system (OS) of a standard mobile phone do not provide privilege for user to access its hardware as well as desired RSSI information. Thus, work in [58] utilized a modified firmware, which allows mobile phone to run Wi-Fi interface in monitor mode and developed tools to process RSSI sample captured on mobile phone in monitoring simple human activities such as walking and phone handling. Meanwhile, work in [59] focused on recognizing 10 different single-handed gestures utilizing the same modified firmware and tools developed in [58] with average accuracy of 0.51 when distinguishing all gestures and is able to achieve average accuracy of 0.60 and 0.72 when reducing to 7 and 4 gestures, respectively. Unfortunately, the OS root access incompatibility, complicated firmware modifications, and low accuracy are the major issues in the real-world applications.

The proposed RF-based DFAR systems in [57–59] utilized the RSS features as per listed in **Table 2** and several combinations of those features for the activities classification. Assume that a wireless network environment consists of a static transmitter node or access point (AP), and a static receiver node or monitoring point (MP). Let $r_i(t)$ denote the RSS of sample i at time t. Assume that $|R_t|$ samples of $r_i(t)$ are captured on a received signal for a sample window, $R_t = r_1(t), \ldots, r_{|R_t|}(t)$, the RSS features of the samples are defined in **Table 2**.

Since works in [58, 59] focused more on hand gestures, Gu et al. [60] proposed an online Wi-Fi RSSI fingerprint-based DFAM concentrated on human activity, which has a flexible architecture and can be integrated in any existing indoor WLANs, regardless the environment conditions. Based on the preliminary results of the human activities impact on the Wi-Fi characteristic study [60], the Wi-Fi RSSI fingerprint can be extracted and exploited to distinguish different activities since each activity has their own RSSI fluctuation patterns.

Feature	Description	Definition
Mean	Represents the static changes in RSS Provides means to distinguish a presence of static person as well as the exact location	$Mean(R_t) = \frac{\sum_{r_i \in R_t} r_i}{\lvert R_t \rvert}$
Variance	Represents the volatility of RSS Provides the estimation on changes in nearby receivers such as movement of person	$Var(R_t) = \sqrt{\frac{\sum_{r_i \in R_t} (r_i - Mean(R_t))^2}{\lvert R_t \rvert}}$
Standard deviation (SD)	Can be used instead of the variance The interpretation of SD and variance is identical	$Std(R_t) = \sqrt{Var(R_t)}$
Median	Represents static changes in RSS. More robust to noise than the mean Let the ordered set of samples $R_{t,ord} = \bar{r}_1, \ldots, \bar{r}_{\lvert R_t \rvert}; i < j \Longrightarrow r_i \leq r_j$	$Med(R_t) = r_{\lceil \lvert R_{t,ord} \rvert / 2 \rceil}$
Normalized spectral energy	Represents a measure in the frequency domain of the RSS Can be used to capture periodic patterns such as walking, running, or cycling	$E_i = \sum_{k=1}^{n} P_i(k)^2$
Minimum and maximum	Both represent extremal signal peaks Can be used to estimate movement and any changes in environment	$Min(R_t) = r_i \in R_t \ with \ \forall r_j \in R_t : r_i \leq r_j$ $Max(R_t) = r_i \in R_t \ with \ \forall r_j \in R_t : r_i \geq r_j$
Signal peaks within 10% of a maximum	Reflections of the obstructed signal strength at a receive antenna Peaks of similar magnitude indicate that movement is farther away Can be used to indicate near-far relations and activity of individuals	$h(r_i) = \begin{cases} 1 & if \ r_i \geq \max(r_1, \ldots, r_{\lvert R_t \rvert}) \cdot 0.9 \\ 0 & else \end{cases}$ $max_{0.9}(r_i) = \sum_{r_i \in R_t} h(r_i)$
Mean difference between subsequent maxima	Similar magnitude of maximum peaks within a sample window indicates low activity in an environment or static activities The opposite will indicate dynamic activities	$R_{max}(R_t) = \{r_i \mid r_i \in R_t, r_{i-1} < r_i \wedge r_i > r_{i+1}\}$ $a(R_t) = \sum_{\substack{\forall r_i, r_j \in R_{max}(R_t); \\ i < j; \\ \nexists r_k \ with \ i < k < j}} \frac{\lvert r_i - r_j \rvert}{R_{max}(R_t)}$

Table 2. Several features considered for RF-based DFAR [57–59].

To reduce the difficulties in distinguishing activities having similar RSSI footprints, such as sitting and standing, the proposed system adopted a novel fusion classification tree-based algorithm. The system has been evaluated through extensive real-world experiments based on six main activities (that are sleeping, sitting, standing, walking, falling, and running) and achieved average accuracy of 72.47% for all activities, thus outperforms Naive Bayes, Bagging, and k-NN classifiers.

Monitoring human activity using RFID technology is often associated with the physical discomfort issues as user needs to wear or carry the RFID devices. However, there exist several studies that implemented the RFID technology in the different way for the device-free activity monitoring [61, 67]. Instead, the RFID devices are attached to the walls, furniture, and daily objects. This approach is known as passive RFID-based DFL. Thanks to the rapid advancement and sophistication in cheap sensing and wireless technology for introducing various RF-embedded devices with an open-source platform such as TelosB [68], IRIS [69], Waspmote [70], etc., that can operate in real-time environment based on the "plug and sense" concept where information like RSS can easily be captured. However, RSS measurements suffer from high uncertainties since the signal profiles tend to fluctuate depending on the environment, thus unpredictably experience interference, complex multipath propagation, and being noise-sensitive. In addition, RSS-based system experiences accuracy and coverage limitation due to the lack of the frequency diversity. Thus, RSS-based approach is only suitable for coarse-grained human activity monitoring.

2.2. CSI-based

Most of the research on Wi-Fi-based DFL utilized the CSI, one of the Wi-Fi features extracted from the physical layer of radio wireless system, for indoor location estimation and human motion and activities monitoring due to its stability and robustness in complex environment compared to RSSI. CSI information are available in commercial wireless devices such as network interface controller (NIC), which is also known as network interface card, network adapter, LAN adapter, or physical network interface. Unlike RSSI value which is usually measured from one packet, CSI value is measured per orthogonal frequency-division multiplexing (OFDM) from each packet and uses the frequency diversity technique to reflect the multipath propagation signals caused by human motion and activity, thus making it suitable for monitoring the fine-grained signals of human activities and motions.

Based on [19, 63], consider a Wi-Fi-based DFL system with NICs continuously measure the CSI variations in every received Wi-Fi frame of multiple wireless channels. Let NTx and NRx represent the number of transmitting and receiving antennas, respectively. Assume that at time t, the frequency domain representation of transmitted and received signals with carrier frequency f is denoted as $X(f,t)$ and $Y(f,t)$, respectively. The relationship of the transmitted and received signals can be expressed as:

$$Y(f,t) = H(f,t) \times X(f,t) \tag{1}$$

where $H(f,t)$ represents the complex-valued channel frequency response (CFR) of the same carrier frequency f and time t. Based on Eq. (1), the CFR depends on the received signal $Y(f,t)$ with noise channel, where the noise channel captured in the measured $H(f,t)$ can be expressed as:

$$H(f,t) = \frac{Y(f,t)}{X(f,t)} \tag{2}$$

The CFR values consist of S metrices of CSI measurement with dimension of $NTx \times NRx$, where S represents the number of OFDM subcarriers. Each CSI matrix represents the CFR value of one received Wi-Fi frame between a pair of $Tx - Rx$ antennas at a particular OFDM subcarrier frequency and time. CSI are usually measured at S = 30 subcarriers and starting from here onward, the time series of CFR values of a particular OFDM subcarrier for a given antenna pair is denoted as CSI stream. For instant, at S = 30, there are 30 × NTx × NRx CSI streams in a time series of CSI values.

Since the radio signals travel from a transmitter to a receiver through multiple paths depending on the surrounding, the measured $H(f, t)$ of a received signal through K different paths can be expressed as:

$$H(f,t) = e^{-j2\pi\Delta ft} \prod_{k=1}^{K} a_k(f,t) e^{-j2\pi f \tau_k(t)} \tag{3}$$

where $a_k(f, t)$ is the complex-valued representation for both attenuation and initial phase offsets of the k-th path, $e^{-j2\pi\Delta f \tau_k(t)}$ is the phase shift on the k-th path with the propagation delay of $\tau_k(t)$, and $e^{-j2\pi\Delta ft}$ is phase shift caused by the carrier frequency offset (CFO) with frequency difference Δf between the sender and the receiver. Any changes in the length of particular path will affect the phase of the Wi-Fi signal travel on that corresponding path.

Figure 3 shows the scenario where Wi-Fi signals transmitted from an AP (Tx) to an MP (Rx) are traveled through different paths, which are the line-of-sight (LoS) path and paths reflected by wall and human body. Let the path of reflected signal due to human body is the k-th path. When the human body moves by a small distance d between time interval 0 and t, the k-th path length changes from $d_k(0)$ to $d_k(t)$. Based on the fact that the radio signal travels at the speed of light, the propagation delay $\tau_k(t)$ experienced by the k-th path can be written as:

$$\tau_k(t) = \frac{d_k(t)}{c} \tag{4}$$

where c is the speed of light, which is related to the carrier frequency f and wavelength λ based on the function $\lambda = c/f$. Thus, the phase shift $e^{-j2\pi f \tau_k(t)}$ of the k-th path can be written as $e^{-j2\pi d_k(t)/\lambda}$, which describes the relationship of the changes in path length by one wavelength with the changes of phase shift of 2π at the receiver subcarrier signal of the given path.

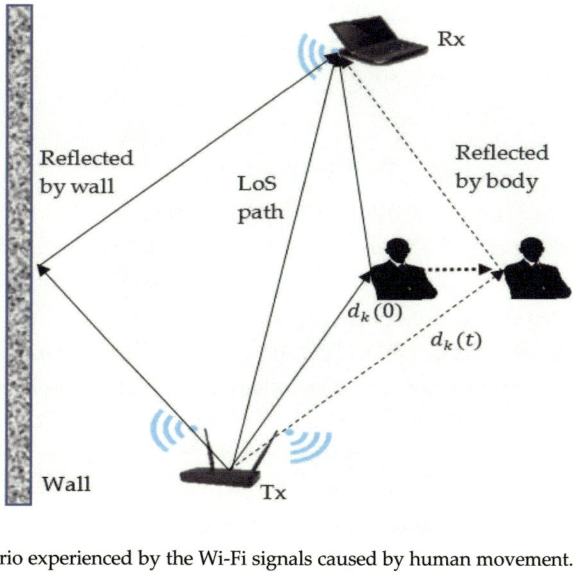

Figure 3. Multipaths scenario experienced by the Wi-Fi signals caused by human movement.

The phase of each path can be precisely measured only if the transmitter is in synchronization with the receiver. Unfortunately, due to hardware limitation and environment variations, the CFO of the commercial Wi-Fi devices, denoted as Δf in Eq. (3), cannot be ignored. The impact of CFOs of devices running on IEEE 802.11n standard causes random variation in the phase of CSI, which allows devices to continuously transmit Wi-Fi frames based on frame aggregation mechanism, thus creating a phase interference scenario. It is difficult to precisely measure even the small phase shift in $e^{-j2\pi f\tau_k(t)}$ under this interference scenario.

To ignore the phase interference introduced by CFO, Wang et al. [63] introduced a CSI-speed model into their activity recognition and monitoring system (CARM), which considers the relationship of CFR power variations instead of CFR phase variation to the human movement speeds. Since the CSI streams of human movements are correlated, it is hard to extract the real trend of CSI caused by the human movement for feature classification purpose. Therefore, works in [5, 19, 63] applied the principal component analysis (PCA) to discover the principal component of the CSI fluctuation pattern caused by human activity motion to be used as features for activity classification. In [5], Li et al. analyzed five features from CSI principal component which are normalized standard deviation (STD), median absolute deviation (MAD), interquartile range (IR), signal entropy, and duration of human motion to recognize seven different human daily activities. By applying random forest-based classification algorithm, work in [5] verified the validity of their proposed human monitoring system in both the LoS and Non-LOS (NLoS) scenarios as 95.43% and 91.4%, respectively. Meanwhile, activity monitoring system based on hidden Markov model (HMM) classifier algorithm proposed by Wang et al. [19, 63] achieved an average recognition accuracy of 96%.

Although undesired noise from the environment may disturb some of the streams, since CSI is measured using OFDM method, other streams which are not affected by the noise still can provide the real trend of CSI information. Since CSI contains more information than RSSI, it is suitable for fine-grained activity monitoring. However, unlike RSSI which is available in almost all wireless devices, CSI only can be obtained from devices with specific NIC cards such as Intel 5300 and Atheros 9390 [19].

2.3. Doppler-based

When wave such as ultrasonic and radio wave is transmitted to moving target, the wavelength of the reflected wave shifts depending on the direction and velocity of the movement. This is known as Doppler effect or Doppler shift. Recently, the principle of the Doppler effect has been proposed by researches in device-free radio sensor network for human activity monitoring and data gathering of real-world environment [25, 65] since the Doppler-based technology has the ability to accurately detect movement and eliminate the stationary noise of the environment [66]. The same principle of Doppler effect is applied to a Doppler sensor, having a beat signal as an output, in which frequency is defined as the difference between transmitted and received waves. Due to its high detection accuracy, work in [25] has deployed a 24-GHz microwave-Doppler sensor for a device-free activity monitoring system to recognize the daily activity of three passive targets with an average recognition rate of 90.6% based on eight different activities.

Based on the Doppler possibility study in [25], assume that a radio wave source at a fixed position transmits a radio wave with frequency f_t and velocity c. An object is moving relatively to the source with velocity $\pm v$. The received wave with frequency f_r can be defined as:

$$f_r = f_t \pm f_D \tag{5}$$

where f_D is the Doppler frequency, which is defined as the difference between frequency of transmitted and received waves. The value of f_D is higher when the object moves toward the source, and lower when the object moves away from the source. Thus, the calculation of f_D can be simplified as:

$$f_D = |f_r - f_t| = f_t\left(\frac{c+v}{c-v} - 1\right) = \frac{2v}{c-v} f_t \simeq \frac{2v}{c} f_t. \tag{6}$$

Let the signal of the transmitted wave S_t with amplitude A_t at time t is defined as:

$$S_t(\mathrm{t}) = A_t \sin\left(2\pi f_t\right) \tag{7}$$

and Δt is the time delay between the transmitted and received signal. The received signal S_r with amplitude A_r at time t is defined as:

$$S_r(\mathrm{t}) = A_r \sin\left(2\pi\left(f_t \pm f_D\right)t - 2\pi f_t \Delta t\right) \tag{8}$$

From Eq. (8), the received signal depends on the object size and its distance from the source. The beat signal S_D with amplitude A_D at time t is then observed to be the output signal of the Doppler source as:

$$S_D(\mathrm{t}) = A_D \sin\left(2\pi f_D t - 2\pi f_t \Delta t\right). \tag{9}$$

From Eq. (9), the amplitude and frequency of the Doppler shift are highly correlated with the range of the object and its motion speed. Thus, any human movement and activities with different speeds will have different Doppler shifts. Those human activities can be estimated and analyzed by extracting the features of Doppler signature in the frequency and time domains.

Work in [65] proposed an in-home Wi-Fi signal-based activity recognition framework for e-healthcare applications utilizing the passive micro-Doppler (m-D) signature classification. A fast Fourier transform (FFT) was used on the cross-correlation product of the baseline and monitored signals to find the exact delay Δt and frequency shift f_D of the strongest signal. This was defined as cross ambiguity function (CAF) and the equation was represented as follows:

$$CAF\left(\Delta t, f_D\right) = \int_{-\infty}^{+\infty} e^{-j2\pi f_D t} S_B{}^H(t - \Delta t) \times S_M(t) dt. \tag{10}$$

where $S_B(t)$ and $S_M(t)$ are the baseline and monitoring signals, respectively. The m-D signature of an activity at a specific time t is defined as the frequency vector $\widehat{f_D}$ induced by the passive target movement at a specific delay Δt. All the recorded Doppler signatures are then concatenated together in a time line history of Doppler signature for the database construction.

Although the constant false alarm rate (CFAR) detection is not suitable for the indoor environment due to the ambiguity peaks and direct signal interference (DSI) problems [65], DSI is an important feature in Doppler-based as it can be used to distinguish different signatures. Instead, a weighted standard deviation is proposed as the indicator to detect the m-D signature without eliminating the ambiguity peaks and DSI. PCA can be applied to reduce the dimension of dataset and eliminate the undesired noise. Finally, the Doppler signature is classified using a sparse representation classifier (SRC) with subspace pursuit (SP) technique, which outperforms the well-known support vector machine (SVM) in terms of classification accuracy and coverage. The sparsity level in SRC can easily be controlled and adjusted, thus making the proposed activity recognition framework a feasible tool, which is very suitable for the real-time healthcare applications, especially for the new users since it is not required to re-training the system.

2.4. PRR-based

It has been proved that RF signal features extracted from RSS and CSI information discussed in Sections 2.1 and 2.2 can be used to distinguish the type of movement as well as recognize the activities performed. However, RSS is sensitive to the shadowing effect and experiences the complex multipath propagation behavior, which makes it only suitable for monitoring coarse-grained activity. Meanwhile, CSI, which provides powerful information suitable for fine-grained activity monitoring, faces hardware issues since the information is only available from NIC embedded devices.

In [66], Huang and Dai presented a novel PRR-based DFL system for human movement recognition under the NLoS scenario based on packet state characteristic from link state information (LSI). The LSI, which contains more physical information such as RSSI, packet delivery rate, packet state, packet delay, packet loss, time arrival, and time interval of the received packet, etc., can be accessed from the network layer. Human movement in the radio network environment will block or reflect the signal and cause significant changes on the signal propagation path. This results in the fluctuation of channel link quality as well as slow fading effect.

By exploring the LSI features such as packet state and packet arrival time, different activities performed by a person in the monitoring area can be identified. Work in [66] exploited the PRR measurement to identify the link state. Assume the i-th window of size w_i at fixed interval L. The packet state is denoted as $s(\mathrm{i})$, and labeled as "1" if the packet is successfully arrived with no error and "0" if the packet is lost or contains an error. The PRR $P(W_i)$ of the link state is defined as the proportion of successfully arrived packets among all transmitted packets and can be expressed as:

$$P(W_i) = \frac{1}{w_i} \sum_{j=L\times i}^{L\times i+w_i} s(j). \tag{11}$$

Consider a wireless network environment in a hallway consists of a transmitter Tx and a receiver Rx as shown in **Figure 4**. When a person is moving into the hallway area, there will be four possible trajectories: walking from Tx to Rx, walking from Rx to Tx, walking from Tx to Tx, and from Rx to Rx. When the person moves into the hallway area, the link state quality tends to fluctuate in terms of the PRR. Different moving trajectories in the hallway will generate different fluctuation patterns of PRR with respect to the person position in hallway, thus the direction of walking can be identified. The distance of moving traces with different trajectories can be calculated using the Euclidean distance equation as in (12) and the walking direction of the traces can be identified using the K nearest neighbors (KNN) algorithm. The Euclidean distance between the PRR of the testing trace P_i and training trace $\overline{P}_i$ can be calculated as:

$$E_d = \sqrt{\sum\nolimits_{i=1}^{n} \left(P_i - \overline{P}_i\right)^2}. \tag{12}$$

Since PRR cannot be used to distinguish the speed of the movement, other link state information known as the received packet arrival time is used to measure the speed. However, the time interval of received packets is highly correlated with the moving speed. Therefore, several parameters, such as autocorrelation function acf, Budget Rate R_B, and expected total latency (ETL), can be applied to the link state-related information in order to classify the different speed [66]. The proposed PRR-based approach introduced in [66] is able to achieve a high accuracy of 95% in recognizing four different movement directions and 44% improvement on the average accuracy in classifying four different speeds compared to the RSSI-based approach.

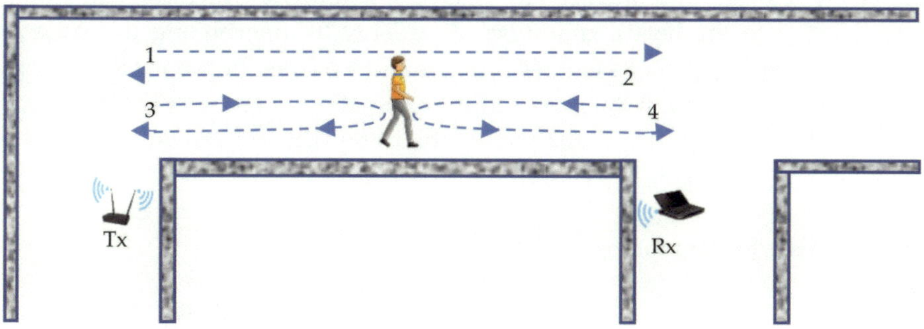

Figure 4. Node deployment in the hallway area.

3. Opportunities and potential applications

DFL for human and activity monitoring is the promising technology for collecting data about the human presence and activity patterns. The technology is much cheaper than the existing traditional monitoring system using video camera. It consists of radio nodes comprising the appropriate sensor array along with computational devices that transmit and receive data wirelessly, and capable of providing information on an unprecedented temporal and spatial scale. The DFL system is an easy-to-install motion tracking system developed based on the IoT to improve the quality of life as well as provide intelligence and comforts to the user especially the disabled. Users, especially family, can respectfully monitor their loved ones who live alone at home, without requiring them to wear devices or change their habits. The system can be integrated with mobile and web apps which allow user to easily monitor their home/office from anywhere, in real time. The system can be made to replace the existing RFID monitoring system which always raises physical discomfort and is less reliable since more than one tag can respond at the same time.

3.1. Remote home healthcare services

In recent years, there has been an increase in the number of patient admission in hospitals worldwide, whether federal or nonfederal, especially in the developed countries due to the increase of older and disabled population [71, 72]. In England, for instance, the older population (aged 65–69) has grown by 34% in 2016 after a decade from 2.2 million in 2006, together with the series of increasing hospital admissions by 57% from 0.8 million, over the same period of time [71]. This causes most hospitals to experience inadequate bed problem to admit patients, thus slowing down the work of medical staff, especially at the casualty department or emergency department (ED). Patients started to complain about the slow services, which lead to bad reputation of the hospital. By implementing DFL system, federal and nonfederal bodies can introduce remote home healthcare services where patients can be monitored and advised from anywhere. These services help patients to improve their function and live with greater independence. Using this system, existing patients are taught to manage their wellness level, and safely manage their medication regimens; meanwhile, medical staff can remotely monitor and estimate the health condition of patients by interpreting the patients' daily routines. In this situation, patients will remain at home, avoiding hospitalization or admission to long-term care institutions. If the daily routine of a patient is abnormal as expected such as too long sleeping or resting in bed, the patient might be sick and should be visited soon for closer examination.

3.2. Ambient assisted living tool

Recent advances in medicine allow people to live longer and healthier compared to the previous generations, which lead to an increase in the number of elder people. Aging brings many challenges to them due to cognitive decline, chronic age-related diseases, as well as limitations in physical activity, vision, and hearing. With an increase in age-related diseases, there will also be a rise in individuals unable to live independently. However, due to the higher standards of living, children nowadays are too busy working to earn money for living and have no time to care for their parents. This leads to an increase in the number of elderly people in the federal- and nonfederal-owned welfare or nursing home; meanwhile, there will be a shortage of professionals trained or care-giver to work with the aging population. Given the fact that most of the elderly people prefer to stay in the comfort of their own homes, and given the costs of private nursing home care, it is imperative to develop technologies that help elderly people to age in place. By implementing the DFL technology as an ambient assisted living tool, family can respectfully monitor their loved ones who live alone at home, without requiring them to wear devices or change their habits. The DFL system can be integrated with mobile and web apps which allow user to easily monitor their home or office from anywhere, in real time. This advantage makes DFL technology very suitable for monitoring persons' activities (especially the elderly, disable people, and patient suffering from Alzheimer's disease) without causing them physical discomfort with the wearable devices or sensors. In addition, it is a challenge for them to remember each day to wear or to activate those devices.

3.3. Smart buildings for home and office

Automatic and monitoring control in "smart" building, i.e., for home or office, was developed based on the IoT and WSN technologies to improve the quality of life as well as provide intelligence and comforts to the user especially the disabled. The DFL technology can be expanded not only for monitoring purposes, but also as an application server that can control and initiate actions as needed. For example, in an office building where few people are working together, the proposed DFL technology can enhance the existing lighting, heating, and air conditioning system by providing information of current environment such as the presence of people, the number of people as well as their location, the body temperature of the occupants, the activity performed by the occupants, the humidity of the environment, etc. If there are too many electronic devices in use or too many occupants in the office which leads to an increased temperature of the room, the building heating system can be adjusted or automatically lowered based on the information provided by the DFL system. If there is no people presence in several areas inside the office especially during lunch break, the lights and air-conditioning in those areas can be automatically switched off. Government as well as private bodies can implement this technology in all their buildings which definitely will reduce the utility cost.

4. Challenges, open issues, and future direction

In the recent years, the RF-based DFL approach has made tremendous achievements and becomes a popular research topic in localization and activity monitoring area. In the previous section, we have provided a review of existing human activity monitoring system based on different approaches. However, there are still significant challenges and open issues worth exploring and require further in-depth research. Moreover, the performance of existing systems can be further optimized, improved, and extended. In this section, we present a list of challenges and open issues together with the possible future research directions to be addressed by the researchers.

Unstructured approaches: Although several theories and models have been presented in the existing human activity monitoring researches, still, there is no general technique, methodological approach, and framework to DFAM. Most of the existing research focused on a particular application and specific technology based on empirical observation result. This topic requires more complete theoretical model as well as its general technique or framework for RF-based activity recognition. Additional in-depth research on the characteristic of human body which relates to the radio signal based on human body model is required. One of our research directions is to deploy the representation learning method such as deep learning method with high recognition rate. Unlike the traditional machine learning algorithm, which required manual feature selection as well as rules definition, deep learning approach is able to learn the correct auto-generated features and accurately predict the correct feature. In addition, although it is a challenging task to implement unsupervised learning technique into the DFL human activity monitoring system, it is worth to be explored.

Inconsistency and unreliability of the sensors: Most of the presented studies used common sensor such as RFID, MEMSIC motes, and other RF-devices used the continuous sensing technique, where the sensor will continuously collect sample for activity recognition. However, this continuous sensing technique is challenging since it depends on the battery lifetime in order to be consistently operated. In addition, various continuous sequences of human performing activity with several periodic variations may result in wrong activity prediction. In order to continuously monitor the human activity without disrupting the system, energy-efficient mechanisms can be implemented to the sensor, where under certain conditions, the sensors can be turned off or put under sleep mode. This technique is known as duty-cycling technique. Only selected sensors are active for sampling at specific state, whereas other inactive sensors are under sleep mode, waiting for any possible state transitions. It has been proven that by using this duty-cycling technique, the battery lifetime can be improved by 75%; however, the recognition latency will increase. Additional research work is needed to compare the performance of activity recognition system in terms of hardware or devices diversity. Some of sensors or devices can be used together for a complete human activity recognition.

Hardware, maintenance, and labor costs: For larger-scale environment, especially for system with finger-printing approaches, the deployment of hundreds of sensors in a building of multiple rooms will obtain good detection accuracy. However, deploying such high density of sensors will affect the overall energy consumption of the building and demand for additional installation, maintenance, and labor costs. If these sensors are powered up using battery, the maintenance and energy requirements should be taken into consideration for the long-term deployment. Thus, it is required to select the best hardware, feature extraction approach, and classification technique to be deployed in the system without the requirement of additional cost.

Noise and interference from other appliances: Recognizing activities in noisy environment, that is, communication channel consisting noisy channel and interferences from other devices running

http://dx.doi.org/10.5772/intechopen.79442

on the same channel, is quite challenging. With the presence of noise and interference due to the inherent volatility of wireless signal, the activity recognition becomes less accurate. Most of the studies are evaluated under controlled condition or laboratory environment, which allowed selected devices to be present in the monitoring environment. Some of the research implementation of frequency diversity technique may help to increase the system accuracy. However, frequency diversity technique is not suitable for indoor environment due to interference from nearby wireless devices. In order to develop the DFL system in the practical or real-world environment, the activity recognition algorithm should be performed in the large-scale area which consists not only the required devices, but other devices running on the same communication channel. Thus, further in-depth research on the noise elimination technique is required to effectively remove the noise of different sources in the radio channel.

Offline classification and training: Most of the presented studies proposed the offline activity classification methods where the data collected by the receiver are being trained and classified offline by the application server. The system performances presented in those studies are based on the offline recognition. In order to build reliable real-world activity monitoring applications, the activity classification and system performance should be performed and evaluated online on the application server. Offline classification process is suitable for application which does not require online recognition such as monitoring daily routine of a person. In this scenario, the data of the daily routine can be collected and stored into the application server and can be processed offline. However, online classification and recognition are required for those applications that interested in specific human activity, duration and sequence of activity, such as fitness coaching, fall detection and remote healthcare. In an ideal and reliable system, the system performance and classifier accuracy can always be improved and optimized as long as the system continuously collects enough data. This will make the system benefit to human centric applications.

Recognizing complex activity: Most of the presented studies focus on the coarse-grained or human basic activities such as walking, running, standing, falling, etc. However, the patterns of these activities are not strong enough to be directly linked to the more complex or fine-grained activities. Human behavior is spontaneous, and they tend to perform multiple tasks at the same time which introduce confusion in the activity recognition process, and sometimes may result in incorrect classification. For instance, it is rather straightforward to detect if the user is lying down on couch but inferring if the user is sleeping or watching television, or fainted is different. Although there exist several attempts in addressing this issue, further research is needed in exploring the information collection of the complex activities recognition and mapping for human-centric application domains, especially in persuasive applications for a behavior or lifestyle change.

Recognizing multiuser activities: It is noticeable that most of the presented studies focus on recognizing activity of a person. In fact, the real-world applications usually involve multiple user presence in environment such as people walking together, queuing in a line, watching television together, family dinner, etc.; however, none of the presented methods are applicable for the situation. This open issue should be further investigated for different application domains.

5. Conclusion

In this chapter, we provided an extensive review on human activity recognition using RF-based DFL technology, targeting human-centric applications such as healthcare, well-being, and assisted living applications. We provided the details information on concept of DFL and DFAM, together with the feature selection approaches based on different signal descriptors and the potential applications. We presented an extensive review on the existing and on-going works qualitatively and discussed on the challenges, limitations, and future research directions relevant to this field. We believe that this DFL technology has great potential in the future, which can benefit humans and will be one of the key areas of research that worth to be explored.

Author details

Shaufikah Shukri[1,2]*, Latifah Munirah Kamarudin[1,2] and Mohd Hafiz Fazalul Rahiman[3]

*Address all correspondence to: shaufikahshukri.ss@googlemail.com

1 School of Computer and Communication Engineering, Universiti Malaysia Perlis (UniMAP), Arau, Perlis, Malaysia

2 Centre of Excellence for Advanced Sensor Technology (CEASTech), UniMAP, Jejawi, Perlis, Malaysia

3 School of Mechatronic Engineering, UniMAP, Arau, Perlis, Malaysia

References

[1] He W, Goodkind D, Kowal P. U.S. Census Bureau, International Population Reports, P95/16-1, An Aging World: 2015, Washington, DC: U.S. Government Publishing Office; 2016

[2] World Health Organization, Fact Sheet: Disability and health [Internet]. 2018. Available from: http://www.who.int/mediacentre/factsheets/fs352/en/ [Accessed: 2018-03-20]

[3] Farber N, Shinkle D, Lynott J, Fox-Grage W, Harrell R. Aging in place: A state survey of livability policies and practices. National Conference of State Legislatures and the AARP Public Policy Institute; 2011

[4] Moeslund TB, Hilton A, Krüger V. A survey of advances in vision-based human motion capture and analysis. Computer Vision and Image Understanding. 2006;**104**:90-126. DOI: 10.1016/j.cviu.2006.08.002

[5] Li F, Al-Qaness MA, Zhang Y, Zhao B, Luan X. A robust and device-free system for the recognition and classification of elderly activities. Sensors. 2016;**16**(12):2043. DOI: 10.3390/s16122043

[6] Yatani K, Truong KN. BodyScope: a wearable acoustic sensor for activity recognition. In: Proceedings of the ACM Conference on Ubiquitous Computing (UbiComp'12); 5–8 September 2012; Pittsburgh, PA, USA. New York: ACM; 2012. pp. 341-350

[7] Sim JM, Lee Y, Kwon O. Acoustic sensor-based recognition of human activity in everyday life for smart home services. International Journal of Distributed Sensor Networks. 2015; **11**(9):679123. DOI: 10.1155/2015/679123

[8] Torres-Huitzil C, Alvarez-Landero A. Accelerometer-based human activity recognition in smartphones for healthcare services. In: Adibi S, editors. Mobile Health: A Technology Road Map. Springer Series in Bio-/Neuroinformatics. Vol 5. Cham: Springer; 2015. pp. 147-169. DOI: 10.1007/978-3-319-12817-7_7

[9] Lu Y, Wei Y, Liu L, Zhong J, Sun L, Liu Y. Towards unsupervised physical activity recognition using smartphone accelerometers. Multimedia Tools and Applications. 2017; **76**(8):10701-10719. DOI: 0.1007/s11042-015-3188-y

[10] Lara OD, Labrador MA. A survey on human activity recognition using wearable sensors. IEEE Communications Surveys and Tutorials. 2013;**15**(3):1192-1209. DOI: 10.1109/SURV. 2012.110112.00192

[11] Tahavori F, Stack E, Agarwal V, Burnett M, Ashburn A, Hoseinitabatabaei SA, Harwin W. Physical activity recognition of elderly people and people with parkinson's (PwP) during standard mobility tests using wearable sensors. In: Proceeding of the International Smart Cities Conference (ISC2), 14–17 September 2017; Wuxi, China. IEEE; 2017. pp. 1-4

[12] Li Q, Stankovic JA, Hanson MA, Barth AT, Lach J, Zhou G. Accurate, fast fall detection using gyroscopes and accelerometer-derived posture information. In: Proceeding of 6th International Workshop on Wearable and Implantable Body Sensor Networks (BSN'09); 3–5 June 2009; Berkeley, CA, USA. IEEE; 2009. pp. 138-143

[13] Su X, Tong H, Ji P. Activity recognition with smartphone sensors. Tsinghua Science and Technology. 2014 Jun;**19**(3):235-249. DOI: 10.1109/TST.2014.6838194

[14] Fei G, Niu J, He Z, Jin X, Pal F. An effective system for detecting family activities based on smartphone. In: 15th International Conference on Industrial Informatics (INDIN'17); 24–26 July 2017; Emden, Germany. IEEE; 2017. pp. 155-160

[15] Li L, Bai R, Xie B, Peng Y, Wang A, Wang W, Jiang B, Liang J, Chen X. R&P: An low-cost device-free activity recognition for E-health. IEEE Access. 2018;**6**:81-90. DOI: 10.1109/ACCESS. 2017.2749323

[16] Kushbu CM, Kurian M. Design and implementation of child activity recognition using accelerometer and RFID cards. International Journal of Advanced Research in Computer Engineering & Technology (IJARCET). 2014;**3**(4);1437-1440

[17] Hekimian-Williams C, Grant B, Liu X, Zhang Z, Kumar P. Accurate localization of RFID tags using phase difference. In: Proceeding of IEEE International Conference on RFID; 2010 Apr 14; Orlando, FL, USA. IEEE; 2010. pp. 89-96

[18] Kellogg B, Talla V, Gollakota S. Bringing gesture recognition to all devices. In: 11th USENIX Conference on Networked Systems Design and Implementation; 2–4 April 2014; Seattle, WA. Berkeley, CA, USA: USENIX Association; 2014. Vol. 14, pp. 303-316

[19] Wang W, Liu AX, Shahzad M, Ling K, Lu S. Understanding and modeling of wifi signal based human activity recognition. In: 21st Annual International Conference on Mobile Computing and Networking (MobiCom'15); 7–11 September 2015; Paris, France. New York: ACM; 2015. pp. 65-76

[20] Abdelnasser H, Youssef M, Harras KA. Wigest: A ubiquitous wifi-based gesture recognition system. In: Proceeding of IEEE Conference on Computer Communications (INFOCOM'15); 26 April–1 May 2015; Kowloon, Hong Kong. IEEE; 2015. pp. 1472-1480

[21] Shukri S, Kamarudin LM, Goh CC, Gunasagaran R, Zakaria A, Kamarudin K, Zakaria SS, Harun A, Azemi SN. Analysis of RSSI-based DFL for human detection in indoor environment using IRIS mote. In 3rd International Conference on Electronic Design (ICED'16); 11–12 August 2016; Phuket, Thailand. IEEE, 2017. pp. 216-221

[22] Qi X, Zhou G, Li Y, Peng G. Radiosense: Exploiting wireless communication patterns for body sensor network activity recognition. In: IEEE 33rd Real-Time Systems Symposium (RTSS'12); 4–7 December 2012; San Juan, Puerto Rico. IEEE, 2013. pp. 95-104

[23] Shi S, Sigg S, Ji Y. Passive detection of situations from ambient fm-radio signals. In: Proceedings of the 2012 ACM Conference on Ubiquitous Computing (UbiComp'12); 5–8 September 2012; Pittsburgh, Pennsylvania. New York: ACM; 2012. pp. 1049-1053

[24] Shi S, Sigg S, Ji Y. Joint localization and activity recognition from ambient FM broadcast signals. In: ACM Conference on Pervasive and Ubiquitous Computing Adjunct Publication (UbiComp'13); 8–12 September 2013; Zurich, Switzerland. New York: ACM; 2013. pp. 521-530

[25] Sekine M, Maeno K. Activity recognition using radio Doppler effect for human monitoring service. Information and Media Technologies. 2012;**7**(2):783-792. DOI: 10.11185/imt.7.783

[26] Lee PW, Seah WK, Tan HP, Yao Z. Wireless sensing without sensors—An experimental approach. In: Proceeding of IEEE 20th International Symposium on Personal, Indoor and Mobile Radio Communications; 13-16 September 2009; Tokyo, Japan. IEEE; 2010. pp. 62-66

[27] El-Kafrawy K, Youssef M, El-Keyi A. Impact of the human motion on the variance of the received signal strength of wireless links. In: Proceeding of IEEE 22nd International Symposium on Personal Indoor and Mobile Radio Communications (PIMRC'11); 11–14 September 2011; Toronto, ON, Canada. IEEE; 2012. pp. 1208-1212

[28] Turner JS, Ramli MF, Kamarudin LM, Zakaria A, Shakaff AY, Ndzi DL, Nor CM, Hassan N, Mamduh SM. The study of human movement effect on Signal Strength for indoor WSN deployment. In: Proceeding of IEEE Conference on Wireless Sensor (ICWISE'13), 2–4 December 2013; Kuching, Malaysia. IEEE; 2014. pp. 30-35

[29] Wang S, Zhou G. A review on radio-based activity recognition. Digital Communications and Networks. 2015;**1**(1):20-9. DOI: 10.1016/j.dcan.2015.02.006

[30] Yurtman A, Barshan B. Human activity recognition using tag-based radio frequency localization. Applied Artificial Intelligence. 2016;**30**(2):153-179. DOI: 10.1080/08839514.2016.1138787

[31] Wang L, Gu T, Tao X, Lu J. Toward a wearable RFID system for real-time activity recognition using radio patterns. IEEE Transactions on Mobile Computing. 2017;**16**(1):228-242. DOI: 10.1109/TMC.2016.2538230

[32] Musa AB, Eriksson J. Tracking unmodified smartphones using wi-fi monitors. In: Proceedings of the 10th ACM Conference on Embedded Network Sensor Systems (SenSys '12); 6–9 November 2012; Toronto, Ontario, Canada. New York: ACM; 2012. pp. 281-294

[33] Lau SL, König I, David K, Parandian B, Carius-Düssel C, Schultz M. Supporting patient monitoring using activity recognition with a smartphone. In: 7th international symposium on Wireless communication systems (ISWCS); 19–22 Sept. 2010; York, UK. IEEE; 2010. pp. 810-814

[34] Shukri S, Kamarudin LM, Ndzi DL, Zakaria A, Azemi SN, Kamarudin K, Zakaria SM. RSSI-based Device Free Localization for Elderly Care Application. In: Proceeding of International Conference on Internet of Things, Big Data and Security (IoTBDS'17); 24–27 April 2017; Porto, Portugal. Setúbal, Portugal: SCITEPRESS; 2017. vol. 2, pp. 125-135

[35] Parlak S, Marsic I, Burd RS. Activity recognition for emergency care using RFID. In: Proceedings of the 6th International Conference on Body Area Networks; 07–08 Nov 2011; Beijing, China. ICST; 2011. pp. 40-46

[36] Buettner M, Prasad R, Philipose M, Wetherall D. Recognizing daily activities with RFID-based sensors. In: Proceedings of the 11th international conference on Ubiquitous computing. 30 Sept–3 Oct 2009; Orlando, Florida, USA. ACM; 2009. pp. 51-60

[37] Kaur M, Sandhu M, Mohan N, Sandhu PS. RFID technology principles, advantages, limitations & its applications. International Journal of Computer and Electrical Engineering. 2011;**3**(1):151. DOI: 10.7763/IJCEE.2011.V3.306

[38] Chaaraoui AA, Climent-Pérez P, Flórez-Revuelta F. A review on vision techniques applied to human behaviour analysis for ambient-assisted living. Expert Systems with Applications. 2012 Sep 15;**39**(12):10873-10888. DOI: 10.1016/j.eswa.2012.03.005

[39] Ananthanarayan S, Siek KA. Persuasive wearable technology design for health and wellness. In: 6th International Conference on Pervasive Computing Technologies for Healthcare (PervasiveHealth'12); 21–24 May 2012; San Diego, CA, USA. IEEE; 2012. pp. 236-240

[40] Avci A, Bosch S, Marin-Perianu M, Marin-Perianu R, Havinga P. Activity recognition using inertial sensing for healthcare, wellbeing and sports applications: A survey. In: Proceeding of 23rd International Conference on Architecture of Computing Systems (ARCS'10), 22–23 Feb. 2010; Hannover, Germany. VDE; 2011. pp. 1-10

[41] Morales J, Akopian D. Physical activity recognition by smartphones, a survey. Biocybernetics and Biomedical Engineering. 2017 Jan 1;**37**(3):388-400. DOI: 10.1016/j.bbe.2017.04.004

[42] Bayındır L. A survey of people-centric sensing studies utilizing mobile phone sensors. Journal of Ambient Intelligence and Smart Environments. 2017 Jan 1;**9**(4):421-48. DOI: 10.3233/AIS-170446

[43] Shang J, Wu J. Survey on human activity recognition systems using RF signals. In McKenzie VD, editor. Mobile Networks: Concepts, Applications and Performance Analysis. Hauppauge NY: Nova Science Publishers; 2017. pp. 109-137

[44] Ma J, Wang H, Zhang D, Wang Y, Wang Y. A survey on wi-fi based contactless activity recognition. In: IEEE International Conferences on Ubiquitous Intelligence & Computing, Advanced and Trusted Computing, Scalable Computing and Communications, Cloud and Big Data Computing, Internet of People, and Smart World Congress; 18–21 July 2016; Toulouse, France. IEEE; 2016. pp. 1086-1091

[45] Yang X, Lü, SH, Zhang M, Wang XD, Zhou XM. A survey on activity recognition using wireless signals. Journal of Software/Ruan Jian Xue Bao. 2015;**26**:39-48

[46] Mitra S, Acharya T. Gesture recognition: A survey. IEEE Transactions on Systems, Man, and Cybernetics, Part C (Applications and Reviews). 2007;**37**(3):311-24. DOI: 10.1109/TSMCC.2007.893280

[47] Turaga P, Chellappa R, Subrahmanian VS, Udrea O. Machine recognition of human activities: A survey. IEEE Transactions on Circuits and Systems for Video technology. 2008 Nov;**18**(11):1473-1488. DOI: 10.1109/TCSVT.2008.2005594

[48] Abdullah MF, Negara AF, Sayeed MS, Choi DJ, Muthu KS. Classification algorithms in human activity recognition using smartphones. International Journal of Computer and Information Engineering. 2012 Aug 27;**6**:77-84. Available: http://waset.org/publications/8520

[49] Peterek T, Penhaker M, Gajdoš P, Dohnálek P. Comparison of classification algorithms for physical activity recognition. In: Abraham A, Krömer P, Snášel V (eds), Innovations in Bio-Inspired Computing and Applications. Advances in Intelligent Systems and Computing, vol. 237. 2014. Springer, Cham. pp. 123-131

[50] Bansal B. Gesture recognition: A survey. International Journal of Computer Applications. 2016 Apr;**139**(2):8-10. DOI: 10.1109/TSMCC.2007.893280

[51] Davila JC, Cretu AM, Zaremba M. Wearable sensor data classification for human activity recognition based on an iterative learning framework. Sensors. 2017 Jun 7;**17**(6):1287. DOI: 10.3390/s17061287

[52] Youssef M, Mah M, Agrawala A. Challenges: device-free passive localization for wireless environments. In: 13th annual ACM international conference on Mobile computing and networking; 9–14 Sept 2007; Montréal, Québec, Canada. ACM: NY, USA; 2007. pp. 222-229

[53] Atzori L, Iera A, Morabito G. The internet of things: A survey. Computer networks. 2010; **54**(15):2787-2805. DOI: 10.1016/j.comnet.2010.05.010

[54] Shukri S, Kamarudin LM. Device free localization technology for human detection and counting with RF sensor networks: A review. Journal of Network and Computer Applications. 2017 Nov 1;**97**:157-174. DOI: 10.1016/j.jnca.2017.08.014

[55] Scholz M, Sigg S, Schmidtke HR, Beigl M. Challenges for device-free radio-based activity recognition. In: Workshop on Context Systems, Design, Evaluation and Optimization; 2011

[56] Sigg S, Scholz M, Shi S, Ji Y, Beigl M. RF-sensing of activities from non-cooperative subjects in device-free recognition systems using ambient and local signals. IEEE Transactions on Mobile Computing. 2014 Apr;**13**(4):907-20. DOI: 10.1109/TMC.2013.28

[57] Sigg S, Shi S, Buesching F, Ji Y, Wolf L. Leveraging RF-channel fluctuation for activity recognition: Active and passive systems, continuous and RSSI-based signal features. In: Proceedings of International Conference on Advances in Mobile Computing & Multimedia, 2–4 December 2013, Vienna, Austria. ACM; 2013. p. 43

[58] Sigg S, Hock M, Scholz M, Troester G, Wolf L, Ji Y, Beigl M (2014) Passive, Device-Free Recognition on Your Mobile Phone: Tools, Features and a Case Study. In: Stojmenovic I, Cheng Z, Guo S. (eds) Mobile and Ubiquitous Systems: Computing, Networking, and Services. MobiQuitous 2013. Lecture Notes of the Institute for Computer Sciences, Social Informatics and Telecommunications Engineering, Vol 131. Springer, Cham

[59] Sigg S, Blanke U, Troster G. The telepathic phone: Frictionless activity recognition from wifi-rssi. In: IEEE International Conference on Pervasive Computing and Communications (PerCom'14), 24–28 March 2014, Budapest, Hungary. IEEE; 2014. pp. 148-155

[60] Gu Y, Ren F, Li J. Paws: Passive human activity recognition based on wifi ambient signals. IEEE Internet of Things Journal. 2016;**3**(5):796-805. DOI: 10.1109/JIOT.2015.2511805

[61] Booranawong A, Jindapetch N, Saito H. A system for detection and tracking of human movements using RSSI signals. IEEE Sensors Journal. 2018;**18**(6):2531-2544. DOI: 10.1109/JSEN.2018.2795747

[62] Kim SC. Device-free activity recognition using CSI & big data analysis: A survey. In: Proceeding of 2017 Ninth International Conference on Ubiquitous and Future Networks (ICUFN'17); 4–7 July 2017; Milan, Italy. IEEE; 2017. pp. 539-541

[63] Wang W, Liu AX, Shahzad M, Ling K, Lu S. Device-free human activity recognition using commercial WiFi devices. IEEE Journal on Selected Areas in Communications. 2017;**35**(5): 1118-1131. DOI: 10.1109/JSAC.2017.2679658

[64] Shi C, Liu J, Liu H, Chen Y. Smart user authentication through actuation of daily activities leveraging WiFi-enabled IoT. In: 18th ACM International Symposium on Mobile AdHoc Networking and Computing; 10–14 July 2017; Chennai, India. ACM; 2017. p. 5

[65] Chen Q, Tan B, Chetty K, Woodbridge K. Activity recognition based on micro-Doppler signature with in-home Wi-Fi. In: 18th International Conference on e-Health Networking, Applications and Services (Healthcom'16); 14–16 Sept. 2016; Munich, Germany. 2016. pp. 1-6

[66] Huang X, Dai M. Indoor device-free activity recognition based on radio signal. IEEE Transactions on Vehicular Technology. 2017;**66**(6):5316-5329. DOI: 10.1109/TVT.2016.2616883

[67] Ruan W. Unobtrusive human localization and activity recognition for supporting independent living of the elderly. In: IEEE International Conference on Pervasive Computing and Communication Workshops (PerCom Workshops); 14–18 March 2016; Sydney, NSW, Australia. IEEE; 2016. pp. 1-3

[68] Memsic Inc., TelosB datasheet, Doc. Part No: 6020-0094-03 Rev A [Internet]. Available from: http://www.memsic.com/userfiles/files/Datasheets/WSN/telosb_datasheet.pdf [Accessed: 2018-03-26]

[69] Memsic Inc., IRIS datasheet, Doc. Part No: 6020-0124-02 Rev A [Internet]. Available from: http://www.memsic.com/userfiles/files/Datasheets/WSN/IRIS_Datasheet.pdf [Accessed: 2018-03-26]

[70] Libelium, Wapsmote datasheet, Document version: v7.2 - 10/2017 [Internet]. Available at: http://www.libelium.com/development/waspmote/documentation/waspmote_datasheet.pdf [Accessed: 2018-03-26]

[71] NHS England. Hospital admissions hit record high as population ages [Internet]. 2016. Available from: https://digital.nhs.uk/article/943/Hospital-admissions-hit-record-high-as-population-ages [Accessed: 2018-03-26]

[72] Yan G, Norris KC, Greene T, Alison JY, Ma JZ, Yu W, Cheung AK. Race/ethnicity, age, and risk of hospital admission and length of stay during the first year of maintenance hemodialysis. Clinical Journal of the American Society of Nephrology. 2014;**9**(8):1049-1402. DOI: 10.2215/CJN.12621213

Section 3

Face and Expressions Recognition

Chapter 7

Access Control in the Wild Using Face Verification

Ricardo Ribeiro, Daniel Lopes and António Neves

Additional information is available at the end of the chapter

http://dx.doi.org/10.5772/intechopen.79520

Abstract

In the past few years, face recognition has received great attention from both research and commercial communities. Areas such as access control using face verification are dominated by solutions developed by both the government and the industry. In this chapter, a face verification solution is presented using open-source algorithms for access control of large-scale events under unconstrained environments. From the type of camera calibration to the algorithms used for face detection and recognition, every stage has a proposed solution. Tests using the proposed solutions in the entrance of a building were made in order to test and compare each solution proposed.

Keywords: face recognition, face detection, access control, unconstrained environment, camera calibration

1. Introduction

Over the past few years, face recognition has become one of the most successful applications in computer vision and pattern recognition. It has received significant attention in several areas, such as law enforcement and surveillance (video surveillance and access control), smart cards (national ID and passports), information security (data management and file encryption), and entertainment (video game and virtual reality), among others [1].

Biometric-based technologies have been developed and implemented over the last century. These systems are the most promising for personal identification. Examples of modes of biometric systems include face recognition, fingerprints, iris scanning, and others [1].

Face recognition as a biometric technique appears to offer several advantages. The lack of interaction of the user is an important advantage regarding these types of systems appointed by [1]. In a fingerprint system, for example, the user needs to place his finger in a designated area, while in a face recognition system, the face images can be acquired passively.

Face recognition systems have, however, some level of complexity as there are some stages that are needed to execute in order to achieve a system with a good performance. **Figure 1** presents these stages.

Within each stage, there are specific operations that can be added in order to achieve better performance results. Right on the start, the image acquisition is a crucial step where there is room for improvement. Later, the face detection and recognition can be performed by specific algorithms which are presented and studied. Finally, two algorithms for face normalization (also known as preprocessing) algorithms, which are mentioned on state of the art articles, are also analyzed for this specific chapter.

State of the art face recognition is dominated by industry- and government-scale datasets. There is a large accuracy gap between today's publicly available face recognition systems and the state of the art private face recognition systems [2]. However, this gap is closing up as better open-source algorithms and datasets with more and better images starts to appear.

Despite the success and high verification or recognition rates, there are still some challenges such as age, illumination, and pose variations. Most of these systems work well under constrained conditions (i.e., scenarios in which at least a few of the factors contributing to the variability between face images are controlled); however, the performance degrades rapidly when they are exposed to conditions where none of these factors are regulated [3].

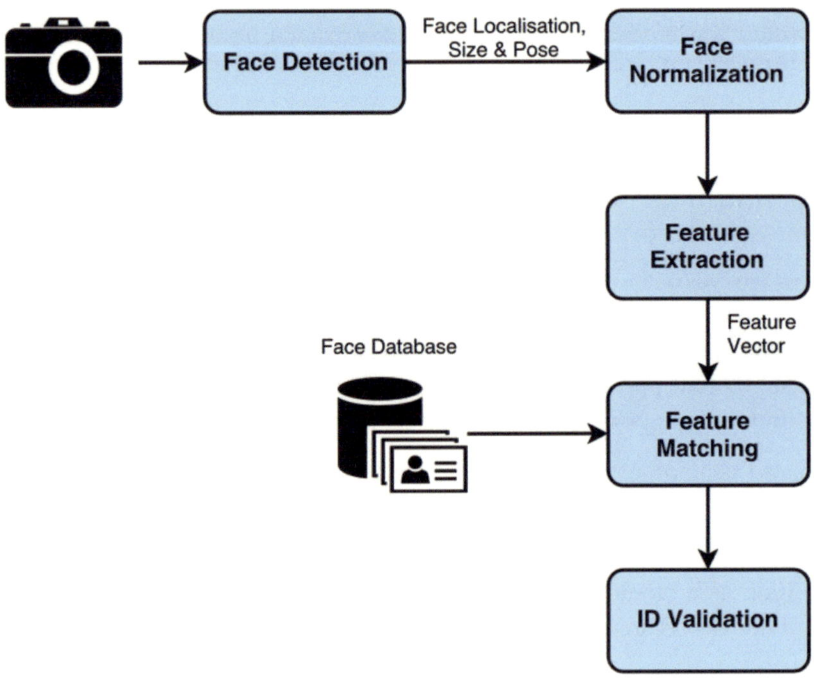

Figure 1. Configuration of a generic face recognition system.

http://dx.doi.org/10.5772/intechopen.79520

Toward exploring this field and the increasing demand of these systems, an access control solution for unconstrained environments using face verification with open-source algorithms is presented in this chapter.

An introductory section is presented that provides a brief introduction to the face recognition system. In Section 2, the proposed solution is described. Later in this section, the major problems for a face recognition system for unconstrained environments are explained. These problems are some of the challenges that are tried to solve in this chapter. The several implemented algorithms are described in Section 3. In Section 4, experimental results showing the effectiveness of the proposed algorithms and the comparison between them are provided. Finally, a summary of the work done, comparison of the different experiments, concluding remarks, and the future work are featured in Section 5.

2. Proposed solution

The proposed solution consists of the creation of a face verification (1:1 match comparison) system using open-source face recognition and detection algorithms in order to implement it in large-scale events with access control, such as sport infrastructures. To access this type of events, it is usually through the acquisition of a ticket/ID card. In order to improve the access control, the ticket access/acquisition is complemented with a face verification system.

The environment of these places is usually outdoors; therefore, the lighting conditions cannot be fully controlled [4]. Thus, the solution involves the use of cameras with adjustable parameters which do not have a proper calibration for these types of environments. An artificial light is also added which helps to compensate the lack or the excess of light in the scene.

As for software, two different programming languages, C++ and Python, are used. The C++ language is used for image acquisition and control of the camera parameters, including the calibration method since the cameras manufacturer only provides a library for the C programming language. Once the image is acquired, it is sent through a socket to a Python script that uses all the computer vision algorithms.

The solution is divided into two stages, registration and verification, that work independently of each other. Each process is divided into five scripts, where camera, facetracker, and NFC scripts are common to both stages. The database and interface scripts have some differences in both stages.

The different scripts are described as follows:

1. *Camera Script*: This script developed in C++ starts the system with the acquisition of images from the outside world. When a person approaches and his/her face is detected, a calibration of the camera parameters is done. Once the camera calibration is finished, the images acquired are sent in real time to the facetracker script.
2. *Facetracker Script*: Once activated, this Python script tracks the face of the person who is in front of the camera. The face is analyzed in order to crop and process only persons looking

toward the camera. When the face cropping and the preprocessing is done, the face image goes through a Deep Neural Networks (DNNs) which gives a 128D vector as output. This vector is compared to the vector acquired on the previous face image and, if the threshold is above the limit set, it will mean that a different person who is appearing in front of the camera, thus sending a warning to the next script. When the comparisons are below the threshold, the output vectors of the DNN are sent to the script.

3. *Database Script*: If no warning is received from the previous script, this script will store the output vectors of the face images. For the verification stage, when it receives an ID from the NFC script, these vectors are compared to the ones that are in the database associated with the ID number. The comparison gives, like in the case of the facetracker, an output value that decides if the person has that card associated with him/her. According to the comparison value, a token is sent to the Interface script. For the registration, instead of comparing the vectors, they are stored in the database associated to the ID number.
4. *NFC Script*: Python script that reads the NFC card reader values. If someone swipes an NFC tag over the card reader, the ID value of that tag is sent to the Database Script.
5. *Interface Script*: This script is used for the communication between the user and the system. It is designed to show images on the screen that gives feedback to the user of what is happening in the system. It tells the user to look at the camera, if he/she had done the registration, and finally a welcome message is displayed if the comparison value presented on the database script is below the threshold or a denying message if the value is above. When the person is in the registration, a wait message is displayed while the vectors are stored and finally it shows a successful registration message.

Figure 2 shows a block diagram of scripts communication.

2.1. Challenges

In order to build a face verification system with these characteristics, an important factor is taken into account: the unconstrained environment where the system is going to be implemented. In a computer vision point of view, some problems related with these kinds of environments appear which are mentioned as follows:

1. ***Head pose:*** At the time of the image acquisition, the viewing direction of the subject may not be toward the camera. These face images may not be the best suitable for the face recognition system.
2. ***Face image resolution:*** As the subject approaches the camera, his/her face starts to be detected. However, if the person is still at some distance from the camera, the face images collected may not have enough resolution for the system.
3. ***Subject motion:*** It is taken into consideration that the subject is in movement and that may cause some blur in the images acquired.
4. ***Face tracking:*** It is crucial that there will be distinction between different subjects especially at the time of the ticket acquisition as if not done correctly, the face images of different subjects may end up in the same person database.

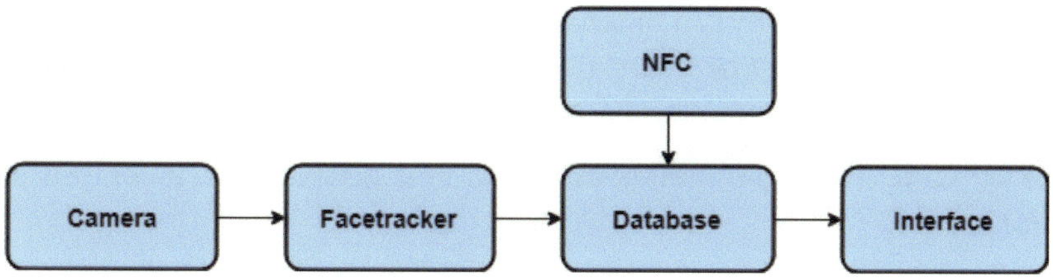

Figure 2. Block diagram of communication between scripts.

5. ***Non-controlled illumination:*** This may be the most difficult challenge to overcome as the cameras may be installed in an outdoor environment and, therefore, different lightning conditions according to the time of the day and the meteorological circumstances.

3. Proposed algorithms

The software developed obeys to some specific steps which are exposed in **Figure 3**.

3.1. Calibration through intensity pixels

In this section, a different type of calibration is proposed to acquire the best digital image for the face verification system.

When using the automatic calibration of the parameters provided by the camera, the whole image is considered when calibrating. Therefore, the region of interest (ROI) that will be acquired by the system can be affected by the light intensity that there is in the background and the image may not have the best quality.

In order to get the most suitable ROI (in this case, the face) for the system, it is attempted to create a calibration focused on this region.

The algorithm proposed is a mixture between the calibration of exposure time and gain.

Since the main goal is to implement the face verification system in an uncontrolled environment, an initial calibration is done using the auto-parameters calibration provided by the camera in order to adapt to the light and environment conditions and to detect the first face for the

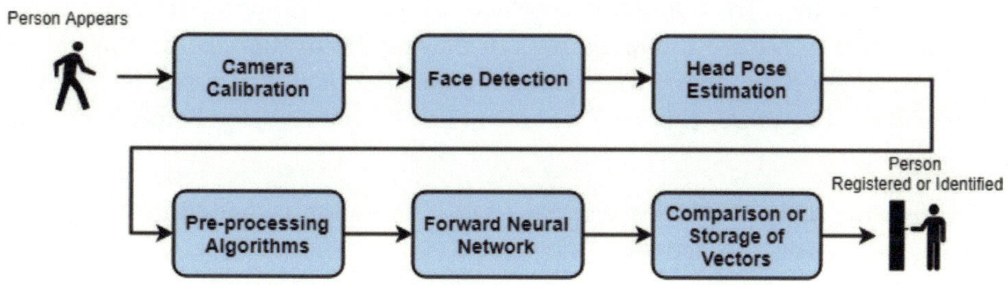

Figure 3. Workflow diagram of the software developed.

use of the calibration. At this point, a timer is set to wait a few seconds, so that the parameters of the camera have the time to be internally changed and established. Exposure time, gain, and white balance are the parameters changed automatically by the camera software.

When a face is found, the auto-parameter calibration is disabled and it continues to the next step of the calibration.

3.1.1. *Mean sample value*

This calibration step is based in the mean sample value (MSV) from the image gray-level histogram of the region where the face is represented. Introduced by [5], the MSV is used to calibrate the exposure time and the gain of the camera.

In this stage, the MSV is calculated through the gray-level histogram of the face region with the equation described next:

$$\mathrm{MSV} = \frac{\sum_{j=0}^{4}(j+1)\,x_j}{\sum_{j=0}^{4} x_j} \tag{1}$$

where x_j is the sum of the gray values in region j of the histogram (in the proposed approach, the histogram is divided into five regions).

It is worth noting that the pixels used for the MSV calculation are only the ones that are inside of the face-bounding box of the largest face found on the image.

A range of values is set for the MSV. If the calculated MSV is in range, between the values 2.1 and 2.5, the camera parameters (gain and exposure) have acquired values. Otherwise, the camera parameters are increased or decreased depending on whether the MSV is below the minimum value or above the maximum value, respectively.

This method has the main advantage that, if the same person appears on different parts of the day, the face images acquired will have very similar intensity values as the gain is calculated to have the same intensity values between a certain range.

3.1.2. *White pixels*

This method addresses the situations when the face of a subject is partially exposed to sunlight which causes that part of the face too bright. To solve this, if a region where the intensity pixels have the maximum intensity found, the camera parameter values are decreased in order to reduce the brightness of that region of the face. In this case, when reducing the camera parameters, the side of the face that is not exposed to sunlight may become too dark. Therefore, the MSV value cannot be reduced far below the minimum value previously.

Figure 4 shows the comparison between parameter calibration provided by the camera and the proposed calibration, respectively.

http://dx.doi.org/10.5772/intechopen.79520

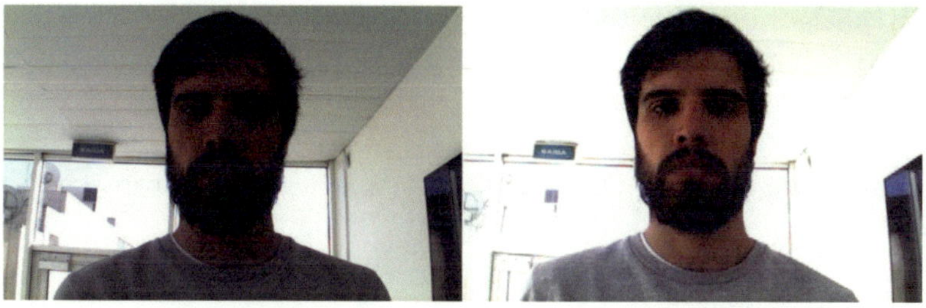

Figure 4. Comparison between the automatic calibration (left image) and the proposed calibration (right image).

3.2. Detection and recognition algorithms

Several algorithms were studied and implemented into the system. Despite these algorithms being state of the art, where the use of neural networks is prevalent in an attempt of closing the gap between the performance of commercial and open-source of face recognition solutions, several other exist in the study [6].

In previous work [7], the Haar Cascades, Local Binary Patterns Cascade (LBP), and Histogram of Oriented Gradients (HoG) algorithms were studied for face detection. The FisherFaces and Local Binary Patterns Histograms (LBPH) algorithms were also studied for face recognition.

3.2.1. Face detection

1. ***Histogram of oriented gradients (HoG)***: *Dlib's*[1] implementation is based on the algorithm presented in [8] that it is used for the face detection stage. It is especially useful as it provides 68 face landmarks that are further used at the recognition step for pose estimation.
2. ***Multi-task cascaded convolutional networks*** [9]: Deep cascaded multi-task framework exploits the inherent correlation between detection and alignment to boost up their performance. It provides five major face landmarks instead of the 64 of *Dlib*. It is, however, more immune to light variations and occlusion.

3.2.2. Face recognition

1. ***Deep metric learning (DML):*** Implementation also provided by *Dlib* library where the network implemented was inspired in [10] that does the face verification. The model trained achieves 99.38% in the benchmark Label Faces in the Wild (LFW) [11]. The input data of the network model for training were two datasets: the FaceScrub dataset [12] and the VGG dataset [13] with about 3 million faces in total.
2. ***OpenFace*** [2]: Face recognition with deep neural networks which achieves an accuracy of about 92% on the LFW [11] benchmark. The training of the neural network was done with the CASIA-WebFace [14] and FaceScrub [12] containing about 500,000 images.

[1] http://dlib.net/

3. ***DeepFace* [13]:** Algorithm inspired in [15, 16]. The CASIA-WebFace is used on training. In LFW benchmark, it achieves 99.2% of accuracy. The implementation used of this algorithm can be found in the github repository.[2]

It is worth mentioning that the *OpenCV*[3] library was used in the image processing and transformation.

3.3. Preprocessing methods

Once the image is acquired, there is still some image processing that may improve the system accuracy toward detection and recognition.

3.3.1. Gamma correction (GC)

Gamma is a very important characteristic in any digital system. In the world of cameras, it defines the relationship between a numerical value of a pixel and its actual luminance. The GC enhances the local dynamic range of the image in dark or shadowed regions while compressing it in bright regions and at highlights [17]. However, this operation is still affected by some level of directional lightning as pointed by [18].

Given a certain gamma (γ), the relation between the gray-level image with gamma correction (I_g) and the original one (I) is given by $I_g = I^{\gamma}$.

As it is possible to analyze in **Figure 5**, the human eye does not relate the detected light with the actual luminance as a "linear" relationship.

Figure 6 presents images with different gamma values, from the highest value to the lowest value (from the left to the right). As it is possible to analyze, the image with a higher gamma is more uniform regarding light.

The ambition then is that using an appropriate gamma value, the images acquired will not be as susceptible to lighting variations.

3.3.2. Contrast-limited adaptive histogram equalization (CLAHE)

CLAHE is an adaption of Adaptive Histogram Equalization (AHE) [19] that was first introduced for contrast enhancement for both natural and non-visual images [20]. This variation that introduced the limitation of contrast started began to be used in the face recognition field [21], which improved the contrast in face images.

Later, it began to see its utility in the facial recognition field, and a variation entitled contrast-limited adaptive histogram equalization (CLAHE) [19] was started to be used.

CLAHE is a preprocessing stage that focuses on improving the contrast in an image. This technique was applied as a preprocessing technique in [21] and it was applied on the face

[2] https://github.com/bearsprogrammer/real-time-deep-face-recognition
[3] https://opencv.org/

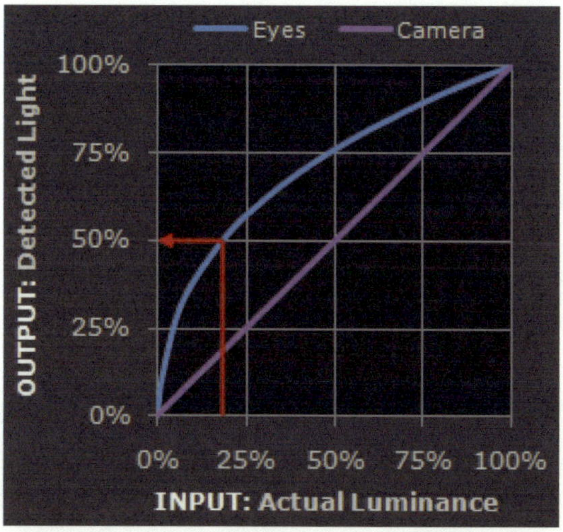

Figure 5. Relation between the detected light and the actual luminance for both eyes (in blue) and camera (in purple) (http://www.cambridgeincolour.com/tutorials/gamma-correction.html).

Figure 6. Face images with different gamma values. From the highest value to the lowest value (from the left to the right) (http://www.cambridgeincolour.com/tutorials/gamma-correction.html).

images in order to highlight the features that describe the face. The results exposed regarding recognition were improved with the addition of this stage.

In this approach, the face image is divided into small blocks, also called tiles, and in each of these blocks, the histogram equalization is applied. However, if any of the histograms calculated is above the predefined contrast limit, the pixels are clipped and distributed uniformly to other bins before applying histogram equalization. **Figure 7** shows a face image before and after the application of the CLAHE, respectively.

3.4. Head pose estimation

In previous work, three degrees of freedom were used for face alignment [7]: yaw, pitch, and roll which are presented in **Figure 8**.

In order to filter some of the input faces in face recognition algorithms, we use these three values to estimate the face position. For each value, a range is defined so that only the faces that are almost frontal to the camera are accepted as input of the face recognition algorithms.

Figure 7. Face image without (left image) and with (right image) the application of CLAHE.

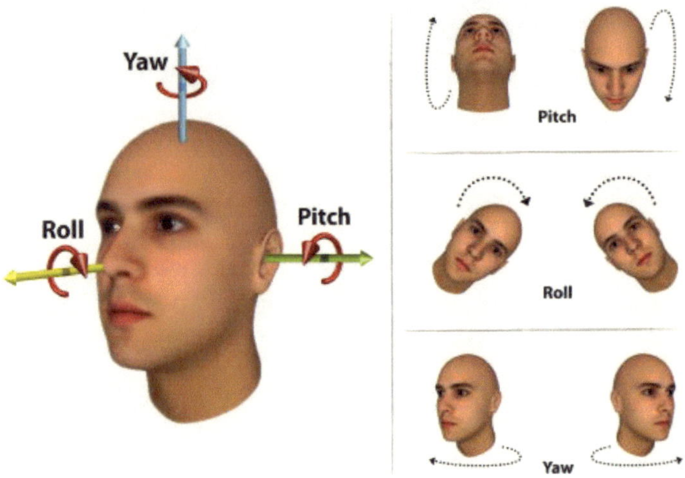

Figure 8. The three degrees of freedom of a human head that can be described by the egocentric rotation angles pitch, roll, and yaw [22].

4. Experimental results

In order to test the algorithms for the proposed solution, an access control system was simulated with face verification at the entrance of the research institute where dozens of people come and go during the day.

4.1. Setup

A prototype was developed with the available material. The prototype incorporates two cameras, an industrial camera and a webcam, on a tripod placed at a height of 1.5 m. Above the camera, an artificial illumination was placed. Since there were no available processing boards during the development of the system, a personal computer (ASUS VivoBook S14), Intel Core i7 8550U, was used instead. Finally, an NFC card reader (RFID-RC522) was connected to read the tag ID of each user both on the registration and verification stages. Also, it is worth mentioning that the PC display was used to show interactive messages explaining what the user should do. **Figure 9** presents the setup of the system.

http://dx.doi.org/10.5772/intechopen.79520

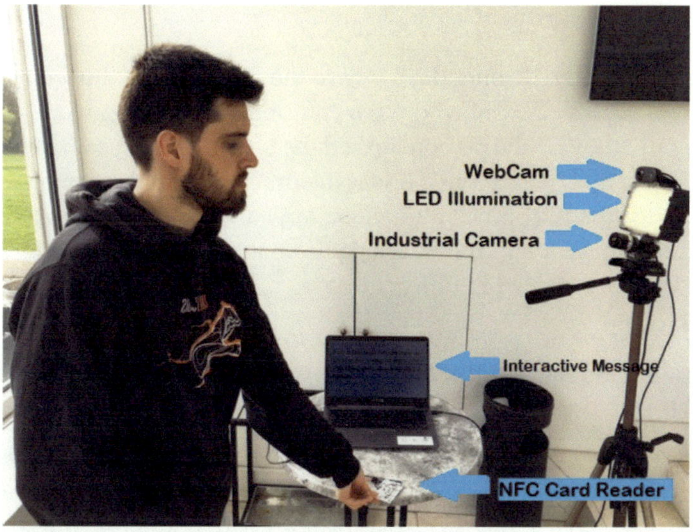

Figure 9. User interacting with the system setup for the experimental results.

4.1.1. Cameras

The cameras used for tests are the IDS UI-1220LE-C (Industrial Camera) and the Logitech C310 (webcam). The purpose of the use of these cameras is to compare the performance between them in this specific system as the webcam does not allow to change its camera parameters such as exposure or gain.

On the other hand, the industrial camera, despite not being the most suitable for this scenario, provides a software development kit (SDK) that enables the complete control of its different parameters. In addition, as the industrial camera does not have a lens integrated, a 4.5-mm lens with manually adjustable aperture is used. Since the system is intended to be implemented at a fixed location, the most suitable lens aperture is defined.

In order to access the image data directly and to process the image captured by the webcam, the Video4Linux API using the OpenCV Video I/O module is used.

As for the industrial camera, an initial procedure is required to prepare the image capture.

In the first phase, the industrial camera is initialized to establish the connection. In order to obtain the image for the system, access to the image data stored in memory is required. To do that, it is necessary to obtain the sensor size as it determines the memory needed to allocate the image.

4.1.2. Illumination

A 168 LED illumination with adjustable intensity is used in order to compensate the excess or lack of illumination. It also eliminates any occlusion that may be caused by external lightning. Another major advantage is its use on darker scenarios where the camera has a substantial exposure time. If the illumination is turned on, the scenario is clearer and the exposure time needed is lower, thus the blur caused by the person's motion in the image is less than without illumination.

4.2. Description of the experiment

The tests were done in three distinct days where the first and the third day were sunny and the second one was cloudy. People who were entering the building were asked if they want to participate in this study. If the person agreed, he/she posed himself/herself in front of the camera and the registration was done (if it was the first time that the person presented in front of the camera). As for the next times the person appeared, the comparison between the face images made on registration and the ones acquired at the time was made. **Figure 10** shows some of the face images acquired in different days.

About 50 people (a big majority of Caucasians from both sexes) participated, and all the participants entered the building at different times of the day which caused different types of directions of lighting in the face images acquired.

The comparisons between the face images registered in the database and the ones acquired next gave output values which were used to construct the receiver operating characteristic (ROC) curves. In total, about 2500 comparison values with both false and true positives were used to construct each curve presented next.

4.2.1. Camera calibration performance

The first test analyzes the performance between the webcam with its automatic calibration and the industrial camera with the calibration proposed. **Figure 11** presents the ROC curve as well as the area under curve (AUC) for this comparison. The HoG and the Openface algorithms were used with both cameras for detection and recognition, respectively.

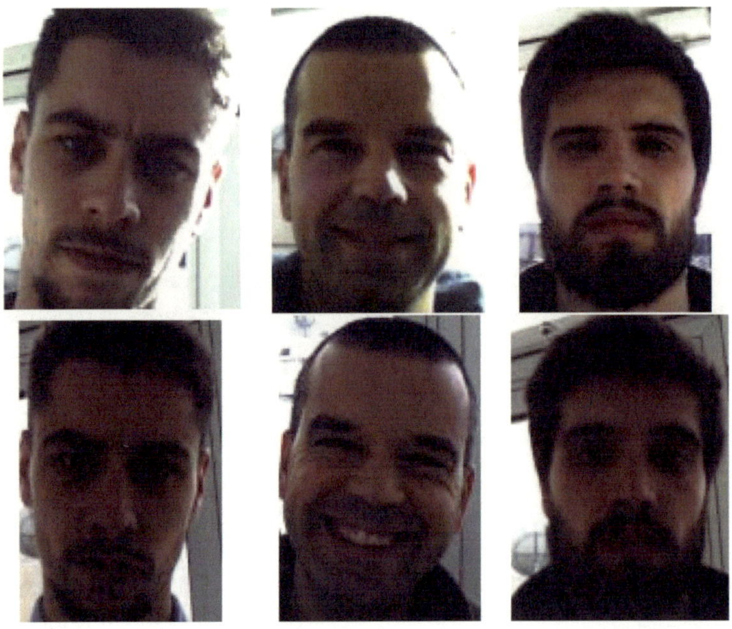

Figure 10. Example of face images acquired in different days with different meteorological conditions.

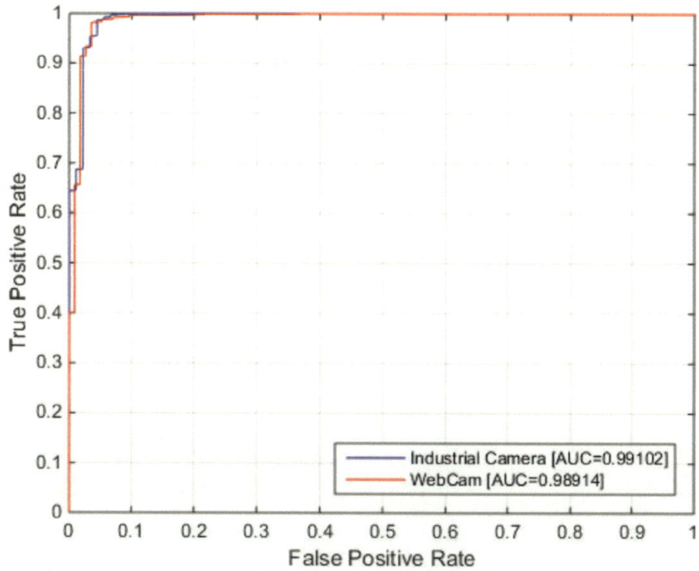

Figure 11. ROC curve comparing the webcam and the industrial camera performance using the same algorithms.

Comparing the AUC resulting from the graphic presented in **Figure 11**, it can be concluded that the proposed method using the industrial camera is better than webcam.

4.2.2. Face detection performance

In this section, the performance of the HoG and MTCNN face detection algorithms is presented. The time that it takes to detect faces in images with dimensions of 752×480 pixels was first measured. Posteriorly, the accuracy of each algorithm using a video recorded at the time of the tests was tested. **Table 1** provides the results for both algorithms.

Analyzing this table, although the HoG algorithm has a lower processing time and less false positives, the MTCNN algorithm has the advantage of detecting faces in profile view and consequently detect more faces for the input of the face verification stage.

4.2.3. Face recognition and preprocessing algorithms performance

Results of the performance of the recognition algorithms tested with and without the preprocessing methods of gamma correction and CLAHE are presented here. As all algorithms are based on neural networks, it is important to point out that, despite using a specific

	HoG	MTCNN
Processing time (ms)	60	121
Total detections	592	740
False positives	1	8

Table 1. Processing times, total detections, and false positives for each face detection algorithm.

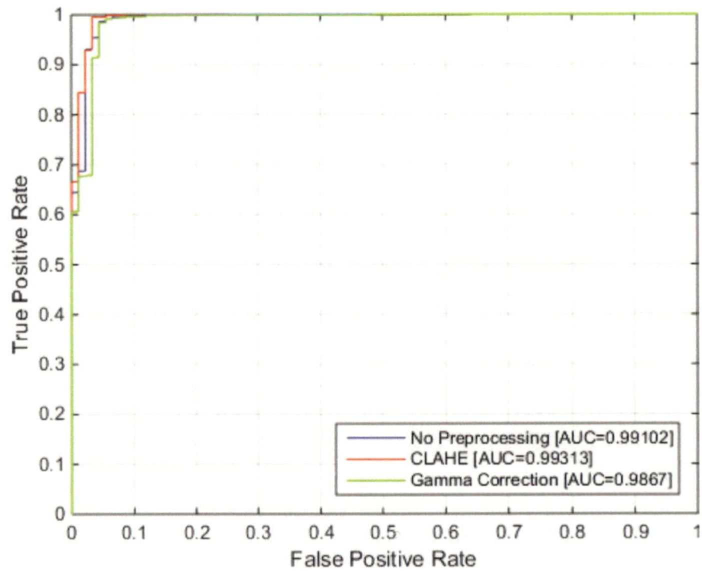

Figure 12. ROC curve presenting the performance of OpenFace using CLAHE, gamma, and no preprocessing methods.

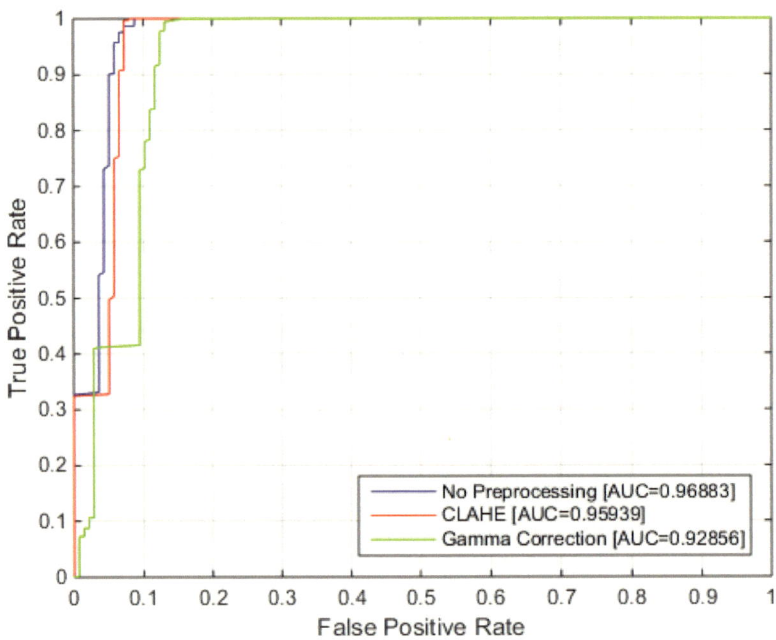

Figure 13. ROC curve presenting the performance of DML using CLAHE, gamma, and no preprocessing methods.

preprocessing method, the network was not retrained. The results might improve if the preprocessing methods are applied to the images that are used to train the neural network.

Figures 12–14 present the algorithms performance using no preprocessing algorithms and comparing its results with the use of CLAHE and gamma correction.

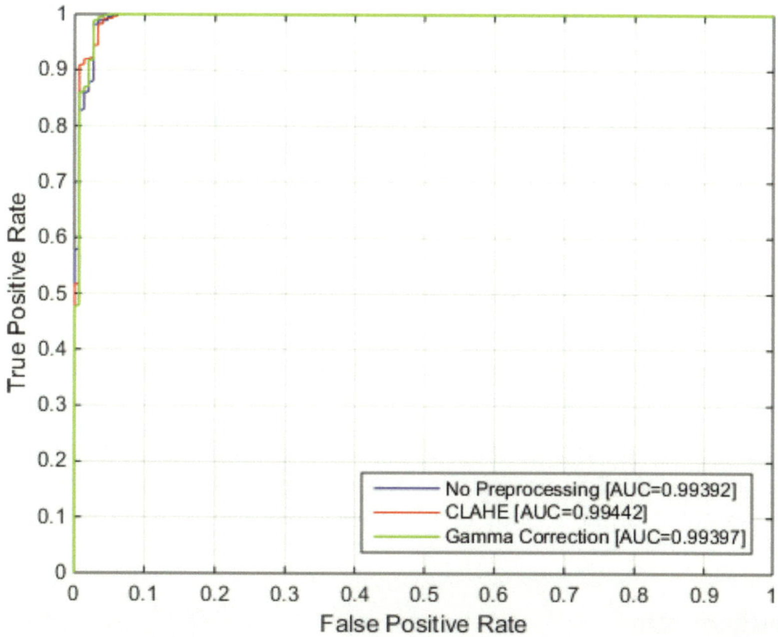

Figure 14. ROC curve presenting the performance of DeepFace using CLAHE, gamma, and no preprocessing methods.

	OpenFace	DML	DeepFace
Forward network runtime (ms)	236	293	110

Table 2. Processing times for forward pass in each network.

Table 2 shows the processing time that takes each face image to forward pass the neural network of each algorithm.

The results obtained using the proposed algorithms for face recognition show that the gamma correction revealed to have a negative impact in OpenFace and DML algorithms. As for DeepFace algorithm, the gamma correction does not have a significant impact on the output.

The preprocessing algorithm CLAHE has a positive impact in all face recognition algorithms used in this work.

Through the analysis in **Figures 12–14** and **Table 2**, the DeepFace is the better algorithm for using in the face verification stage. The DeepFace is two times faster than the other proposed algorithms and the AUC is higher.

5. Conclusion

This chapter presented a face verification solution and studies where algorithms and cameras are appropriately used under uncontrolled environments. Regarding the camera and its calibration, the industrial camera had a better performance compared to the webcam as the calibration method presented focus on the best face image that can be acquired. As for software, both detection algorithms presented a good performance. Despite that, MTCNN seems to have the best performance as it detects faces where subject is in the profile view. In relation to the recognition and the preprocessing algorithms, CLAHE algorithm had a positive impact in all the recognition algorithms as for the gamma correction had a negative impact. It is believed that the results would improve if the preprocessing technique was applied in all the face images used for the training of the neural network. Unfortunately, the training of these types of neural networks takes over a day using powerful GPUs which are difficult to access. Despite that, the overall performance of the system was satisfactory and, from now on and according to the experiments, the best solution for this system is the use of an industrial camera, MTCNN for face detection, CLAHE for preprocessing, and DeepFace for the face verification stage.

The future work goes through the implementation of the solution in larger scales where more people would use it. Until then, the training of new neural networks using the preprocessing techniques is presented, and the study of new alternatives for cameras is on the agenda.

Acknowledgements

This work is partially funded by National Funds through the FCT—Foundation for Science and Technology in the context of the project UID/CEC/00127/2013.

Author details

Ricardo Ribeiro*, Daniel Lopes and António Neves

*Address all correspondence to: rfribeiro@ua.pt

Institute of Electronics and Informatics Engineering of Aveiro, Aveiro, Portugal

References

[1] Zhao W, Chellappa R, Phillips PJ, Rosenfeld A. Face recognition: A literature survey. ACM Computing Surveys. 2003;**35**(4):399-458

[2] Amos B, Ludwiczuk B, Satyanarayanan M. OpenFace: A general-purpose face recognition library with mobile applications. Technical Report. CMU-CS-16-118. CMU School of Computer Science; 2016

[3] Jafri R, Arabnia HR. A survey of face recognition techniques. Journal of Information Processing Systems. 2009;**5**(2):41-68

[4] Olszewska JI. Automated face recognition: Challenges and solutions. In: Ramakrishnan S, editor. Pattern Recognition - Analysis and Applications, Chapter 4. Rijeka: InTech; 2016

[5] Neves AJR, Cunha B, Pinho AJ, Pinheiro I. Autonomous configuration of parameters in robotic digital cameras. In: Lecture Notes in Computer Science (Including Subseries Lecture Notes in Artificial Intelligence and Lecture Notes in Bioinformatics). 2009. pp. 80-87

[6] Wood R, Olszewska JI. Lighting-variable AdaBoost based on system for robust face detection. In: Proceedings of the 5th International Conference on Bio-Inspired Systems and Signal Processing; SciTePress Digital Library; Algarve, Portugal. 2012. pp. 494-497

[7] Lopes D, Neves A. A study on face identification for an outdoor identity verification system. Vol. 27. Lecture Notes in Computational Vision and Biomechanics. 2017. pp. 689-699

[8] Dalal N, Triggs B. Histograms of oriented gradients for human detection. In: Proceedings–2005 IEEE Computer Society Conference on Computer Vision and Pattern Recognition, CVPR 2005; 2005. pp. 886-893

[9] Zhang K, Zhang Z, Li Z, Qiao Y. Joint face detection and alignment using multitask cascaded convolutional networks. IEEE Signal Processing Letters. 2016;**23**(10):1499-1503

[10] He K, Zhang X, Ren S, Sun J. Deep residual learning for image recognition. In: 2016 IEEE Conference on Computer Vision and Pattern Recognition (CVPR) [Internet]. 2016. pp. 770-778. Available from: http://ieeexplore.ieee.org/document/7780459/

[11] Huang GB, Ramesh M, Berg T, Learned-Miller E. Labeled faces in the wild: A database for studying face recognition in unconstrained environments. University of Massachusetts Amherst Technical Report. 2007;**1**:07-49

[12] Ng HW, Winkler S. A data-driven approach to cleaning large face datasets. In: 2014 IEEE International Conference on Image Processing, ICIP 2014; 2014. pp. 343-347

[13] Parkhi OM, Vedaldi A, Zisserman A. Deep face recognition. In: Procedings of the British Machine Vision Conference 2015 [Internet]. 2015. pp. 41.1-41.12. Available from: http://www.bmva.org/bmvc/2015/papers/paper041/index.html

[14] Yi D, Lei Z, Liao S, Li SZ. Learning Face Representation from Scratch. 2014. Available from: http://arxiv.org/abs/1411.7923

[15] Schroff F, Kalenichenko D, Philbin J. FaceNet: A unified embedding for face recognition and clustering. In: Proceedings of the IEEE Computer Society Conference on Computer Vision and Pattern Recognition. 2015. pp. 815-823

[16] Wen Y, Zhang K, Li Z, Qiao Y. A discriminative feature learning approach for deep face recognition. In: Lecture Notes in Computer Science (Including Subseries Lecture Notes in Artificial Intelligence and Lecture Notes in Bioinformatics). 2016. pp. 499-515

[17] Engineering C. Gamma correction technique based feature extraction for face recognition system. International Journal of Computational Intelligence and Informatics. 2013;**3**(1):20-26

[18] Bebis G, Boyle R, Parvin B, Koracin D, Remagnino P, Nefian A, et al. Illumination normalization for color face images. Advances in Visual Computing. 2006;**4291**(2):90-101. Available from: http://www.springerlink.com/content/y74g332844240075/

[19] Zuiderveld K. Contrast Limited Adaptive Histogram Equalization. In: Graphics Gems. Academic Press; 1994;474-485. ISBN: 9780123361561. Avaliable from: http://www.sciencedirect.com/science/article/pii/B9780123361561500616

[20] Pizer SM, Amburn EP, Austin JD, Cromartie R, Geselowitz A, Greer T, et al. Adaptive histogram equalization and its variations. Comput Vision, Graph Image Process. 1987; **39**(3):355-368

[21] Benitez-Garcia G, Olivares-Mercado J, Aguilar-Torres G, Sanchez-Perez G, Perez-Meana H. Face identification based on contrast limited adaptive histogram equalization (CLAHE). In: Proceedings of International Conference on Image Processing, Computer Vision and Pattern Recognition; 2011

[22] Arcoverde Neto EN, Barreto RM, Duarte RM, Magalhaes JP, Bastos CCM, Ren TI, et al. Real-time head pose estimation for mobile devices. Integrated Computer-Aided Engineering. 2014;**7435**:467-474. DOI: 10.1007/978-3-642-32639-4_57%5Cn

Chapter 8

Detecting Micro-Expressions in Real Time Using High-Speed Video Sequences

Radu Danescu, Diana Borza and Razvan Itu

Additional information is available at the end of the chapter

http://dx.doi.org/10.5772/intechopen.76155

Abstract

Micro-expressions (ME) are brief, fast facial movements that occur in high-stake situations when people try to conceal their feelings, as a form of either suppression or repression. They are reliable sources of deceit detection and human behavior understanding. Automatic analysis of micro-expression is challenging because of their short duration (they occur as fast as 1/15–1/25 of a second) and their low movement amplitude. In this study, we report a fast and robust micro-expression detection framework, which analyzes the subtle movement variations that occur around the most prominent facial regions using two absolute frame differences and simple classifier to predict the micro-expression frames. The robustness of the system is increased by further processing the preliminary predictions of the classifier: the appropriate predicted micro-expression intervals are merged together and the intervals that are too short are filtered out.

Keywords: micro-expression spotting, image differences, affective computing, random forest classifier, detection

1. Introduction

Automatic facial expression analysis has been extensively studied in the last decades, as it has applications in various multidisciplinary domains, ranging from behavioral psychology, human-computer interaction, deceit detection, just to name a few. In the last years, a new research field has drawn the attention of computer vision researchers: micro-expression analysis.

Micro-expressions (ME) were discovered by Paul Eckman [1] and his colleagues in the early 1970s while analyzing facial expressions in order to recognize concealed emotions. Eckman defined various facial cues that can be used for deceit detection: micro-expressions, squelched expressions, and facial asymmetries and various parameters related to the dynamics of the expression. Nowadays, automatic expression and micro-expression analysis have a strong impact on a variety of applications. As an example, in the United States, within the SPOT program [2], airport employees are trained in ME recognition in order to detect the passengers with suspicious behavior. MEs are short facial expressions (with a duration between 1/5 and 1/25 of a second) that usually occur when people try to hide their feelings (either consciously or unconsciously). A micro-expression can be defined by its time evolution, its amplitude, and its symmetry. There are three key moments in the elicitation of a ME: onset (the moment when the ME starts), apex (the moment of maximum amplitude) and offset (the moment when it fades out).

Recently, the automatic analysis of ME has received the attention of researchers in the computer vision field. Besides the difficulties posed by facial expression detection and recognition in general, micro-expressions bring several other challenges. First of all, as MEs are involuntary, data are very hard to gather. However, several ME databases are available [3–5], but they only contain video sequences captured in controlled scenarios. Another difficulty is related to data labeling, as this is a time-consuming and subjective process. As a result, some ME databases [5] classify the expressions only into three categories: positive, negative, and surprise. Finally, MEs are very fast movements and are visible only for a limited number of frames. Therefore, high-speed cameras and accurate motion and tracking algorithms are required in the analysis of ME.

In this chapter, we propose a fast and robust micro-expression detection framework based solely on the movement magnitudes that appear on certain regions of the face. Although numerous works tackled the problem of micro-expression recognition, micro-expression detection has only been addressed recently. However, in real world applications, we argue that ME detection is more valuable than the recognition process.

First of all, the emotion recognition is a complex and fluid problem and psychologists still have not reached a consensus on a taxonomy of emotions and the way they are represented on the face. Eckman proposed a taxonomy with six universal emotions: *anger, disgust, fear, happiness, sadness,* and *surprise*. However, recently, the idea of emotion universality has received much criticism [6]. In practice, more complex emotion classification schemes are used, such as Plutchik's Wheel of Emotions [7] or Parrot's classification scheme [8]. Parrot emotion taxonomy [8] identified more than 100 emotions and classified them into a tree-based structure (primary, secondary, and tertiary emotion levels).

Another problem related to micro-expression recognition is the elicitation of emotion. All the micro-expression data available to this day are captured in (highly) controlled environments: the subjects are asked to watch video sequences with high emotional valence, without moving their head and try to suppress the expression of any emotion. However, using this methodology, the subjects are often impacted by the research technology and pure emotions are not produced, only blended emotions. To solve this problem, Eckman suggests using trained actors in Stanislavski acting technique [1]: in which emotion expression is generated based on actor's conscious thought and past experiences.

Finally, due to micro-expression's short duration and low amplitude, human often fail to perceive them. In fact, in their first study, Haggard and Issacs [9] stated that micro-expressions cannot be perceived with the naked eye.

The proposed algorithm is envisioned to be integrated into a computer-aided emotion analysis system: the detection module determines the frames in the video sequence where the emotion appeared and the psychologist analyzes these frames in order to recognize (a more nuanced) emotion.

The proposed algorithm determines if a ME has occurred at a certain time moment, while the recognition process establishes the type of the micro-expression. For the detection part, we use a sliding window to iterate over the movement variations of the video sequence and we compute the minimum and maximum response for each window position. The resulting feature vector is fed to a classifier in order to determine if a ME occurred at the center of the window. The raw result from the classifier is further processed in order to filter out false positives and to merge responses corresponding to the same ME.

This work has the following structure: in Section 2, the recent advances in the field of ME detection and recognition are presented. The outline of the proposed solution is illustrated in Section 3 and detailed in Section 4. The experimental results are presented and discussed in Section 4. Finally, this work is concluded in Section 5.

2. State of the art

Although automatic ME detection and recognition is not as widely studied as macro-expression analysis, with the recent advances in computer vision, several works addressed this problem. A ME analysis framework usually consists of three main tasks: (1) the selection of the relevant face regions, (2) the extraction of spatiotemporal features, and (3) the detection and recognition of ME using machine learning algorithms.

The first module is related to the selection of the facial areas where the MEs are more likely to occur. The Facial Action Coding System (FACS) [10] is a methodology used to classify facial expressions based on the muscles that produce them and it is used by trained human practitioners. For the automatic ME analysis, the face is usually segmented according to the most prominent facial elements (eyes, mouth corners, and nose) [11–13], or a complex deformable model is used to divide the face into more precise regions [6, 14]. Another approach is to split the face into n equal cells [15, 16].

As MEs are brief facial movements, their analysis requires robust spatiotemporal image descriptors. Various descriptors have been used in the literature: Local Binary Patterns in Three Orthogonal Planes (LBP-TOP) [6], 3D histogram of oriented gradients (HOG) [11, 12], dense optical flow [14], and optical strain [15]. Finally, using the appropriate features, ME can be classified using supervised [6] or non-supervised [11, 12] machine learning algorithms.

Several works perform both ME detection and recognition. In [17], the authors propose a general micro-expression analysis framework that performs both micro-expression detection and recognition. The detection phase does not require any training and exploits frame difference contrast to determine the frames where movement occurred. First, the authors define 36 facial cells based on the position of three facial features (the right eye inner corner, the left eye inner corner, and the tip of the nose). Two types of features are extracted for the detection process: Histogram of Oriented Optical Flow and LBP histograms; these features are extracted from each facial cell and concatenated into the final feature vector. Finally, the detection module uses histogram differences and thresholding to spot micro-expressions in the high-speed video sequence. The recognition algorithm implies a face alignment preprocessing step. Also, Eulerian motion magnification is used to emphasize the motion magnitude. Next, the classification features are extracted and concatenated from each one of the 36 facial cells: (LBP-TOP, Histogram of Oriented Gradients on Three Orthogonal Planes and Histogram of Image Gradient Orientation on Three Orthogonal Planes). A linear support vector machine classifier is used to recognize the micro-expression type.

In [16], micro-expressions are detected and recognized using optical strain and LBP-TOP motion descriptors. The face region is divided geometrically into 25 rectangular cells, and the feature vector is defined by concatenating the optical strain information and LBP-TOP information from each cell. Finally, a support vector machine classifier is used to both detect and recognize the micro-expressions.

Deep learning and convolutional neural networks in particular have recently received an increasing attention from the scientific literature. Several recent works also tackled the problem of micro-expression detection and recognition from a deep learning perspective. In [18], a convolutional neural network is used to locate 68 features on the subject's face. Based on the position of these landmarks, several regions are defined on the face and the histogram of oriented optical flow (HOOF) is extracted from each facial cell. Finally, the features from all the cells are concatenated and the support vector machines are used to determine the frames in which micro-expressions occurred. In [19], convolutional neural networks and long short-term memory recurrent neural networks (LSTM networks) are used to recognize the micro-expressions. First, a convolutional neural network is trained using the video frames from the beginning of the micro-expression sequence and the onset, apex, and offset frames. The learned features are finally fed to LSTM network to recognize the type of the micro-expression.

As stated earlier, the main problem in micro-expression detection and recognition is the gathering of a representative dataset. **Table 1** describes the micro-expression databases available.

The Polikovsky dataset [13] was captured at a frame rate of 200 fps and involves 10 University students (5 Asian, 4 Caucasian, and 1 Indian). Its main drawback is that the emotions are posed: the students were asked to perform seven basic emotions with low amplitude and go

Dataset	Posed/genuine	Image resolution	FPS	Annotation
Polikovsky [13]	Posed	640 × 480	200	Action units
CASME [3]	Genuine	1280 × 720, 640 × 480	60	Action units 8 emotions
CASME II [4]	Genuine	640 × 480	200	Action units 8 emotions
SMIC [5]	Genuine	640 × 480	100	3 emotions

Table 1. Distribution of the ME types in the CASME-II and SMIC-E databases.

back to the neutral state as fast as possible. Therefore, some difference between these expressions and genuine micro-expressions might occur.

However, some datasets that contain genuine micro-expressions were developed. The following methodology was used to elicit emotions: the users were asked to watch several videos with high emotional valence and try to hide or suppress all their facial expressions that might occur during the experiment. In order to create a high stake situation (as micro-expressions only occur when people have something to lose), some kind of penalty was imposed: if the subjects failed to hide their expression, they would have to fill in a very long and boring questionnaire.

The SMIC [5] database contains 168 micro-expression video sequences labeled with only three emotion classes: positive, negative, and surprise. The dataset was collected using 16 subjects. In addition, 10 subjects were used to capture video sequence at a regular temporal resolution (25 fps) with both visual and near-infrared cameras. For the task of micro-expression detection, a new version of the SMIC dataset was published, which contains longer micro-expression sequences (their average duration is 5.9 s).

The CASME II [4] dataset contains video sequences captured at 200 fps of 35 subjects. In total, 247 micro-expressions were elicited. The database was captured in highly controlled laboratory environments and is labeled with eight emotion classes. The CASME-II dataset also contains some samples (annotated with the "repression" label) that correspond to squelched expressions. Squelched expressions also appear when humans try to conceal their feelings, but there are some major differences between squelched expressions and micro-expressions. First of all, squelched expressions are not complete in terms of temporal parameters: the subject usually becomes aware that expresses an emotion and tries to hide it, by rapidly going to the neutral state or with another emotion (often a smile). Micro-expressions occur involuntary and unconscious, are complete emotions (they have a clear onset, apex, and offset) and their duration is shorter.

The main drawback of all the data available to this day is that all the data are captured in unnatural conditions: the subjects are asked to keep their head fixed and not to make any (macro) facial movements.

3. Solution outline

Figure 1 shows the outline of the proposed solution.

The method analyzes the motion variation that occurs across the high-speed video sequence. Two absolute image differences are computed: the difference between the current frame t and the frame t-ε (that describes the noise variation) and the difference between the current frame and the previous frame at distance $\Delta t/2$ (that describes the motion information).

The main issues that need to be addressed in detecting the micro-expressions are related to their short duration and low amplitude; therefore, this task requires sensible and robust motion descriptors. In **Figure 2**, we depict several frames within some micro-expression sequences.

Ideally, the features used to detect micro-expressions should be based on dense optical flow. However, this descriptor is very hard to compute and extract on the face area: the zone is

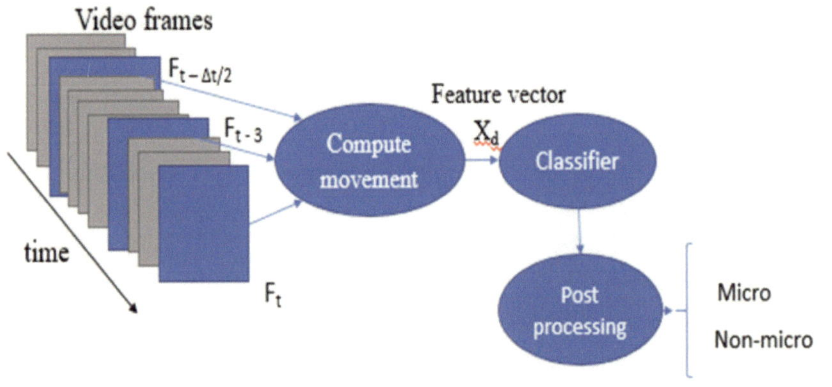

Figure 1. Solution outline.

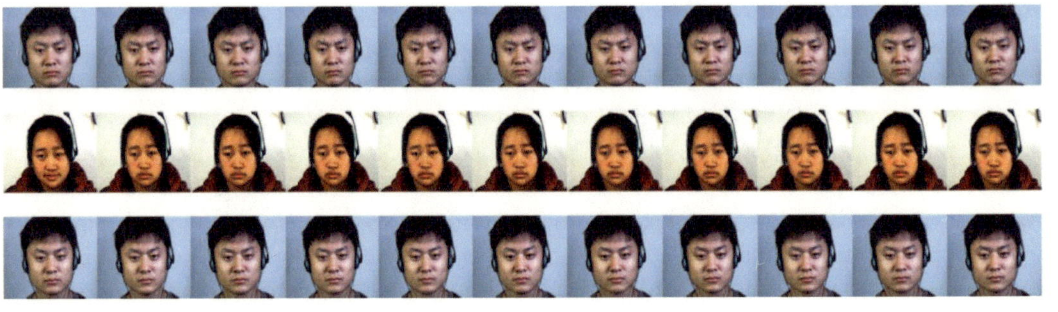

Figure 2. Some samples belonging to micro-expression sequences. First row: an example of a negative ME sequence, second row: an example of a positive ME sequence, third row: an example of a surprise ME sequence. (Raw frames from CASME II database [4] (©Xiaolan Fu)).

mostly homogenous and the micro-expression movement amplitude is too low. We argue that, under these conditions, the dense optical flow is impossible to detect at the pixel level. In addition, dense optical flow computation is slow and requires high computational resources.

The movement magnitude is computed by pixel-wise division of the second difference image by the first difference image. Next, the mean magnitude variation around the most prominent parts of the face (eyebrows, eye corners, mouth corners, and chin) is computed and a classifier is used to determine if a ME occurred at the current frame t. Finally, the response of the classifier is further processed in order to increase the robustness of the solution.

4. Solution description

In this section, a detailed description of each module is presented. First, we describe the regions of interest used to detect the micro-expressions and the computation of the motion detection features. Next, we detail the classification process and the post-processing model used to improve the algorithm's performance.

4.1. Selection of relevant face regions

Our proposed solution analyzes the movement magnitude variation in regions of interest. We defined 10 equally sized regions of the face that correspond to the positions of the muscles that are most used in facial expressions. The selection of the muscles used during a ME was based on the facial action coding system methodology. A first step is to use a general off the shelf facial detector, based on constrained local models [20] to detect 68 facial landmarks. The 10 cells (regions of interest) used in our solution are selected based on the detector results. Therefore, three cells in the upper area correspond to the left frontalis, procerus, and right frontalis muscles (the eyebrows area). Two cells are positioned around the eye corners, corresponding to orbicularis oculi muscles, two cells around the mouth corners and nostrils that overlap the orbicularis oris and zygomatics muscles. The last cell around the chin area overlays the mentalis muscle. The cell dimensions, height and width were chosen heuristically to be half the mouth width. The 10 cells that are analyzed by the ME detection and recognition algorithm are illustrated in **Figure 3**.

4.2. Feature extraction

Our solution relies on a simple method for the estimation of motion variation during a ME. We use Δt to denote the average ME duration (expressed in number of frames) for a given dataset. The facial movements that occur during consecutive frames are very low, as the ME video sequences are captured with high-speed cameras at a high frame rate.

We consider noise as a normalization factor, due to the fact that the movement magnitude for an ME has a very low intensity. Two absolute difference images are computed for each frame t:

1. ΔME (the difference between the frame t and the frame $t-\Delta t/2$).
2. $\Delta\varepsilon$ (the difference between the frame t and the frame $t-\varepsilon$); the resulting images are presented in **Figure 4 (a)** and (b). The $\Delta\varepsilon$ image describes the noise that occurs at frame t.

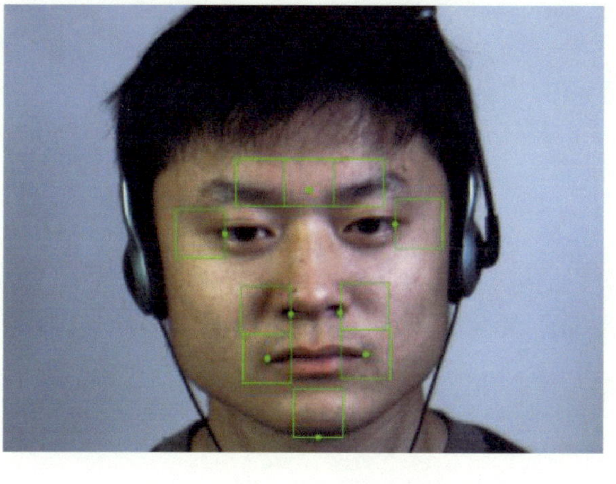

Figure 3. Facial regions of interest. Ten regions of interest are selected around the most prominent facial areas, where the MEs are likely to cause muscle movements.

(a) Δε (b) ΔME (c) M

Figure 4. Frame movement computation. (a) Difference between the current frame and the previous frame at three frames distance. (b) Difference between the current frame and the t the frame t - $\Delta t/2$. (c) Movement magnitude.

The first difference image ΔME describes the movement variation that occurred within the $\Delta t/2$ interval. Due to the fact that there is little to none facial movement within the interval of ε frames in a high-speed capture system, the $\Delta\varepsilon$ image is considered a neutral reference image and it is used as a normalization factor. In the reported results, ε was set to 3; this value was determined through trial-and-error experiments. Therefore, the movement magnitude M (**Figure 4(c)**) at each frame t is computed as:

$$M = \frac{\left|I_t - I_{t-\frac{\Delta t}{2}}\right| + 1}{\lceil I_t - I_{t-\varepsilon} \rceil + 1}, \tag{1}$$

where I_t represents the frame at index t.

The average value of the M image within the region of interest is computed for each of the 10 face cells (regions of interest). For example, **Figure 5** illustrates the average value of the M image for the middle eyebrow region.

We iterate through the responses for all the cells by using a sliding time window. A feature vector is created using the minimum and maximum values within the time frame and will be further analyzed by a classifier in order to detect if a ME has occurred. For each cell, we compute the

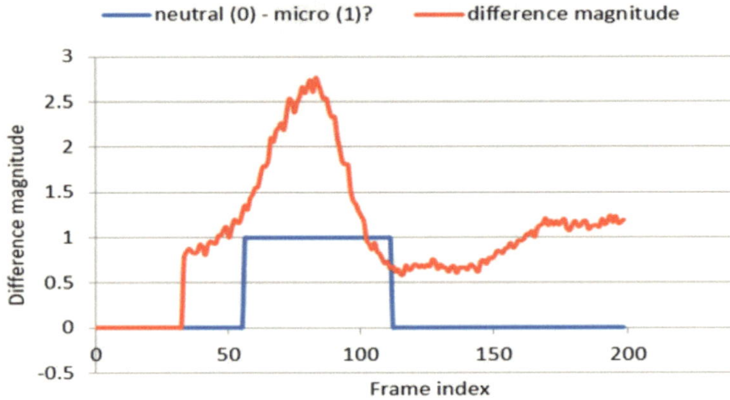

Figure 5. Difference variation of the middle eyebrow face cell. The ground truth labeling of the ME sequence is marked with a blue step, and the difference variation is depicted in gray.

average minimum and maximum value within the sliding window and we concatenate them to the feature vector. The dimensionality of the feature vector is 20 (10 cells × 2 values per cell).

$$feature_t = \|_{c_i \in cell}\left(\max_{t \in sz}\langle MM_t[c_i]\rangle,\ \min_{t \in sz}\langle MM_t[c_i]\rangle\right), \tag{2}$$

where $\langle MM_t[c_i]\rangle$ represents the average value of the M image within the region of interest c_i, at frame t and || represents the concatenation operator.

We convolved the input frame image with the Laplacian kernel in order to make the algorithm more robust to illumination changes and to eliminate the lighting bias:

$$\mathrm{L} = \begin{bmatrix} -1 & -1 & -1 \\ -1 & 8 & -1 \\ -1 & -1 & -1 \end{bmatrix} \tag{3}$$

The image filtered with the Laplacian kernel is presented in **Figure 6**. The results obtained using the raw difference images and the Laplacian filtered difference images are discussed in Section 5.

4.3. Classification

The extracted feature vectors are used as input for a classification algorithm that will determine the state (ME or non-ME) at each frame t. We performed the classification using two classifiers: decision tree and random forest classifier.

Decision trees [21] use structures similar to graphs to determine classification rules, meaning that they are non-parametric supervised learning algorithms. A decision tree's structure contains internal nodes that represent "tests" on an attribute, whereas each edge will represent the outcome of the tests. The leaves in the tree represent the encodings of the class labels, while the classification rules are represented by paths from the root of the tree to each leaf. Decision trees are computationally efficient (the prediction step is logarithmic in the number of data instances used to train the tree), easy to interpret and visualize and require little or no data preprocessing. Their main disadvantage is that the learning algorithm can generate an over-complex tree, meaning that it does not generalize the data well and can usually lead to overfitting.

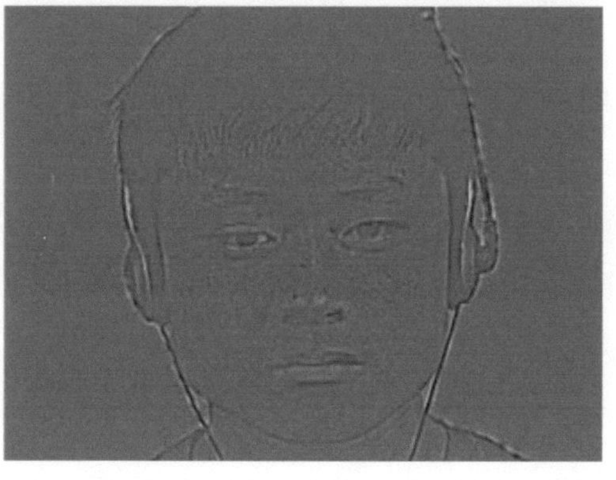

Figure 6. Laplace filtering.

Random forest classifiers, also known as random decision forest classifiers, [22] are ensemble learning methods for classification, regression, that were designed to cope with the problem of overfitting that occurs in decision trees. These classifiers generate multiple decision trees at training time and the final class label is the mode (the label that appears more often) of the classes of the individual trees. The prediction accuracy is improved by fitting a different number of decision trees on subsets of the dataset and uses averaging to improve the prediction accuracy and to better control overfitting.

4.4. Postprocessing

The preliminary result (R_t) obtained from the classifier is further analyzed in order to filter out false positive and to determine the time frame of the ME (onset, apex, and offset moments). R_t contains the predicted classes (0—non-ME class and 1—ME class) for each frame from the input video sequence. We make the assumption that the preliminary result vector should contain agglomerations of ME class predictions around the apex frame of a ME, and the singular predictions of ME class correspond to false positives. Therefore, we first determine all the contiguous intervals that contain only ME class predictions. The intervals that are too close to each other (their distance is less than $\Delta t/4$) are merged together, and next, all the intervals that are too short (their width is lower than $\Delta t/10$) are considered false positives as filtered out. The remaining intervals are considered ME intervals and their centroid is selected as the apex frame of the ME.

The raw response of the classifiers on an input video sequence and the filtered response of using the proposed algorithm are depicted in **Figures 7** and **8**. The plot is also marked with the ground truth onset, apex, and offset frames.

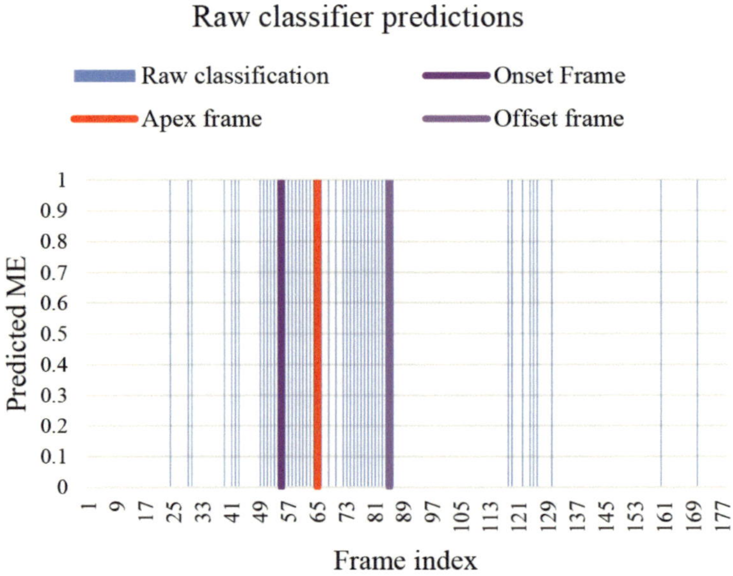

Figure 7. Raw classifier prediction. The predictions are depicted in blue vertical lines; the ground truth onset and the apex and, offset frames are depicted in violet, red, and yellow respectively.

http://dx.doi.org/10.5772/intechopen.76155

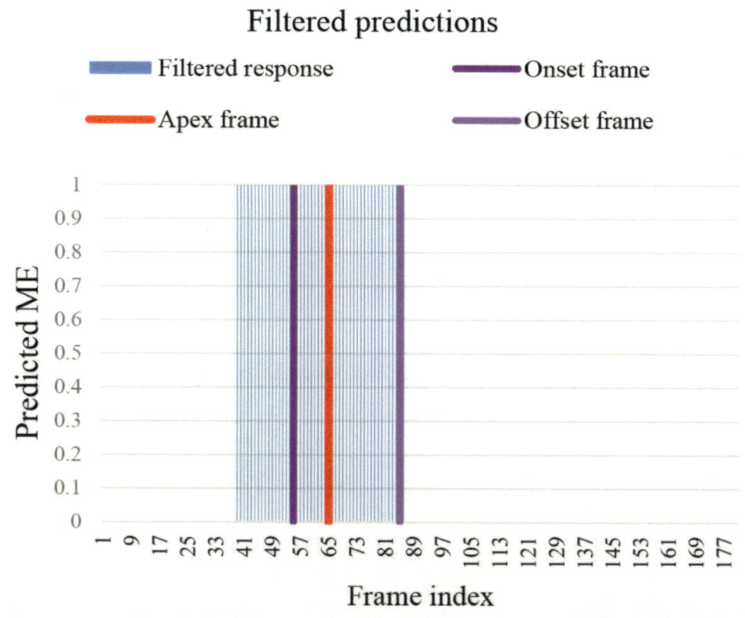

Figure 8. Postprocessing of the classifier result. The retained classifier predictions are depicted in blue vertical lines and the ground truth onset, apex, and offset frames are depicted in violet, red, and yellow respectively.

The classifier response if further post-processed in order to filter out false positives and to merge the positive responses which belong to the same ME. The first step is detecting all the disjunctive ME intervals and then merging together the intervals that are too close to each other. In the last step, the size of each interval is analyzed, and the intervals that are too short are ruled out (Algorithm 1). The middle of each predicted ME interval represent the apex frames.

Algorithm 1: ME detection and postprocessing

Parameters:

minMicroSz: the minimum size in frames of a ME ($\Delta t/4$ in our experiments).

maxDist: the maximum distance between two clusters to be merged ($2\Delta t$ in our experiments).

```
Find the predicted and disjunctive ME intervals: I = {(s0, e0), (s1, e1), …, (sn, en)}
doMerge ← True.
while doMerge do.
    doMerge ← False
    for i = 1 to length(I) do
        m1 < − (ei-1 − si-1)
        m2 < − (ei − si)
        if (m2 − m1) < maxDist then
            merge(Ii, Ii-1)
            doMerge ← True
            break
```

Algorithm 1: ME detection and postprocessing

```
            end if
      end for
end while.
for i = 1 to length(I) do.
      if (e_i – s_i) < minMicroSz then
            remove(I_i)
      end if
end for.
```

In the above mentioned algorithm, the predicted ME intervals are described as a list of frame pairs (s_i, e_i) denoting the start and end frames of each interval.

5. Experimental results

The proposed solution was trained and evaluated on the CASME II [5] database. This dataset contains 247 video sequences of spontaneous micro-expressions, captured from 26 participants. The mean age of the participants is 22.03 years, with 1.6 standard deviation. The video sequences were captured by a high-speed camera (200 fps), with a resolution of 640 × 480 pixels. The video sequences are labeled with the onset, apex and offset moments, and with one of following ME types: happiness, disgust, surprise, repression, and tense.

Two types of evaluation strategies are used in the specialized literature: *leave one sample out cross validation* and *leave one subject out cross validation*. The first evaluation technique randomly selects some video sequences for the evaluation, while the latter randomly selects some subjects which were not used in the training process and uses all the samples belonging to the selected subjects for evaluation. Leave one subject out cross validation is more generic, as the classification algorithm hasn't "seen" the subject. For the evaluation part, we used "leave one subject out cross validation" (LOSOCV).

To label the data for detection module, a sliding time window is iterated through the video sequence. If Δt is the average micro-expression duration (67 frames), and t_{apex} is the ME ground truth apex frame, the current frame t is labeled using the following rule:

- If $t \in [0, t_{apex} - \delta \cdot \Delta t]$ or $t \in [t_{apex} + \delta \cdot \Delta t]$, then the frame t is labeled as non-micro-expression frame (neutral frame or macro-expression);
- If $t \in (t_{apex} - \delta \cdot \Delta t, t_{apex} + \delta \cdot \Delta t)$, then frame t is considered a ME frame.

The scale factor δ was heuristically set to 0.25 through trial and error experiments. The main idea regarding this value is that we do not want to label all the frames from the micro-expression interval as micro-expression frames, so we decided that only half the frames from the ground truth micro-expression interval, centered on the apex frame, to be labeled as micro-expression frames—as there should be a higher movement variation within this region.

Table 2 shows the performance of the algorithm on the CASME II dataset. TPR stands for True Positive Rate, FPR for False Positive Rate, FNR stands for False Negative Rate, and TNR represents the True Negative Rate. The metrics are defined as follows:

$$\mathrm{TPR} = \frac{\mathrm{TP}}{\mathrm{TP} + \mathrm{FN}} \tag{4}$$

$$\mathrm{FNR} = \frac{\mathrm{FN}}{\mathrm{TP} + \mathrm{FN}} = 1 - \mathrm{TPR} \tag{5}$$

$$\mathrm{TNR} = \frac{\mathrm{TN}}{\mathrm{TN} + \mathrm{FP}} \tag{6}$$

In the abovementioned equations, the following abbreviations are used: *TP*—true positive samples, *FP*—false positive sample, *FN*—false negative sample and *TN*—true negative sample.

The best results are obtained using the Laplace filtering of the input image and a random forest classifier.

Our method is better than recent state-of-the-art methods. In **Table 3**, we present the comparison of the proposed solution with other state of the art works. ACC stands for accuracy, FPR stands for false positive rate and TPR stands for true positive rate.

Feature	Classifier	TPR (%)	FPR (%)	FNR (%)	TNR (%)
Raw pixels	Decision tree	68.18	0.25	31.81	99.74
Raw pixels	Random forest	72.72	0.15	27.27	99.84
Laplacian	Decision tree	76.19	0.06	23.80	99.93
Laplacian	**Random forest**	**86.95**	**0.012**	**13.04**	**99.87**

Table 2. Performance on the CASME 2 dataset.

Method	Features	Performance
[3]	LBP-TOP	ACC: 65.49%*
[5]	LBP-TOP	N/A
[16]	Optical strain, LBP-TOP	ACC: 74.16%*
[17]	Frame differences	TPR*: 70%
Our solution	Frame differences	TPR: 86.95%

Methods marked with an asterisk * were evaluated on SMIC [3] database. To detect the micro-expressions, most of the works were only evaluated on SMIC database. Therefore, the numerical comparison with these methods might not be relevant.

Table 3. Comparison with state-of-the art works.

The execution time of the proposed solution is approximately 9 ms on a fourth generation Intel i7 processor.

6. Conclusions and future work

In this chapter, we presented a fast and robust method for the detection of subtle expressions from high-speed cameras. The method analyzes the movement variations that occur in a given time frame using image differences. Two classifiers were used and evaluated to determine if a ME occurred at a given frame t. In order to ensure the robustness of the algorithm, the raw response of the classifier is further post-processed in order to filter out false positives and to merge the predictions that belong to the same ME zone. The proposed method is fast, robust, and it achieves a high positive rate, while maintaining the false-positive rate low.

As a future work, we plan to gather more data for the training process so that more data variation is present. Till this day, all the micro-expression data are captured in highly controlled environments: artificial lighting conditions, the subjects are not allowed to move their heads freely and must keep a near-frontal pose etc. We plan to gather a different dataset, in which the emotion elicitation technique is quite different (for example, interrogation scenarios) and the users are allowed to act naturally. Of course, under this modified settings, the 3D head pose must be taken into account.

Also, we intend to use motion magnification in order to accentuate the magnitude of the facial movement during a micro-expression and so to increase the algorithm's performance.

Finally, the proposed detection algorithm will be integrated into a full micro-expression analysis framework, which is capable of also recognizing the type of the micro-expression that occurred.

Acknowledgements

This work was supported by the MULTIFACE (Multifocal System for Real Time Tracking of Dynamic Facial and Body Features) of the Romanian National Authority for Scientific Research, CNDI-UEFISCDI, Project code: PN-II-RU-TE-2014-4-1746.

Conflict of interest

The authors declare no conflicts of interest.

http://dx.doi.org/10.5772/intechopen.76155

Author details

Radu Danescu*, Diana Borza and Razvan Itu

*Address all correspondence to: radu.danescu@cs.utcluj.ro

Technical University of Cluj-Napoca, Cluj-Napoca, Romania

References

[1] Ekman P. Telling Lies: Clues to Deceit in the Marketplace, Politics, and Marriage. New York: W. W. Norton & Company; 2009

[2] Wikipedia. SPOT (TSA program) [Online], April 28, 2017. Available: https://en.wikipedia.org/wiki/SPOT_(TSA_program)

[3] Rautio H. SMIC—Spontaneous Micro-expression Database, University of Oulu [Online]. April 12, 2017. Available: http://www.cse.oulu.fi/SMICDatabase

[4] Yan W-J, Wu Q, Liu Y-J, Wang S-J, Fu X. CASME database: A dataset of spontaneous micro-expressions collected from neutralized faces. In: FG. IEEE; 2013. pp. 1-7

[5] Zhao G, Liu Y-J, Chen Y-H, Fu X. CASME II: An improved spontaneous micro-expression database and the baseline evaluation. PLoS One. 2014;**9**(1):e86041

[6] Nelson NL, Russell JA. Universality revisited. Emotion Review. 2013;**5**:8-15

[7] Plutchik R. The Nature of Emotions. American Scientist. Archived from the original on July 16, 2001. Retrieved April 14, 2011

[8] Parrott W. Emotions in Social Psychology, Key Readings in Social Psychology. Philadelphia: Psychology Press; 2001

[9] Haggard EA, Isaacs KS. Micromomentary facial expressions as indicators of ego mechanisms in psychotherapy. In: Gottschalk LA, Auerbach AH, editors. Methods of Research in Psychotherapy. Boston, USA: Springer; 1966. pp. 154-165

[10] Ekman P, Friesen W. Facial Action Coding System: A Technique for the Measurement of Facial Movement. Palo Alto: Consulting Psychologists Press; 1978

[11] Pfister T, Li X, Zhao G, Pietikainen M. Recognising spontaneous facial micro-expressions. In: 2011 IEEE International Conference on Computer Vision (ICCV); Barcelona; 2011

[12] Polikovsky S, Kameda Y, Ohta Y. Facial micro-expressions recognition using high speed camera and 3D-gradient descriptor. In: 3rd International Conference of Crime Detection and Prevention; 2009

[13] Polikovsky S, Kameda Y, Ohta Y. Facial micro-expression detection in hi-speed video based on facial action coding system (FACS). IEICE Transactions on Information and Systems. 2013;**E96**(1):81-92

[14] Godavarthy S, Goldgof D, Sarkar S, Shreve M. Macro- and micro-expression spotting in long videos using spatio-temporal strain. In: Automatic Face & Gesture Recognition and Workshops (FG 2011); 2011

[15] Liu Y-J, Zhang J-K, Yan W-J, Wang S-J, Zhao G. A main directional mean optical flow feature for spontaneous micro-expression recognition. IEEE Transactions on Affective Computing. 2016;**7**(4):299-310

[16] Liong ST, See J, Phan RC-W, Oh YH, Le Ngo AC, Wong KS, Tan SW. Spontaneous subtle expression detection and recognition based on facial strain. Signal Processing: Image Communication. 2016;**47**:170-182

[17] Li X, Xiaopeng HONG, Moilanen A, Huang X, Pfister T, Zhao G, Pietikainen M. Towards reading hidden emotions: A comparative study of spontaneous micro-expression spotting and recognition methods. IEEE Transactions on Affective Computing. 2017. http://ieeexplore.ieee.org/document/7851001/

[18] Li X, Yu J, Zhan S. Spontaneous facial micro-expression detection based on deep learning. In: 2016 IEEE 13th International Conference on Signal Processing (ICSP). IEEE; 2016. pp. 1130-1134

[19] Breuer R, Kimmel R. A deep learning perspective on the origin of facial expressions. arXiv 674, preprint arXiv:1705.01842 2017

[20] Cox M, Nuevo J, Saragih J, Lucey S. CSIRO Face Analysis SDK. AFGR; 2013

[21] Quinlan JR. Induction of decision trees. Machine Learning. 1986;**1**(1):81-106

[22] Ho TK. Random decision forests. In: Proceedings of the Third International Conference on Document Analysis and Recognition. Vol. 1. IEEE; 1995. pp. 278-282